The Book of Prayers

By: Only A. Guy

The Book of Prayers

Published by Only A. Guy Publishing

Cover Art and Editing By Whyte Lady Designs L.L.C.

www.onlyaguy.com
www.facebook.com/onlyaguy
www.twitter.com/onlyaguy1

ISBN 13: 978-0-9847382-2-9
ISBN: 0-9847382-2-9

Printed in the USA.

Table of Contents

Are You Sure? You Can Know For Sure!

Introduction 1

Are The Decisions We Make That Important?

The Right Plan For Your Life & How To Find It, Get to It, & Live "In" It

From Here to There

How I Came Into The Right Path And How I "Know" It!

Awakening To Truth (God IS The Truth)

Why Does This Occur?

We Are Not So Perfect After All

How An Enemy Of Our Soul Is Allowed To Creep In

The Spiritual Realm Is Real

... It's God's Fault, What Kind Of God Would..., And The List Goes On!

The KEY

The Truth, The Whole Truth And Nothing But The Truth!

This Is Extremely Important!

Who You Are And How A Person Can Be Separated From God And
     Not Realize It!

Let's Take It From The Top!

God Made A Way!

The First Step In Finding His Purpose And Plan For Your Life Is To
     Go To Him!

The Feeling Of Unworthiness In His Presence

Is Hell Real?

Knowing You Are Speaking To the God Who Created You!

Some Major Stumbling Blocks, Pit Falls, And Wrong Beliefs About
     "Getting Into Heaven"

How to Move Past Any Stumbling Blocks

How To Ask Jesus Christ Into Your Heart

If You Have Already Asked Jesus Christ Into Your Heart

Some Basic Reasons People Think They Are Saved But Are Not

Prayer Of Salvation 15

Thanksgiving For Salvation 15

    Nail It Down

    Assurance Of Salvation

    New Beginnings

    Feelings

    What If I Sin Again After Asking Jesus Into My Heart?

    To Our New Brothers And Sisters In Christ

    Restoration

    Restored Walking In The Light With Our Lord In The Mind of Christ

Entering The Holy of Holies/Entering Our Heavenly Father's Presence 24

    How Do We Enter In With GOD? According To His Biblical Pattern!

    Oh But I Know How To Worship Already!

    According To Pattern

    Struggles Will Pursue You

The Journey Begins 25

    A Few Steps To A Successful And Joyful Time With GOD

The First Things First (On This Side of the Veil) 26

    The Earthly Realm

    An Overview of Where you are Headed

Important!!! 30

Why Does God Tell Us NO 30

    "Moving on" In The Holy of Holies

    Leaving the Holy of Holies

Why Pray? 33

    The Lord's Principle Of Prayer

    Difference Between John 14:14 and John 16:23

    Hindrances Can Block You From Receiving Your Deliverance

    Biblical Grounds For Sickness, Disease, Demons, Etc.

    Prayer Makes The Difference

Asking For His Wisdom 39

Physical Healing 39

Praying Against the Root Cause, Not the Symptom

Putting the Word of God into Action

Importance of Forgiveness & Repentance for Judging 41

Finances 42

Confirmation by Two or Three Witnesses 44

Curses 44

Power of Your Spoken Word 44

Prayers

Daily Prayer 47

Prayer of Spiritual Doors 47

Prayer For The Release Of Resentment & Bitterness 47

Prayer For The Help Of The Lord 48

Daily Prayer For A Child 49

Prayer For Those Who Bless The Poor 49

Prayer For The Forgiveness of Sin 50

Prayer For The Forgiveness Of Others I 50

Prayer For The Forgiveness Of Others II 50

Prayers For The Breaking Of Curses 50

Prayer For Binding and Banish Demonic Spirits 52

Prayer To Apply The Blood Of Jesus 53

Prayer To Be Filled With The Holy Spirit 53

Binding the Enemies Eyes and Ears Prayer 54

Prayer To Wear The Full Armor of God 54

Prayers For the Protection Of The Angels 54

Psalms 91 Prayer Of Protection 55

Demons Can Follow Unaware 55

Prayer Against Demons That Follow

Unrighteous Agreements 56

Prayer To Destroy Unrighteous Agreements

Deuteronomy 28 Prayer Of Blessing 56

Numbers 6:23-26 Prayer Of Blessing 57

Daily Prayer To Commit Your Life To The Lord.......................... 57

Prayer For God's Presence To Be With You................................. 57

Prayer for Clarity 58

Prayer For Mind Cleansing.. 58

Prayers of Blessing 58

Luke 21:36 Prayer Of Watchfulness.. 59

1 Thessalonians 5:23-24 Prayer Of Sanctity................................ 59

Isaiah 40:31 Prayer To Renew Strength....................................... 59

Ephesians 1:17-23 Prayer For The Spirit of Wisdom 59

Ephesians 3:16-21 Prayer For Inner Strength 61

Prayers of Spiritual Warfare From The Psalms 61

    Psalms 35

    Psalms 61

    Psalms 64

    Psalms 32

    Psalms 51

    Psalms 67

Jabez Prayer 64

Bind Mind To The Will Of God 64

Romans 12 Prayer for Grace & Patience in Tribulation 64

Hearing God's Voice Prayer.. 65

Testing The Spirits.. 65

Remove Any Deception 65

Traveling Mercies Prayer.. 65

The Prayer For Judges... 66

Pastor's Prayer... 67

Hospital Prayer... 68

Prayer For Inmates 69

Malachi 3: Praying God's Promises For The Tither..................... 70

Prayer For A Person Who Has Lost A Loved One 71

Prayer For A Person Grieving The Loss Of A Loved One 71

Comprehensive Daily Prayer..72

Prayer To Bind & Banish Strongmen (General) 81

Prayers To Bind & Banish Strongmen (Specific) 82

    Spirit of Rejection

    Spirit of Anti Christ

    Spirit Of Error

    Seducing Spirits

    Spirit of Bondage

    Spirit of Death

    Spirit of Divination

    Dumb And Deaf Spirit

    Familiar Spirit

    Spirit of Fear

    Spirit Of Pride

    Spirit Of Heaviness

    Spirit Of Infirmity

    Spirit of Jealousy

    Lying Spirit

    Perverse Spirit

    Spirit Of Whoredoms

Prayer Of Spiritual Warfare...98

Hedge of Protection Prayer 100

Communion Prayer...104

Destroying Generational Curses..105

Bondage Breaking Prayer..105

Shattering Strongholds On Self..106

Shattering Strongholds On Others..107

Prayer For Peaceful Sleep I 108

Prayer For Peaceful Sleep II..109

Bedroom Blessing 110

Prayer For Physical Healing I...111

Prayer for Physical Healing II 113

Prayer For Physical Healing III 115

Prayer For Victory In Jesus.. 115

Prayer for God to Empower Medication and Remove Adverse

    Side Effects of Medications 115

Prayer Of Repentance 116

Prayer For Forgiveness Of Others 116

Baptism of the Holy Spirit 117

Prayer for Wisdom 118

Prayer for Israel.. 119

Prayer for America.. 119

Prayer for World Leaders... 120

Prayer for the Lost 121

Prayer To Abide In His Love.. 121

Psalms 107:20 Prayer.. 122

Job 22:27-28 Prayer 122

Prayer Over Buildings, Churches, Restaurants, Houses 122

Prayer For Cleansing A Home. 122

Prayer To Destroy Curses 123

Cancellation of Witchcraft or Prayers of Manipulation.............. 124

Breaking Word Curses Spoken Over Yourself and Others.......... 124

Prayer for Our Children in School 125

Prayer To Keep Us From Harm 125

Prayer For A Person Experiencing Loss Of A Loved One 126

Prayer To Receive Forgiveness & Cleansing Of Sins 126

Casting Out Evil Spirits 127

Prayer For The Covering Blood of Jesus 127

Prayer For Rendering The Enemy Harmless & Unable To Return............. 128

Loosing Angels For Protection 128

Prayer for Finances 128

Prayer To Release Guilt... 129

Prayer For Freedom 129

Praise the Lord 130

Prayer To Let Go of Resentment & Bitterness 130

Prayer For Children With ADD/ADHD 131

Prayer To Clean Out A Room, Church, Building 132

Prayer To Clean Out Churches, Restaurants, Public Buildings 132

Prayer Of Deliverance 133

Prayers For Spirit, Soul, And Body 134

    The Spirit Of Man

    The Soul Of Man

    The Body Of Man

Prayer For Your Divine Purpose 136

Prayer For The Word of Provision 137

Prayer of Impartation 137

Prayers Of Priestly Blessing To Anoint a Brother or Sister in Christ 138

Prayer of Worship 139

Prayer of Acknowledgement, Submission, and Position 140

Prayer To Stop Evil Spirits that Follow 141

Prayer To Stop Evil Spirits Transferring, Influencing, and Manifesting 141

Prayer To Bind Demonic Spirits From Answering Wrong Prayers 141

Prayer To Call On GOD 141

Parents Prayer for a Teenager 142

Prayer For Release From Addiction for the Believer 143

Prayer To Humbe Yourself Before The Lord 144

Prayer For Members of the Armed Forces 145

Prayer For You To Know God's Plan Regarding Marriage 146

Prayer For Peace In A Troubled Marriage 146

Prayer For The Restoration Of A Marriage 147

In A Pinch Prayer 148

Prayer to Help Against Anger 149

Affirmations And Lists

Importance of Affirmations 151

    Affirmations For You

    Affirmations For Our Children/Grandchildren

    I Am In Christ Affirmations

Names of God 159

The Word of God; A Scriptural Reference By Subject 165

    Concerning Us And GOD'S Gifts

    Concerning Our Strength To Overcome Sin

Healing Scriptures List 171

Financial Success Scriptures List 173

A Believer's Scriptural Authority Against Demonic Spirits 174

Sin List 181

Demon List 183

ARE YOU SURE? YOU CAN KNOW FOR SURE!

"I knew you before I formed you in your mother's womb..." "Yes, I have loved you with an everlasting love; therefore with loving-kindness have I drawn you." (Jeremiah 1:5, 31:3)

INTRODUCTION

You shall know the Truth and the Truth shall set you free. We need to stand free and to know what true freedom is. Life is full of many choices and there is a sure path *(Jeremiah 6:16)* we can take. We all have to make decisions in various areas of life on a daily basis. Unfortunately there are those things in this life that "appear as one thing" when they are actually something totally different. The truth about something can determine whether we make the right choices in this life. Truth is not something that is relative to just one situation and then changes to fit another situation. Truth is constant, never changing. Having a working knowledge of what Truth really is and how to walk in the Truth will help you to make the right decisions in your life.

"Multitudes, multitudes in the valley of decision!" Joel 3:14 NKJV

As you go through this life you will need to recognize the Truth in order to see clearly so you understand what is truly happening and why. In turn this will help us to understand and reason clearly. We need to be sure of the path (course) we are on and realize that there is only one way meant for us.

ARE THE DECISIONS WE MAKE THAT IMPORTANT?

Absolutely, the course you're on, the decisions you select will lead you somewhere eventually. There used to be a saying that all roads (paths) lead to Rome. This is not true! All roads do not lead to Rome. Some roads are dead ends. Other roads or paths in this life seem to be right but end up a waste of time. Some roads in this life lead people down paths *(Jeremiah 18:15)* they may wish they had never taken (regret, sorrow, even death). The stark reality is that we go through "this" life only once. That is a vital statement. We all want the best for our lives and others. Most people go through life trying to stay up with their perception of "life" and trying to get it right along with the flow (ways) of humanity and its challenges. Sometimes our decisions can tend to weigh us down even when they are not all that serious. That is not to say that some aren't!

THE RIGHT PLAN (COURSE) FOR YOUR LIFE AND HOW TO FIND IT, GET TO IT, AND LIVE "IN" IT

Like a car going down the road, we don't want to end up in a ditch or as with boats, shipwrecked! That is what this message is about, finding and staying "in" that sure path for your life. Wouldn't it be sad to be thinking that things are really going well and believing things are okay when actually you could be headed straight for trouble or in it and not realize it?

FROM HERE TO THERE

It is important to start out on the right path. Then it is important to stay on the right path. Finally it is important to end up at the correct and final destination point. *(2 Tim 4:7)* If you start in a straight line and your destination is a few miles up ahead and you get off just one degree then you will end up quite a ways from your intended destination and most likely not finish the course.

HOW I CAME INTO THE RIGHT PATH AND HOW I "KNOW" IT!

You might say at this point, "How do you know this?" A change so pervasive and strong came into my life when I was about five and a half years old. I experienced something so life enriching and powerful that I have to share and help others know that Truth. Ever since then, I have walked in the Truth, experienced Truth and found out that Truth is a Person. He is very real! He desires us to have a loving, and caring relationship with Him. Truth has a Name, His Name is Jesus. It is in a relationship with God's Son, Jesus Christ, which we experience and learn about Him. He is committed in His love and faithfulness toward us. Literally and figuratively speaking, it is God Who places and keeps our feet on His path in life. He is the One who designed and created your life, He knows all of the situations and circumstances you will ever encounter. He has a plan on how to deal with each situation or circumstance that arises. He is in control of His creation. When you hook up with Him, then you are on the correct path! (*Psalms 119:35, 119:105,* and *Proverbs 2:9*) He desires to bless you, enrich you, causing you to prosper in all areas of the life He has designed for you. He desires to help you, and encourage you. Those that find Him and enter in with Him will never be sorry.

AWAKENING TO TRUTH (GOD IS THE TRUTH)

There is only one True Truth. Even God's Word to us declares that God is Light and in Him is no darkness (deception or lies). When a person has the Truth opened up to them; then they can say the Truth has been revealed. True revelation can only come through those who have a relationship with God through Jesus Christ. The Truth will not only reveal new aspects about God but He will also open up new insights, wisdom, and revelations about life, self, and others around you and the way you perceive. Things will change because the touch of the Creator changes all who choose Him. This will happen because you are being transformed into His likeness.

WHY DOES THIS OCCUR?

We were originally made in His likeness, and in the likeness of His Precious Son, Jesus the Christ. We are of His design and He knows what is best for each of us. Notice I said He knows what is best for each of us. Usually we think we know what is best for us, this is called pride. When we think that way then we get in trouble! That is why the human race is so far away in their relationship with God, instead of knowing God, they are seeking "paths to enlightenment" but leaving God their Creator out of their thinking, their life, being blind themselves but thinking they truly see. They are those who continue stumbling down a mental path of self deception. We think we "have to" do things our way because we think we know best. In all actuality we simply need to come to God for all our needs. We need God all the time! It is God's persistent love for us and mercy that helps us endure the hardships of this life.

The help or revelation God gives us is to see and understand what is also missing in our lives or where we fall short. We are then able to realize "the condition that our condition is in!" This revelation from our Heavenly Father is not given to us to condemn us or beat us but as a loving Father He helps us see our need, where we fall short and need

His help, which without, we would never be able to make it! Our true need is to come to Him and embrace Him and all He has for us, Him and Life Eternal through His Son Jesus Christ. Our Heavenly Father dearly loves us! Yes, He loves and cares for you! Even when we were in darkness (ignorance) and opposed to Him, He loved us and gave His life for us! That my friend is True Love!

WE ARE NOT SO PERFECT AFTER ALL

Revelation will always affect our realization. Most people perceive everything going on in their life as good, good enough, close enough, near perfect, or perfect. Either way it is common for most people to settle for what seems to work well or is comfortable. Being comfortable or being at ease can be a major deception. Falling short of a mature or complete outcome by thinking you are "close enough to what it should be" is essentially saying "Well that's good enough for me" or "that's the way it should be." Our perception about the way life is going can be a lie that we readily accept. For example, "Everything seems to be flowing smoothly so why upset things by changing it now!" Most people think that if life is going good it has to be a "God thing!" Wrong!

HOW AN ENEMY OF OUR SOUL IS ALLOWED TO CREEP IN

Many people believe there is a God and for them that is "good enough." No, it is not enough! To just believe there is a God does not insure anything except that God "is" or "was" in their thinking somewhere, somehow, at sometime and I will deal with Him later when I have the time, things are okay, "I'm okay", or "I am too busy for this stuff now."

Friend, I have lived long enough to see people make that mistake. Things can so easily drive you away from God and His Truth: distractions, accidents, weddings, and even a death of a loved one. You don't know the day, the hour, minute or second your life can be taken from you! The Truth is that God's Word tells us that there is more to just believing that God "is". God tells us in His Word, *"Thou believest that there is one God; thou doest well: the devils also believe, and tremble." (James 2:19)* When all is said and done, these devils, or fallen angels, deceiving and lying spirits sent out to deceive mankind by God's enemy Satan, are not going to be in Heaven with God, they will be in a place set aside for them by God and this is not a good place to be!

THE SPIRITUAL REALM IS REAL

The spiritual realm is a real unseen existence, alive and active. There is a war going on of Satan, and his demonic spirits (evil), against God, and His angels, and praying saints (good). This war is for the possession of your soul; mind, will, and emotions. It is also about dominating the unredeemed spirit of that person.

There are many lies out there. Let me give you insight how these work to draw you away from God and the relationship He desires to have with you, and His plan for your life in Him.

> Lie #1.   All people will be forgiven and be in Heaven. God will surely forgive me without Jesus in my life.
> Lie #2.   There is no God or Devil.

3

Lie #3.　There is no Heaven or Hell.

Lie #4.　The Bible was just a book written by men.

Lie #5.　Religion was thought up by a man or men to control the masses.

Lie #6.　Man evolved.

Lie #7.　 believe some of the Bible is true and I don't take it so literal; I am okay.

Lie #8.　I can get to Heaven on my own good behavior or merit.

Lie #9.　I am good and I will be good and help others. (This is called "works.")

Lie #10.　I believe in God but I don't think I need to ask Jesus into my heart, because there are many ways to Him.

Lie #11.　I believe there is a God. I believe in God. This "cross" or "Jesus" thing is not for me.

Lie #12.　I believe in God, and His Son and what Jesus did. I am good, and that is good enough!

Lie #13.　I believe Jesus was just a Prophet sent by God.

Lie #14.　How can Jesus' Blood save anyone? ...that's a bloody religion. Do you expect me to teach my children that?

... IT'S GOD'S FAULT, WHAT KIND OF GOD WOULD..., AND THE LIST GOES ON!

The devil gives people excuses and reasons to believe God does not exist or that He is far off. The devil is also trying to persuade people into thinking they don't need God or that He is a weak God.

The devil, Lucifer, is a created being, a fallen Cherub, angel, who became twisted on the inside. "How art thou fallen from heaven, O Lucifer, son of the morning! How art thou cut down to the ground, which weakened the nations!" (Isaiah 14:12) The only power the devil has is the power you give him over yourself by believing his lies. These lies are like a trap, or a snare that take people captive. The devil, the enemy of God, and his evil followers on this planet are always trying to draw you and me away from our Heavenly Father, a relationship with Him, and His plan for our lives. Most people don't even realize when they are deceived or ensnared, that is how slick (devious) the devil is. The most dangerous thing I see in people that allows this deception to occur is pride. Pride is blindness to God and the reality that we need Him! Pride tells us that we can do things without God's help or intervention. That is dangerous. Through pride we become blinded, set in our minds and hearts to go another way (stiff necked), with a bad attitude (hard-hearted) and rebellious (against or opposing God). When blinded like that we can believe a lie or think we are okay even when we are not. God is the turning point, the turning around place, is in Him! We need God's help! We need God!

The Key

As for me and you, the key is to know and have a relationship with our Heavenly Father. This is not an option, nor an opinion, but Truth (which is greater than a fact)! Experienced Truth!!! We must realize that God is real and He has thoughts, feelings, power, and is pure love. God is pure in thought, intent, and motive! He is for us! He is telling you "I truly love you, come to me." God loves us and knows best for us. Anything else is a lie rejecting Him.

The Truth, The Whole Truth And Nothing But The Truth!

You cannot just have a part of God's Word or Truth. We must have the entire Truth. Just to believe that God is, is not enough! God's Word to us states, "As you believe in your heart AND confess with your mouth that Jesus Christ is Lord, then you are saved."

To be "saved" means that a conversion or a God-produced change takes place in a person due to Jesus Christ being received into your heart. I truly believe that there is a higher percentage of church members who believe that they are truly saved yet lack a true conversion.

This Is Extremely Important!

When you receive Jesus Christ into your heart, His character, and the power of God, will bring change into your life! Sometimes it is experienced and seen quickly and at other times it is not as evident.

Conversion can be defined as a change that takes place in our heart or spirit-man, through the Spirit of God. We are born into this world, separated from God, due to sin. We become awakened or "made alive" to God through the intervention of His Holy Spirit in our lives, moving us to repentance. Repentance is the turning away from our sinful nature, by acknowledging it in the presence of God's Holiness, where we see we fall short of being Holy like GOD, and then turning to God and receiving His help, mercy and grace, to empower us to change to God's ways and likeness. This is can only be done through the Holy Spirit as we submit or yield, to allow, this change to take place in us. The Holy Spirit helps us to see this need to receive Jesus Christ as Savior, who takes away our sins and to receive Him as Lord, to help us live a life right unto God. At this point, by an act of faith on our part (believing that God is and trusting Him), we ask Jesus Christ into our heart (inner man) as Savior and Lord. This is the process of giving our lives to and receiving Jesus Christ as our Savior and Lord. We are now born into the Kingdom of God as his dear sons or daughters!

After receiving Jesus Christ into your heart a "desiring" to remain in that relationship with Him will come alive or exist in you. Therefore you will "know" He lives in you! So please take your time reading this book.

You say that you believe? Then you are in a wonderful position or place! Rejoice in that, but do not stop reading. Let God's TRUTH confirm that to you as you read.

Who You Are And How A Person Can Be Separated From God And Not Realize It!

You are a spirit being in a body, with a mind, will, and emotions. These three parts, the mind, the will, and emotions make up your human soul. When Jesus is Savior in your life the "true" you, the spirit-man, will express itself through the soul into the world around you. Therefore when all things are in their correct God-given order then (God in our spirit-being) moves through our soul via His Holy Spirit; expressing Himself to the world through us; making known His Presence, His Love, and His Way. However, if Jesus is not Savior and Lord in your life then what ever thought pops up tends to rule and express itself, directing your life.

For example, let's take a light bulb with no electricity; it may be good and functional. It may exist but it does not shine forth shedding light. Now if that light bulb was a human being, not having experienced God, it would not know what it is missing, thinking life is okay, thinking that "this is life just the way it ought to be!" You know in life, light bulbs when placed in a light socket brings forth light, else it is thrown away! I thank God He didn't cast me out or throw me away! God saw me in my state of need and made a way for me through His Son Jesus Christ. God wants to come into your life, like electricity to a light bulb that is not perfect, to love you and get you connected to Him. He wants to shine in us and through us in a darkened (blinded and ignorant to God) and dying world that truly needs Him. The only thing we have to do is make the right choice (*Deuteronomy 30:19, Joel 3:14*) to come to Him, repent showing true regret of sin and being away from Him, acknowledge we need Him, and ask His Son Jesus Christ into our heart, which will allow that connection in our lives, then we will start to shine with God's Life and Light!

"The spirit of man is the candle of the Lord, searching all the inward parts of the belly." (Proverbs 20:27). What do candles do? Like light bulbs, they are meant to bring light to the room they are in. Light, in this case, brings revelation of what is in the room and understanding can then takes place. Just like a light being turned on in a darkened place, you will then see and understand exactly what is before you concerning God and this world. Ignorance (darkness) flees when God's Light comes in.

LET'S TAKE IT FROM THE TOP!

Here is the problem. When we are born, we are born in our human nature separated from God and the Truth of God, due to a spiritual fall or separation of Adam, the first man, from God; therefore our minds from one generation to the next, are corrupt, shaped by sinful (separating from God) tendencies. There is a veil of this sinful blindness or darkness that keeps us from seeing and understanding the Truth. Darkness can mask Truth out if we don't know Truth. We therefore cannot perceive the Truth on our own. When we belong to God through Jesus Christ, the Spirit of God helps to order and direct our thoughts. However, on our own, with misguided minds (with wrong or bad perceptions), we think we are okay. We think we can do anything right, apart from God, but in all actuality, we are deceived. We must have God, (like a light in a dark room) in us to even begin to understand how far off base we are or how bad we have missed what is really going on. God is not coming to us to condemn us but to reveal Himself and invite us to share with Him in His most wonderful Life and Light. Without the Truth and Light of God we will not understand why the world – those people fallen or separated from God, act and do the things they do. If you listen to what people say you can clearly hear their words justifying their actions and giving a clear broadcast of the darkened heart and mind they live in. God didn't make us robots. Instead, God gave us a choice, and it is up to each one of us to walk with Him or apart from Him. Thank God He didn't leave us, nor forsake us in that condition, but has provided a way back to our Heavenly Father through His Son Jesus Christ. Jesus said, *"I am the Way, the Truth, and the Life: no man cometh unto the Father, but my Me." (John 14:6)*

GOD MADE A WAY!

Jesus is the Way back to our Heavenly Father. The Word of God clearly states that our life is hid in Him. So if you want to find your purpose and fulfillment in this life, you can only find it in a relationship with our Heavenly Father through Jesus Christ. In God's eyes, everybody has value and worth. We must realize that we are God's creation and He loves us. He has also given us great potential, a purpose, and has a plan for our lives. Even if you were conceived outside of marriage; you are not an accident! The Lord tells us through His Word, *"I knew you before I formed you in your mother's womb..."*, Jeremiah 1:5. *"Yes, I have loved you with an everlasting love; therefore with loving-kindness have I drawn you..."*, (Jeremiah 31:3).

THE FIRST STEP IN FINDING HIS PURPOSE AND PLAN FOR YOUR LIFE IS TO GO TO HIM!

The way to God is through His Son, Jesus Christ. "For God so loved the world, that He gave His only begotten Son, that whosoever believeth in Him should not perish, but have everlasting life." (John 3:16)

It is that simple! For many people that is too simple. Most people "feel" they are not worthy and therefore do not want to go to God or cry out to Him. Others are blinded by pride and don't even realize it, self-sufficient not wanting to acknowledge a need for help. That is the fallen nature of mankind lying to you. The truth is that you are God's precious creation and He longs for you to come to Him! Other people feel or reason that they have to work to earn entrance into Heaven or some way "qualify" to get on "God's good side" so He will allow them into Heaven. That is not God's way and it will fail!

God tells us very clearly that He loves us. He then tells us that all have sinned and fallen short of His glory. Yes, even at one point in time, I, the person writing this book, was lost in sin, separated from God, but yet while Jesus was on the cross He counted it (you and me) as joy set before Him to die on that cross, for my sin and yours, which separated us from Him (Jesus) and God the Father. Jesus has made the Way (Path) back to God the Father. For this very reason God so loved you that He sent His only Son Jesus Christ as the perfect (substitute) sin offering to die on the cross for you and me.

> ..."I am the Way, the Truth, and the Life: no man cometh unto the Father, but by Me." (John 14:6)

Only Jesus' life sacrificed and His Blood could make atonement, pay in full, for our sins before our Heavenly Father! This was the only sacrifice acceptable to God the Father for our sins. This selfless act of love on God's part, through His Son, made a Way for us back to Him so we could once again enter into a relationship with Him. He so longingly desires for us to be with Him! Jesus Christ made it possible for you and me to become

7

accepted back into a place of fellowship with God, our Heavenly Father. Our part is to accept this gift of His love. Jesus paid the only acceptable price for our sins, so that we would no longer be separated by those sins from our Heavenly Father. It is now up to us individually to receive that gift. *(Romans 5:18)*

God did not plan to have you come on this earth just to watch you grow old and die. God cares about you! You are His creation! He desires a relationship with you here and now. Yes. I said a relationship! Yes, it is possible; I speak from that relationship even now, because that is where I live, move and have my being, which is in that relationship with Him!

> *"Looking unto Jesus the Author and Finisher of our faith; Who for the joy that was set before Him [that is you and me] endured the cross, despising the shame, and is set down at the right hand of the throne of God." (Hebrews 12:2)*

THE FEELING OF UNWORTHINESS IN HIS PRESENCE

Sometimes we realize God's awesomeness and we "feel" unworthy to be in His Presence or to go to Him, due to His true love and character. The truth is that when we become His dear children through Jesus Christ, we are made worthy and restored to Him. God desires us to do more than just ask Jesus Christ into our heart and become converted. We are to continue in an ongoing relationship with Him. Even in maintaining our relationship with Him, He knows that we need His help and He is faithful to us to supply it! This is not a come to Him "one time" deal! He desires for us to grow closer to Him, getting to know Him through an ongoing and continuous basis. As we mature and grow in Him many things in our lives will be seen for what they truly are, but remember, God already knew that those things were in your life before you chose to give your life to Him. Our Heavenly Father wants to reveal things to us so that we can see the lies that we have been told and believe. He wants us to be set free in areas of our lives where we are deceived (believe a lie and thinking we are okay). In other words, we come to Him and exchange whatever the darkness is, for the Truth and receive a fresh new way of thinking and living causing you and me to be changed, therefore coming closer to Him. He has taken the first step! It is now up to us to respond by taking the next step by accepting this gift of Eternal Life through Jesus Christ.

IS HELL REAL?

Yes! Most people do not take God seriously enough at His Word and that is sad. I was walking along one day and God quickly brought back into my mind an incident of a man who had driven his car to a wooded area. The man got out of his car, went up into the woods, and using a gun, killed himself. The man had a history of drugs and work-related problems. I was walking along the street where I lived one day, and I asked the Lord, "Is the man in Hell, Lord?" The Lord clearly and recognizably said, "Yes". At that moment, I was looking down toward the sidewalk and God gave me a vision of a dark hole. I saw this man stretching upward, trying to reach up and get out of this pit. Pain soared up out of this opening from him. This man was in pain! Fear and torment were easily seen on his face. I was allowed to experience a slight measure of it myself, it was horrible! I saw fire race up through him. The man screamed. The agony of the moment raced ever so briefly through me! Just as fast as I saw it and experienced it, it went away, and more was to come. A feeling of dread as to what might come next followed. I was left without words. I asked the Lord if this man had ever asked Jesus Christ into His heart. And the Lord said, "No". The man had been led down this darkened road through drugs and self-means (ideas and choices). The man was in excruciating torment. I remember thinking, "Oh God, if he had only asked Jesus Christ into his heart as his Savior and Lord, and had that relationship in his life, then he would not be there today." Physically we live this life only once and death marks the end of it. We each need to have our own relationship with our Heavenly Father through Jesus Christ! Those that do not follow God through receiving Jesus Christ as their Savior and Lord, AND do not obey His will are the same people who are actually saying to God that they desire to do their own thing. They are therefore in rebellion against Him, and are following the way of the devil.

All of this is plainly depicted throughout God's Word in *Psalms 9:17*. God's Holy and Righteous children will not be subject to the same place in eternity as the children of wrath. The children of wrath are those who will experience God's wrath in a place set aside for them, the devil and his kind, a place called Hell and the Lake of Fire! They have chosen it for themselves; no one forced them into opposition against God. We have all been given a free will by God and the right to make our own decision (choice); to receive Jesus Christ as our Savior (Who takes away our sins), and Lord (Who leads us in Life Eternal).

KNOWING YOU ARE SPEAKING TO THE GOD WHO CREATED YOU!

God has given all who choose to come to Him through His Son, Jesus Christ, Eternal Life. This brings all of humanity to the place where each of us must individually make a choice to receive Jesus Christ, God's only Son, into our heart. There is only One Way back to God (YHVH), some people use the name Jehovah here but that is not an exact Hebraic rendering of the Name of God the Father. So we know Who we are speaking of I want to give you some background now. The True Heavenly Father, decided what Way was the only acceptable Way, Himself. He didn't come and ask man's advice, being God! He decided and made the one and only acceptable Way back to Him. That Way is through His Son Jesus the Christ. We need to understand that "Jesus" was the Name of the human form; the man, or house, the spirit of the man Jesus would dwell in when He came to Earth) God the Father chose for Him. "Christ" is the Holy Spirit. Jesus was indwelt with the Holy Spirit and in-filled with the Holy Spirit (Ruach Ha Kodesh) of God (YHVH), Know the Truth and the Truth (Who is a Person, the Holy Spirit) will set you free! Jesus Christ is therefore called the Messiah (Yeshua). Who is alive forever more!

So as you can see clearly the Way back to God is not "Buddha", not "Mohammad", and not Allah, a false god. Messiah(Yeshua-Jesus Christ) is the Only True, acceptable sacrifice and therefore the Only True Way back to God our Heavenly Father.

9

Notice that when your mom called for you she did not use another name. For sake of the conversation let me be called "Sam". When you come into my place of work you don't say you are looking for "Joe" if you are trying to see me and talk with me, you ask for Sam.

It is sad to say, but many are deceived thinking that "YHVH" and "Allah" are one in the same. Not so! Many are being deceived with a demonic doctrine and are being given a bill of false peace, false unity, and a false sense of safety. Many are being sold out to the guise of "political correctness". Many are being taught that Allah is another name for the True God of Heaven. This Is Not So! To tell someone Allah is God is a LIE and is straight from the "father of lies", the devil or Satan himself! We are being confronted with a lie right to our face by the devil in the name of peace, a false peace and must be armed with the Truth so we are able to make the right choice. Choose Life, Jesus Christ as Savior and Lord, or choose death in a false god. The line is clearly drawn and seen. We do not bow to the false god Allah, but we choose Life, in Jesus Christ!

These words are not to attack the Muslim, for they too are sons of Abraham through Ishmael, son of the Egyptian bond servant Hagar, who was cast out from Abraham's camp. When their provisions had run out Hagar cried to the Lord, *"... and lift up her voice, and wept. And God heard the voice of the lad, and the angel of God called Hagar out of heaven, and said unto her, What aileth thee, Hagar? Fear not; for God hath heard the voice of the lad where he is. Arise, lift up the lad, and hold him in thine hand; for I will make him a great nation." Genesis 16:16-18.* God took care of Ishmael by providing water springing up in the desert. This verse prophetically implies that the sons of Ishmael may come to the Living Waters, of Jesus Christ (Yeshua), through repentance, and by accepting and receiving, Jesus Christ (Yeshua), as their Messiah, Lord and Savior.

God the Father, Lord Jesus Christ, and the Holy Spirit are the True and Living God, the Truth, the Life, and the Way, longsuffering, and compassionate, Creator of all things that exist. All things consists and are held together by Them. Jesus Christ has the fullness of the God-head. He is the Truth. He is Life Eternal. He is the Light of men. He is the One you need to be trusting and receiving, the One you should be following and pouring your life back to. Jesus Christ is the Only True Way back to your Heavenly Father.

Our Heavenly Father, through His Word to us in *2 Corinthians 5:18* says, *"But all things are from God, Who through Jesus Christ reconciled us to Himself* [received us into favor, brought us into harmony with Himself] *and gave to us the ministry of reconciliation* [that by word and deed we might aim to bring others into harmony with Him]." AMP

Verse 19, "It was God [personally present] *in Christ, reconciling and restoring the world to favor with Himself, not counting up and holding against* [men] *their trespasses* [but canceling them], and *committing to us the message of reconciliation* (of the restoration of favor)." AMP

We each have a free will to choose or not to choose Eternal Life (with God). We choose Eternal Life by asking His Son, Jesus Christ, into our heart, and allowing Him to change

10

us from there outward! *John 3:16* clearly states, *"For God so loved the world that He gave His Only begotten Son that whosoever believeth in Him shall not perish but have Eternal Life."* Perish means to die, death, spiritual death, being separated from God eternally. Thank God that it is not His desire for us to be separated from Him. Instead God so loved us that He made a Way back to Himself through Jesus Christ.

Psalms 49:8 says, "For a soul is far too precious to be ransomed by mere earthly wealth. There is not enough of it in all the earth to buy eternal life for just one soul, to keep it out of hell."

SOME MAJOR STUMBLING BLOCKS, PIT FALLS, AND WRONG BELIEFS ABOUT "GETTING INTO HEAVEN"

- Many do not believe God at His Word, and that Jesus Christ is alive even in the flesh, today. God, through His Word to us, clearly states that Jesus Christ appeared after His death and resurrection to: Mary, two men on the Damascus road, to the disciples in a room, and to countless others. Was this just as a spirit? No! Did He actually come in the flesh? Yes! Let's look at the evidence recorded in God's Word. Thomas, a disciple of Jesus Christ, was not with the other disciples the first time they saw Jesus after the crucifixion and resurrection. When the other disciples reported the appearance of Jesus to Thomas, he doubted this occurrence! When Jesus appeared a second time to the disciples, "doubting Thomas" was there and not only saw Him but also TOUCHED the nail-scared places in Jesus' hands. Thomas commented saying, "My Lord, my God!" *(John 20:28)*. Wow! You cannot ask for any greater witness or testimony than that! Jesus resurrected and alive in the flesh! Many other people also saw Him ascend into the clouds out of sight.
- Many have not confessed Jesus as their personal Savior, the One True awaited Messiah. He came in the flesh, died on the cross, and God raised Him from the dead: spirit, soul, and body. As you believe in your heart and confess with your mouth then you will be saved, that is, born into the Kingdom of God as His dear son or daughter. It only takes simple childlike faith (belief and trust) to enter into God's Kingdom.
- Many think they are good and that they have done good works, therefore God will let them into Heaven on that basis. "I am good." There are tons of people who for various reasons think that because of their right standing (reputation) in the community, by being a member of a church, rightfully justifying their actions before themselves with good deeds or works they have done "for God", that they are in good-

standing with God. These people think they will be in Heaven one day. They may even think that God wouldn't dare do anything but accept them. **WRONG!** This is a wakeup call folks! Just because you do good works or think you are the way you should be it is not enough. You might be saying "I did this..., I did that..., I prayed..., I talk with God..., and I have this understanding with God..., I will make God..., I have a certain degree from this Seminary, I was ordained by Pastor Billy, I was an Elder at ..., or I was a Deacon at ..., or I was a Bishop at ..., I cut the grass at church, or I helped widow Jenkins." Sorry, that will not get you into Heaven. *(Titus 3:3-7)*

- Many think that by reading the scriptures they can obtain an entrance into Heaven. The Holy scriptures of God are from the Spirit of God. God by His Holy Spirit breathed the scriptures into men who have penned the various books of the Bible for over thousands of years. Just picking up God's Word and reading the scriptures does not change your heart. That would be like trying to obtain entrance into Heaven through "intellectual ascent", which is also a type of "works" or trying to gain entrance into Heaven by "doing" something good (i.e., to achieve your way into Heaven). The Word of God clearly states that man's own righteousness is as dirty rags. *(Isaiah 64:6)* God's Word says in *John 5:37-40, "And the Father Himself, which hath sent me, hath borne witness of me. Ye have neither heard His Voice at any time, nor seen His shape. And ye have not His Word abiding in you: for whom He hath sent Him ye believe not ye search the scriptures for in them ye think ye have eternal life and they are they which testify of me. And ye will not come to Me, that ye might have life."* (That "life" means Eternal Life in the Heavenly Father, through His Son, Jesus Christ.) One of the purposes of the scriptures is to testify of Him. The Word of God was designed to be received into your spirit, and that can only take place by the aid of God's Spirit, the Holy Spirit. The Holy Spirit quickens (makes understood) what God is speaking to us in our mind. The process works like this: the Holy Spirit communicates to our spirit-man who in turn communicates to our mind (soul) the things of God. (God's revelation and understanding then comes forth.) *"The spirit of man is the candle of the LORD, searching all the inward parts of the belly." (Proverbs 20:27)*

- Many think they can enter by their own merit or ability. Our righteousness (right-ness before God) without Jesus Christ is as dirty rags. *(Isaiah 64)*. The only Righteousness acceptable to God comes through Jesus Christ by means of His shed Blood. As the verses above in *John 5:37-40*, infer, we desperately need to go to Him; the One Who has Life and is Life. Do not let your personal problems with God and His Word hinder you in going to Him. We need to accept Him at His Word and know that He has our best interest at heart! In the beginning was the Word and the Word was with God and the Word was God *(John 1:1)*. God and His Word are inseparable! The Word is as much a part of Him as Jesus His Son and His Holy Spirit is. The Word was made flesh and dwelt among us, the Son of God, Jesus Christ. *(John 1:14)* Only through Jesus Christ and His Blood can we be deemed as right before God.

HOW TO MOVE PAST ANY STUMBLING BLOCKS

- KNOWING you can have Eternal Life! It is written in God's Word to you and me in I John 5:13, that you can know you have (now) Eternal Life. That means exactly what it says "you can know" or you can be sure that once you ask Jesus Christ into your heart, He is there and with you! This restored relationship only comes through Jesus Christ, our resurrected and living Savior. There is no other way back to the Father, but through His Son. Only through Jesus Christ can a man's life be redeemed. God tells us this in His Word and God is not a liar, unlike man. He does what He says. He is Who He says He is. *(Hebrews 6:18)* God is love. *(1 John 4:16)* You can absolutely trust God! I have experienced that during 100% of my relationship with Him in these last 42 plus years and so have countless others who have experienced His Mercy, His Faithfulness, and Loving Kindness!

- If you truly desire Him and seek Him, He will not turn you out! Wow! What a statement!!! There is no rejection or messing up! God is not looking for a chance or excuse to "whack" you. Get rid of that earthly thinking! When that type of thinking arises just know that it does not come from God. Don't worry about making a mistake. God looks at and knows your heart. He loves you dearly. So, don't argue with Him! Dear child, God loves you and through Jesus Christ He has made a clear-cut way to back to Him. There is no other path, way, or whatever you might call it, back to the Heavenly Father. *(Hebrews 12:13)*

- There are no excuses for not coming to Him! "For He saith, I have heard thee in a time accepted, and in the day of salvation have I succoured (helped) thee: behold, now is the accepted time; behold, now is the day of salvation." (2 Corinthians 6:2)

HOW TO ASK JESUS CHRIST INTO YOUR HEART

- First, by an action of faith. We go to God, believing and trusting that He is all that He has said He is, and will do for us all He has said He will do through His Son, Jesus Christ.
- Second, by acting upon that belief. ("a step of faith") In accordance with your faith, we believe and trust God, and ask Jesus Christ to come into your heart. (He will just as He has promised!)

You can receive Jesus into your heart now by praying and trusting God at His Word. God knows the desire of your heart and is ready to come and live in you and through your spirit. He will not turn you away. This is the way to taste and see, and know (and continue to know) that the Lord is good!

I ask you to get in a place now, where you will not be disturbed, so you can get quiet in the privacy of your own mind with Him. How do you know He is there with you? He is omnipresent, which is an attribute of God. He can be with someone in China and be with you here at the same moment in time. Trust me, I know what I am telling you. It's a God thing! Be determined to block out all interferences, get still, quiet, and serious with God. Tell God you are serious about what you are about to pray. Will He hear you? Absolutely! He loves you, you are His creation. He has been waiting on you to come to Him and He is listening to you right now!

IF YOU HAVE ALREADY ASKED JESUS CHRIST INTO YOUR HEART

Even if you have previously prayed a prayer asking Jesus Christ into your heart, asking Jesus into your heart again is not wrong before God. I encourage you to say the following prayer and say it with meaning in your heart (sincerely or in your best effort). This will only strengthen you in Him because it demonstrates your commitment to the Lord. That is your faith and heart's determination!

SOME BASIC REASONS PEOPLE THINK THEY ARE SAVED BUT ARE NOT

- They do not believe Jesus Christ is risen from the dead and is alive today: spirit, soul, and body.
- They have not confessed Jesus as Lord and Savior before man.

We can lead you through the prayer part but you will need to believe and confess Jesus Christ as Savior and Lord yourself! Then confess Him as your Savior and Lord before another person. Please pray with me now focusing your heart's desire to be His Kingdom child!

PRAYER OF SALVATION

Heavenly Father, I come to You now, I acknowledge You as God, creator of Heaven and Earth. Heavenly Father I confess that I am a sinner. I have sinned against You. I believe in my heart that Jesus Christ is Your Son and You sent Your Son to Earth, and that he was born of a virgin. I believe that Jesus Christ is the One true sacrifice for my sins. I believe that Jesus Christ was crucified on a cross as a sacrifice for the sins of the world, sins which have blinded me and separated me from You. I believe, Heavenly Father, that You sent Jesus Christ to personally die for me. I believe Jesus Christ, Your Son, took upon Himself all of my sins and the sins of all mankind. I believe Jesus, who knew no sin, became sin for me that I may receive Eternal Life. I believe Heavenly Father; You raised Jesus Christ from the dead and He is alive and well, seated at Your Right Hand in Heaven. I now repent (turn) from my sins and choose to follow and obey Jesus Christ as my Lord and Savior. I ask You Jesus Christ to be the Lord of my life and to lead me in all areas of my life. Jesus Christ I receive You as my Lord and Savior with all my heart and believe that You are my King and My God. Lord Jesus Christ, fill me with Your Holy Spirit, and use my life as a willing vessel. Heavenly Father, I ask that my life glorify You. Thank You Heavenly Father for my salvation by faith in Jesus Christ and the Truth of Your Word,
In Jesus' Name, Amen

For those who just can't seem to say that prayer, try saying this prayer first:

Heavenly Father, I come to You and ask You in Jesus' Name to set me free from any wrong thoughts, fear, doubt, unbelief, believing any lies, any lies of the enemy, the devil, or demonic spirits, any thoughts that I have that are hindering me now in coming to You. I ask You, Father God, to deliver me now of all hindrances to becoming Your born-again Kingdom child, in Jesus Christ's Holy Name. I resist the devil and all his demonic spirits must flee and leave my presence. Lord God, remove the lies and the hindrances and help me so I can say the above prayer of salvation in earnest from my heart! I ask You to force out, drive out, and bind all evil things far away from me.
In Jesus' Name. Amen

Now, go back and choose to say the prayer before this last one, with all of your heart, soul and being!

If you prayed the prayer asking Jesus Christ into your heart as your Savior and Lord, and you meant it, then you need to realize that the Living God, Creator of Heaven and Earth now lives within you! That is awesome! God is awesome!!!

After saying the Salvation Prayer, thank God for what He has done for you!

THANKSGIVING FOR SALVATION

Thank You Heavenly Father, God. I love You, and thank you Jesus, and thank you Holy Spirit. Thank You. Lord thank You for all that You have done for me by making me Your son/daughter through the shed Blood of Jesus Christ. Thank You, Lord Jesus for taking all of the sins, the guilt, the shame, and the weight of all burdens of those sins from my shoulders. Cause me Lord to live and move in Your ways, to hear and know

You all the days of my life, and walk with You in Your Righteousness forevermore! Lord Jesus Christ, teach me what it means to abide (live) in You, and You in me, no matter what this world (fallen/corrupt life) or the devil throws at me. Your "Will" be done in and through my life as a light, so other people may come to You and know You!

In Jesus' Name. Amen

Continue to praise Him! Get some praise and worship CD's or music and celebrate Jesus!

NAIL IT DOWN

The next best thing you can do is to immediately talk to someone, or call someone, another believer in Christ, and tell them what you have just done! The Word of God tells us to tell others. This allows you to confess the Name of Jesus before man, and it also strengthens you in Him. Write what you just did on a piece of paper, date it, sign it, put it in a special place, and go out and celebrate it!

Please note, the devil will come, either sooner or later, and try to get you to believe you didn't become God's child or that this was not real to begin with. The devil will use anybody or anything to do this! Not everybody is going to agree with or like what you just did, and there are reasons for that. Don't let that stop you! They need to hear it. It might be the very testimony they have waited for, or that God uses you to bring them into His Kingdom. However, if at first they don't agree, don't be discouraged. They have been living in darkness a long time. It is not up to you to change that. That is the work of the Holy Spirit!

You are a new creature in Christ, celebrate, rejoice and be glad. Then go forth and never deny Jesus as being Your Savior and Lord.

ASSURANCE OF SALVATION

I am going to pray for you the reader, "Heavenly Father, I ask You in the Name of Your Son Jesus Christ, to continue to affirm this new believer in Christ with a strong sense of Your Presence in and upon their life. I ask You Lord to reveal to each of these who asked Jesus into their hearts, that their sins are as far from them as the East is from the West, gone, never to return to them again. I ask Lord that Your Holy Spirit speak to, minister, and guide each one of these people in a definite way, according to Your plan for their lives. Heavenly Father, I pray that You grant them a deep inner peace and resolve in their entire being, that they can know that they have entered an Everlasting Blood Covenant with You, a covenant where You said You would never, never, never, leave them nor forsake them. *(Hebrews 13:5-6)* Also Father, teach them to know they can depend on You. Lord, I ask that Your Kingdom come and Your Will be done in each of their lives. Heavenly Father, strengthen them, cause them to Hear and Know Your Voice, keep them from all harm and tricks of mankind, keep them from the Devil and his fallen angels, teach Your Kingdom children, and grow them in Your love, wisdom, power, and by the leading of Your Holy Spirit. Lord God, place within them strongly, the desire to become a praise and a glory unto You all the days of their lives. Lord, empower them to praise and glorify You, in Jesus Christ's Holy Name, I ask all of

these things according to Your Will and Your Word in the *Book of John, Chapter 14, verses 13 and 14.*
In Jesus' Name. Amen"

Now start getting acquainted with God the Father, God the Son, and God the Holy Spirit, His Word, and His Ways.

- Read His Word (Start in the Book of John, one chapter a day). The Book of John is included in this book.
- Pray: Lord Jesus, reveal to me what I am reading in Your Word.
- Pray (communicate with Him). Set aside a time for just you and Him! Talk to Him as you go through your day. He is interested even in the small things in your life!
- Have fellowship and communion with Him. Love Him with all your heart, soul, mind, strength, and obedience.
- Fellowship with other true believers. Father God has other children we can fellowship with. (Other brothers and sisters in Christ!)
- Study the Word to prove yourself and be approved unto the Lord, so you may walk in His precepts, principles, and ways as He reveals them to you. (1 Corinthians 2:13 and 1 John 2:27)
- Share Jesus and your new life (experiences) in Christ with others.

NEW BEGINNINGS

You are now "born again" into the Kingdom of God, restored to Him. When this occurs, the Spirit of God, the Holy Spirit, enters into you when you relinquish your spirit to God through the act of believing God, turning from your sinful nature, to trusting God, and then by an act of faith, asking Jesus Christ into your heart as Savior and Lord of your life. This allows God's Holy Spirit to come into you and place the seal of God's redemption upon your heart (inner man).

And last but not least the Word of God is clear in *Mark 16:16, "He that believeth and is baptized shall be saved; but he that believeth not shall be damned."* Baptism is the outward sign of the inward work of the heart, your heart. You will also need to find a Christian brother or sister in Christ who has been baptized, to baptize you.

"And baptism, which is a figure [of their deliverance], does now also save you [from inward questionings and fears], not by the removing of outward body filth [bathing], but by [providing you with] the answer of a good and clear conscience (inward cleanness and peace) before God [because you are demonstrating what you believe to be yours] through the resurrection of Jesus Christ." 1 Peter 3:21 (AMP)

FEELINGS

Some people do feel something at this point and some people don't. Don't worry about that! If you meant it then don't question it! What you have to really come to terms with is that now you have Him "in" you! It is settled, a "done deal". You have been in this world a long time operating and being tuned to worldly ways of thinking, feeling, and doing. I call that "the flesh." Realize this, our walk with God is not about our thoughts - logic or rationalization, what we do for a living, and it is not about our feelings. Our walk now is to be focused in a faith-based realm wherein we have a "trust and obey" relationship with our Heavenly Father. It may take some time to get your thinking, feelings, and emotions turned around, or ordered by God's Ways, Word and Spirit, but they will come with God's help, as we diligently seek Him. Give yourself time! I have been there and I am still walking by faith. This is not a fast or speedy "microwave" process. Give yourself and God time. I know what I am talking about!

DO NOT WORRY! (Matthew 6:25-34)

(Worrying is a sin anyway.) I know what I have experienced in my walk with the Lord! You will want to get more of the Word in you, and spend more time in prayer with Him. You will want to spend more time with His children (other believers in Christ, your new family, your brothers and sisters in Christ). Your target or goal is to get to know Him and spend more time in His Presence. Allow Him to bring change in Your Life.

Just as the natural person needs natural food to grow; now you will want to feed your spirit-man spiritual food and drink to continue to grow. Feed before Him in prayer on the Book of John. Ask Him to reveal His Word and Himself to You! Ask Him questions and keep a journal, expectantly waiting for His answers. Even today I thirst and hunger for more of God. The Word of God says you will find Him if you seek Him with all your heart, all your soul, and all your being. God desires you to draw near to Him, and in doing so, He promises to draw near to you! In doing so you will continue to grow into the likeness of His dear Son, Jesus Christ. God will reveal Himself to you.

WHAT IF I SIN AGAIN AFTER ASKING JESUS INTO MY HEART?

After becoming one of His dear children you will still make mistakes and get into sin. Hopefully you will not sin as often as time goes and you mature in Christ. Just in case you do then know that the Word of God in 1 John 1:9 says, "If we confess our sins, He is faithful and just to forgive us our sins and to cleanse us from all unrighteousness." Once we confess our sins, they are gone, never to be remembered by God (Jeremiah 31:34). He will never bring up confessed sins, nor hold them against us. His mercy and grace is sufficient. We are not to deliberately sin. He will deal with you and deliver you from that. Ask the Lord to take all the guilt and shame, wrong memories, and urges away from you. He loves you!!! He will never, never, never, leave you nor forsake you! So, don't bring up past confessed sin that has been forgiven. All you are doing is beating yourself up. God has cast forgotten it. He might be saying to you, "What are you talking about?" If you have confessed your sin with true regret (a true repentant heart). He has already forgiven you, and He wants you to forgive yourself! God doesn't want us focused on sins. He wants us to be Him (God) conscious. *"Finally, brethren, whatever things are true, whatever things are noble, whatever things are just, whatever things are pure, whatever things are lovely, whatever things are of good report, if there is any vir-*

tue and if there is anything praiseworthy — meditate on these things. The things which you learned and received and heard and saw in me, these do, and the God of peace will be with you." Phil 4:8-9 NKJV

Now where is our focus suppose to be now Mr., Miss, or Mrs. New Creature in Christ?! Not sin! Not demons! On Him and His goodness. Yes!

It is Written God's final authority on the matter is given to us through His Word in 1 John 5:13 as follows "These things have I written unto you that believe on the Name of the Son of God; that ye may know that ye have Eternal Life, and that ye may believe on the Name of the Son of God." See, there it is! You can know! Very plain and very straight forward. Now receive that Truth, and believe on the Name of the Son of God, and receive Him into Your heart.

After asking Jesus Christ into your heart, He now lives within you. You can now walk in total confidence knowing for sure that He is in you! Jesus said, *"You shall love the Lord your God with all your heart, with all our soul, and with all your mind,' This is the first and great commandment. And the second is like it: 'You shall love your neighbor as yourself."* (Matthew 22:37-39) We need to always continue to ABIDE in Jesus Christ by seeking Him through,

- prayer,
- fellowship with other believers where God is the center of attention (we are the "church") this should include praise and worship,
- time with Him in His Word (the Bible),
- telling others about Him – what experiences we have had with Him (witnessing),
- Praise and Worship of the Lord – a time when we exalt God from our heart!

God desires an ongoing and growing relationship with us! This is the place, in Him, you are to "be" from now on, and not stray from! Jesus Christ is our resting place in God! Finally, continue to believe in, trust in, lean on, rely on, and cleave to the Lord Jesus Christ with all of your heart growing in Him, *(Proverbs 3:5-7). "When I passed by you again and looked upon you, indeed your time was the time of love; so I spread My wing over you and covered your nakedness. Yes, I swore an oath to you and entered into a covenant with you, and you became Mine,"* says the Lord GOD. Ezek 16:8.

Having Jesus Christ in your heart is the difference between having a Relationship with God which is Life and a religion which is not a relationship with God. It is the Holy Spirit within us that allows this close knit interaction with God, hearing Him, knowing Him, not just a knowing of Him, and maturing in Him. Religion is only a band aid, not Eternal Life. We desperately need a Relationship with God. This only comes through asking Jesus Christ into our hearts, then getting to KNOW Him! He is ready and willing to bring you in to an intimate relationship, and then a daily walk with Him. God wants to spend time and Eternity with you. You can know for sure He is always with you when you are awake or asleep, moment by moment! Jesus said, *"I am the Way, the Truth, and the Life: no man cometh unto the Father, but by Me." (John 14:6)*

Now, that you are His child by asking Jesus Christ into your Heart Now, that you have been born into God's Kingdom through asking Jesus Christ into your heart, you are His child. As a child of God you need to feed your spirit on God's spiritual Word! We want to encourage you to read, meditate, and pray on the Gospel of John. The Lord says in His Word to us that if we will ASK, when seeking Him, that He will give it to us. Here is the way I remember it;

A
sk and it will be given to you.

S
eek and you shall find.

K
nock and it will be opened unto you.

This comes from *Matthew 7:7*. He also says that we have not because we ask not, so ask the Lord to teach you and give you understanding of what you are reading in His Word and to place His Word in your heart so that you will grow in Him! We also encourage you to read from the books of *Proverbs* and *Psalms*. Ask the Lord to reveal Himself and what He wants you to learn or possess in His Word to you daily. Don't ever quit reading the Word of God. Why? After He lays one foundation and area of Life into you then He desires to reveal more of Himself in the same or different areas of growth or maturity. We are the Temple of the Holy Spirit. Let us always be humble, that is, seeing that we always need God, no matter how we think or feel. This attitude will never fail you. Continue always to **ASK.** God really loves it when we come to Him!!! He doesn't condemn us, go to Him humbly, do not be afraid, He knows our hearts and what is best for us!

TO OUR NEW BROTHERS AND SISTERS IN CHRIST

> *"The Lord Bless you and keep you, the Lord make His face shine upon you and be gracious to you; The Lord lift up His countenance upon you, And give you peace" Numbers 6: 24-26.*

The Lord bless you in your rising up, your laying down, your going out, your coming in, all that you put your hands to, to prosper for the Lord and His Kingdom, angels be about you to guard and protect you, and yours in your leisure, in your work, and as you go in life.
In Jesus' Name. Amen

Trust in the LORD with all your heart, And lean not on your own understanding; In all your ways acknowledge Him, And He shall direct your paths. Do not be wise in your own eyes. *"Fear the LORD and depart from evil. It will be health to your flesh, And strength to your bones" Proverbs 3:5-8* NKJV

Speak to the Lord as you go through your day. From the time your eyes open, right on through till they shut at night. Abide in Him and obey in these little things of the Lord all the days of your life! Enjoy your journey with the Lord!

RESTORATION

Restoration is to be brought back to our position and condition before the foundation of the world when we were chosen. At our spiritual birth into the Kingdom of God through Jesus Christ, we were immediately made the righteousness of God in Christ. We were justified, cleansed and redeemed from the curse of the Law of sin and death. We were purchased with the Precious Blood of Jesus Christ, made His Own and adopted into His family. We are given the mind of Christ as we were reconciled to God and given the Ministry of Reconciliation as ambassadors of the Kingdom of God. We have been by grace justified and made whole.

We were restored to that place in God, before the fall, in which Adam fell from dominion into sin consciousness, where Adam saw his own nakedness before God. This means there was a point in time however before Adam had "fallen" into sin consciousness. At this point before Adam's fall mankind did not need restoration back to God. The time I am referring to, even before Adam, was the laying of the foundation of the world. Even before that scripture states that BEFORE the foundation of the world the Lord knew us, meaning we had an interactive relationship with Him, He knew us and we knew Him. In restoration, we are brought back into that vital relationship of knowing Him again. This is the place the Lord wants us to realize that in Christ, we are, in Him.

It is all about Him, God, Jesus. It is all about knowing Him Face to Face, knowing Him and His Ways. The Word says Moses knew His Ways, and the children of Israel knew His "acts". God's "acts" are great and wonderful but not as near as He is! We are seated in the Heavenly Places with the Lord, BE STILL, and know that He is God, He is in control. Do not fret, nor squirm, do not get up out of your protected Heavenly position and get back into the "Adam" mind set trying to figure things out, that is Adam thinking. We are to possess and have the mind of Christ! The devil is defeated! LET GOD! Let God arise and defeat your enemies and heal you. The Word of the Lord says to Call Upon the Lord. Let God be God, so you are healed, made whole, and restored in all areas. Whatever ails you take it to God in prayer, confessing God's Word believing! Stop that mind set! (Gal. 5:1) That is why Jesus shed His Blood for you in the first place, restoration to the Heavenly Father! That is whole, that is complete in: spirit, soul, and body!

Be restored and don't let anyone rob you of your inheritance! Know Whose you are, Who you are, where you came from, where you are. Know you are seated in the Heavenly Places with your Lord and where He is leading you, speaking to you now! Just BE, learn to be content in Him as you were before the foundation of this world were formed, in Him! We are to become Ambassadors of Christ and His Kingdom reconciling men and women to Christ. We are also called by the Lord to be Restorers of the Breach between mankind and God. God through the Holy Spirit desires to restore other's spirit, mind, desires, will, emotions, and body in to that divine creature we are to be.

RESTORED WALKING IN THE LIGHT WITH OUR LORD IN THE MIND OF CHRIST

Let this mind be in you who was also in Christ Jesus, Who, being in the form of God, did not consider it robbery to be equal with God, but made Himself of no reputation, taking the form of a bondservant, and coming in the likeness of men. And being found in appearance as a man, He humbled Himself and became obedient to the point of death, even the death of the cross. Therefore God also has highly exalted Him and given Him the name which is above every name, that at the Name of Jesus every knee should bow, of those in heaven, and of those on earth, and of those under the earth, and that every tongue should confess that Jesus Christ is Lord, to the glory of God the Father.

"But what things were gain to me, these I have counted loss for Christ. Yet indeed I also count all things loss for the excellence of the knowledge of Christ Jesus my Lord, for whom I have suffered the loss of all things, and count them as rubbish, that I may gain Christ and be found in Him, not having my own righteousness, which is from the law, but that which is through faith in Christ, the righteousness which is from God by faith; that I may know Him and the power of His resurrection, and the fellowship of His sufferings, being conformed to His death, if, by any means, I may attain to the resurrection from the dead" Philippians 3:7-11

"Trust in the LORD with all your heart, And lean not on your own understanding; In all your ways acknowledge Him, And He shall direct your paths. Do not be wise in your own eyes; Fear the LORD and depart from evil. It will be health to your flesh, And strength to your bones. Honor the LORD with your possessions, And with the first-fruits of all your increase; So your barns will be filled with plenty, And your vats will overflow with new wine" Proverbs 3:5-10

Recommended Reading: "Chosen For Greatness" by Kelley Varner

Entering The Holy of Holies/Entering Our Heavenly Father's Presence

How Do We Enter In With God? . According To His Biblical Pattern!

In the Old Testament, *Exodus 25 - 27*, our Heavenly Father set forth a pattern for the Tabernacle, in which He would dwell, the place of worship and coming to know Him. Today, we are that Tabernacle dwelling with the Holy Spirit; the place of worship is in our hearts. Most people think of worship as going to a place or building to lift hands and sing to God. True worship is an intimate relationship and exchange with God the Father, the Son and the Holy Spirit. This can only take place in your innermost being, a place called your heart or spirit man.

Oh But I Know How To Worship Already!

I am continually learning and growing in God. To say that I know, is to cut myself off from continued learning with God. This also restricts or retards growth with the Father, Son, and Holy Spirit. As Christians we are to be constantly maturing in the Lord. When we think all is done, we have just put ourselves on the sidelines. Don't limit God by this prideful attitude of "I already know this (whatever it is)."

According To Pattern

With God all things are done according to pattern, His pattern, His way. God has set this pattern for prayer forth, God's way not ours, else it will fail somewhere down the line. How wonderful it is to be rapture into His awesome Presence, to a place where you are not aware of time and space anymore. You will be consumed with nothing but HIM. In Him we live and move and have our being. A friend once told me to pray before I pray. Entering in with God is not about you, it is all about Him! Death to self will take place. The more you enter in with Him, the deeper you will go and there will be more of Him and less of you. The flesh, or worldly, ways are not allowed to go in with God and are left out, that is called death to self. In other words the deeper you go with God the more opportunity you will have to be changed into His likeness. This is where we are putting off the old man and the old man's ways, the character and nature, and in turn putting on the new man with Christ's character and nature; an exchange takes place. It is there with Him that we are transformed into His likeness or image. The more you surrender to God the more you desire to be with Him. You exchange your agenda, life, etc., and in turn receive and choose to keep and walk in His Life, His Character, His Ways, His Thoughts, His Peace, His Order and His timing, which is called "being in Him" or "abiding in Him". To sum it up you will learn to let go of anything that hinders you in this earthly existence so you can get still before Him and into His Presence. In this stillness you will get to know Him. You will also learn to allow Him to position you for a deeper "letting go" and true stillness before Him. Deeper intimacy will occur. Realize however this is not a "microwave" type experience. When you allow Him to position you, realize that learning is about to take place!

Let go of the earthly, be still before Him, and know that He is God. Intimate time with God starts here, a Life giving exchange and getting to know Him!

At this point in prayer I sing a song which echoes the longing and heart-felt desire to be with God. You will be drawn through the veils that separate you from God. Along the way, with the Holy Spirit, during this time, with the Lord, these hindrances, or veils, and their effects should tremendously decrease. You will start becoming more aware that you are coming before a great and all powerful God, who loves you!

STRUGGLES WILL PURSUE YOU

Struggles will pursue, and try to entangle, you as you go further into God's Presence. They will try to keep you or draw you out but there are some easy techniques I will share with you that He wants you to learn so you can continue on in this time, with Him. All the time you are in prayer you will be developing and growing "in Him", and should become more dependent upon Him. Remember this: God wants you there with Him too! It is a privilege to come into His Presence. In Him abides His deep enriching peace which passes all understanding.

THE JOURNEY BEGINS

A FEW STEPS TO A SUCCESSFUL AND JOYFUL TIME WITH GOD

At first, I strongly suggest that you have a prayer closet, a place where you and a few others can go so you will not be disturbed. My prayer closet is downstairs in a secluded place, yet it is still not impervious to noises. I have found in the past that the days and the times the Lord calls me into this type of prayer are when things are quiet around the house. The kids are out, and my spouse is not home from work. I leave the cell phone upstairs where I cannot hear it. You might set the ringers on the phones to "off." I usually unplug the downstairs phone. Sometimes, things will happen, like the dog will bark, or there will be some incredible "boom", or noise. Just realize you must stay on track with the Lord! Be determined! The flesh of loved ones will rise up and you will be interrupted. The Devil will stir up problems during this time to disrupt or keep you out of this intimate time with the Lord. When interruptions occur you will have to either ask the Holy Spirit to take you back where you were or start over. Simply know that you love these people and animals. Do not let it disturb you! Love them and let the disturbance go. Continue to enter in with God, press in! We will talk about how to deal with those outer distractions and "self" during this time of communion with the Holy Spirit, the Lord Jesus Christ and our Heavenly Father. Whatever you do, stay on course! One obvious course of action is to lovingly inform those around you of what you are doing, that this time is set aside to be with the Lord. Unless the house is burning down, or someone is seriously hurt, then they are not to interrupt you until you emerge from your prayer room. Whatever happens don't get into sin, it isn't worth it! LOVE above all! If someone calls, let it ring or tell a family member to take a message. If someone comes to the front door, either tell family members to not answer it or let others know you are not to be disturbed. How you handle it is between you and the Lord, but do it graciously! If God called you to get with Him, He comes first! Know this, if someone is hurt or in pain, go to them and help them! God understands!

I will say from experience that God directs me when I am to come to Him in this deeper way. So far it hasn't been every day. For me, this helps my time with Him continue to be a privilege and not a ritual, a relationship and not a religion, a joy and not tiresome.

THE FIRST THINGS FIRST (ON THIS SIDE OF THE VEIL)

THE EARTHLY REALM

When you are clean or have prayed and are cleansed of sin, strongholds, bondages, demonic spirits, curses, evil or wrong prayers, assignments coming against you, unrighteous agreements have been destroyed, controlling prayers, instruments of unrighteousness driven out, evil principalities, powers, and rulers in high places severed from you, you have been cleansed by the Blood, and have the Armor of God on, you are protected by the Blood, then you are ready to begin to approach the Lord Jesus Christ and our Heavenly Father. Personally I ask the Lord according to *John 14:14* to loose His angels around me and to keep out all demonic spirits from coming anywhere near me, the house or the land, as the last thing I do before entering in with Him. You are now ready to start a walk with the Holy Spirit which will lead you into the Holy Place to meet with our Messiah and then from there to the Holy of Holies to be with our Heavenly Father.

AN OVERVIEW OF WHERE YOU ARE HEADED

There are several areas we will go through from here to the Holy of Holies.

Preparation For Entering In

By prayer we need to confess our sins, repent, and ask for forgiveness. Continue to get cleaned up as I mentioned in the section, "The Earthly Realm." At this point we have been cleansed by the cross and washed in the Blood of Jesus. The atmosphere spiritually clears and we are ready to center our hearts deeper on the Lord by entering into praise and worship.

- We will enter His Gates with Thanksgiving in our heart.
- We will enter His Courts with Praise
- We will enter the Holy Place

Where the Shew Bread is; Jesus is the bread of Life. Where the Candlesticks of Light or Illumination are; the Holy Spirit is the Light of men and women. Where the Altar of Incense is; true Worship and Exchange, and a deeper intimacy occurs in this place with Him. Prayers of the heart arise as He places them on your heart. Intercession may occur here.

There is a transition that occurs, a transferring into the Holy of Holies. This is the place we meet with our Heavenly Father. This is the time when you are drawn into God's Presence. You don't just go in of your own accord! God the Father draws you in past the veils of the flesh, mind, emotions, distractions, hindrances, things, cares, riches, and pleasures of this world. You are coming into the presence of an awesome GOD, HE is to be feared and reverenced!

Now that we have heard about it, it's time to go there.

Time to Go There

After praying, getting cleaned up, and asking the Lord to loose angels about you and the house it is time to "enter in." I usually start out by speaking to the Holy Spirit. "Holy Spirit I ask You to pray to my Lord in Heaven, lead me and guide me into the Holy Place and then into the Holy of Holies."

In the Name of Jesus, I command my spirit, mind, and will; my emotions, ego, libido, imaginations, and subconscious areas; the mind of the flesh, and all other areas of my life down to the obedience of Christ within me.

"Holy Spirit I ask You to pray to my Lord in Heaven to remove from me any hindrances, any obstacles, double mindedness, duplicity, anything in my life or on the throne of my life that does not belong. f there is anything or area in my life that is not totally submitted to the mind of Christ, I give You permission and ask You to cause these areas and/or things to come down now to the obedience of the mind of Christ within me, in Jesus Christ's Holy Name. Speaking in Tongues may manifest itself here and would be entirely appropriate.

"Holy Spirit I ask You to pray to my Lord in Heaven that the mind of Christ arise in me, over all areas of my life, and over the throne of my life.

Holy Spirit I ask You to pray to my Lord in Heaven, to remove anything that would hinder me from coming into total oneness, and knowing You, and having intimate exchange with My Heavenly Father, the Son, and You the Holy Spirit, from where I am now with You, and through the time You want me to have in the Holy of Holies, **Amen**. Speaking in Tongues may manifest itself here and would be entirely appropriate.

Holy Spirit I ask You to pray to my Lord in Heaven, to lead me now into the Holy Place and then on into the Holy of Holies. Keep me focused upon You, Your Voice, the Lord Jesus Christ, and my Heavenly Father, while all the time keep me "in Your Presence" throughout this prayer, **Amen**

Preparation For Entering In ("after" the Outer Court)

At this point I start to give thanks and praise to the Lord Jesus Christ.

- We will enter His Gates with Thanksgiving in our heart.
- We will enter His Courts with Praise.

This is where I sing and if you want to dance to Him it is proper.

"I enter Your Gates with thanksgiving in my heart, I enter Your Courts with praise, this is the Day that the Lord has made I will rejoice for You have made me glad. You have made me glad, You have made me glad, I will rejoice for You have made me glad, my Lord and Savior. You have made me glad. You have made me glad, I will rejoice for You have made me glad ... I may not have sung it right but He likes it from the heart!

Hallelujah. Thank You Jesus. Praise You Lord. Speaking in Tongues may manifest itself here and would be entirely appropriate. Continue to praise and worship Him. "Hallelujah", "Thank You Jesus."

We Will Now Enter The Holy Place.

His Presence should be evident by now. His Presence may be felt. You may experience His Presence as a light tingling, or as a strong anointing throughout your body or in an area of your body. If not, then ask Him, "Heavenly Father, I ask You to fill this room with Your Presence." or "Heavenly Father, I ask You to cover me with Your Presence."

Holy Spirit I ask You to pray to my Lord in Heaven, to take me now into the Holy Place. If you have the gift of tongues this is also an appropriate time and place to give utterance as the Spirit of the Lord leads. This is when you meet with the Lord Jesus Christ. Holy Spirit I ask You to pray to my Lord in Heaven, cause me to hear and know my Lord's Voice. I speak aloud saying, "Lord Jesus You are the Bread of Life, the Life and the Light of men." Speaking in Tongues may manifest itself here and would be entirely appropriate.

Then be quiet and listen, be still, no talking!

He might speak your name. He will respond to you. He speaks to me identifying Himself as the "I AM." He wants us to speak this back to Him, so I say that back to Him out loud, "Lord Jesus You are the I AM." He may next say, "I Am That I Am", so I speak that back to Him, "You are the I Am that I AM." Thank You Lord!, Thank You Jesus! During this time I may be led to speak in tongues and giving thanks out loud to Him. Thank You Jesus!

Again it is important to mentally be still and allow the Holy Spirit to guide you. Continue to exalt the Name of Jesus, "Thank You Lord, Thank You Jesus. Thank You Lord, You have brought me into the Holy Place, You are the Life and You are the Light. Thank You Jesus. Thank You Lord, You always identify Yourself to me. Thank You Lord." (He identifies Himself as the "I Am", "The I Am That I Am." He identifies Himself as the "Life" and "the Light." Mainly He identifies Himself as the "I Am." He may say after that, "I knew you before the creation of the Earth, before the foundations were even laid." He has a plan and purpose for your life, and calls you "son." (Since I am not a female I must assume by previous words of knowledge to women that He says to them, "daughter.")

You will know that it is Him because when He speaks His Voice goes through your entire being. You will "know that you know" in your inner man, it is Him. His Peace will fill you when He speaks. He will tell you He loves you. He wants you to know that He loves you. Sometimes He will say, "I Am the Great I Am, The Creator of Heaven and Earth, the Creator of all things." Then thank Him. Thank You Lord! Yes Lord!

The peace of God will flood your entire being when you are with Him. Thank You Lord You are the Bread of Life and in You is Light. You are the Candlesticks of Light, the Illumination, the Light of the Holy Spirit, bringing us Life and Light; wisdom, insight, understanding, revelation and realization. I usually end up being led by the Spirit into tongues, and then entering into a deeper worship, praise, and adoration which is a type of prayer, or incense lifted up to our Heavenly Father; therefore fulfilling the part of the prayer concerning the Altar of Incense.

Now is the time where we are transitioning more out of the flesh and we are being positioned by the Holy Spirit to be taken into the Holy of Holies. Notice I said "taken" into the Holy of Holies. We do not enter the Holy of Holies of our own accord or ability. God initiates, the Holy Spirit moves, and we respond to Him, He moves into, through, and past the veils into His Most Holy Presence.

Lord I worship You! I praise You! I exalt Your Holy Name. At this point I may even be quickened to sing or speak, both or neither. I usually worship the Father with a song. "I Worship You, Almighty God! You're my Joy and Strength! I Worship You, Almighty God! I Praise Your Name." I might repeat this song from my heart, or praise Him, "Father God, Heavenly Father, You're my Joy and Strength!" Worship may even turn into tongues.

Deeper Adoration And Awe Of Our Heavenly Father Begins
"I love You Lord, Daddy God, Heavenly Father.' "You created the Heavens and Earth, in You there is no shadow of turning." "Thank You Lord, thank You Daddy God." Speaking in Tongues may manifest itself here and would be entirely appropriate.

Heavenly Father I come to Your Throne of Grace through the Precious Blood of Jesus Christ. Holy Spirit quicken me and into the Holy of Holies, quicken me to my Heavenly Father's Voice. Speaking in Tongues may manifest itself here and would be entirely appropriate.

Be Still. Be Quiet. Wait!
Then Do Not answer out loud when He speaks He will then speak to me saying something like, "son!" "Be still" or "I am doing a work in you". He will answer you however he sees fit. Answer Him with the mind of Christ, not your human voice out loud for you have the mind of Christ. If He says to "be still", then be quiet! That is when it gets hard for me. I want to "do" something or say something.

Our "do" is to believe and receive from Him in stillness, even when we don't think or feel He is doing anything, TRUST and OBEY! This will stretch you! He will release you when His work in you is done. Allow Him to stretch you!

Pray silently through the mind of Christ. "Yes Father." Usually He responds with, "I love you" or "I love you son!" My response back to Him by the mind of Christ is, "Yes Lord, I love You!" or "Heavenly Father, I love You!"

In the Holy of Holies we are no longer concerned about our earthly existence, what happens next, what time it is, or how long we have been with Him, not even how much time there is left.

If your thoughts start drifting then the quality of "being with" the Father will be diminished. You are allowing yourself to be distracted, is what it boils down to.

Quick Recovery From Drifting Or Distractions Of The Mind

Pray, "Holy Spirit I ask You to pray to my Lord in Heaven to quicken me back to where I was with my Heavenly Father and His Voice. Speaking in Tongues may manifest itself here and would be entirely appropriate. You must come to the realization and reality that "the mind" Your Heavenly Father desires you to have is one of being with Him, existing in Him as one, and that all else does not matter! He comes first. All the worries and concerns of the natural life pales; they are insignificant! Whatever goes on out there, in the flesh life you must learn to truly trust Him with it all! God tells us in *John 12:24, "Verily, verily, I say unto you, Except a corn of wheat fall into the ground and die, it abideth alone: but if it die, it bringeth forth much fruit"* KJV. Your life is hid in Christ! We have to learn that God, is in control. Let go, trust Him with all of your existence, be still, and know that He is God. This an intimate knowing, not just a knowing of Him! This is where we are changed into His Likeness!

I have found in the past, that when He has called me to get into the Holy of Holies, that He has orchestrated the entire event, all things around it, even before entering in, during, and after. He then calls you to "Come." Our response is to obey, go to Him immediately!

IMPORTANT!!!

Now if your child gets hurt, you know you have to attend to that! If your child is sick, you know you have to attend to that! If your child is hungry, you know you should attend to that! This is why I try to preclude these things and serve others before getting into this prayer time. In case you have to leave to attend to an emergency, you might say to the Lord, "Lord, I am sorry I have to go." Just realize that He knows what is going on already! So don't beat yourself up or be hard on yourself. He will not hold that against you. Then go! Tell Him you love Him on the way out the door! Remember the people or person you are now going to needs your attention, love, and understanding! Later pray and if He lets you, return to your place of prayer, else do not be upset!

I could comment on how the enemy loves to plague God's children with distractions during prayer time. I find that a dog barks or people come in, and they have forgotten I go downstairs and get in to prayer, distractions may try to disturb me in this quiet time. Again, good communication prior to going into this time of prayer will often stop those problems from occurring. Mute the phone or place the answering machine on silent mode, and when all else fails "unplug it as need be." God is most important! When He says "Come", then it is time to "come" and immediately move to the place of prayer. I usually ask Him that morning or during the day if He wants me to come into the Holy Place and Holy of Holies when I get home tonight. He will let you know! He may confirm it through His Presence coming on you or He might simply say "NO."

WHY DOES GOD TELL US NO

Sometimes He answers "no" because He knows we need our physical and mental rest, as well as spiritual rest. He knows we need to cultivate relationships of family, friends, church, and those in the world he is drawing to Him, through us. So, here again, God knows what is best for us! This does not mean we can't pray and ask Him questions or intercede for others during these other times.

- Trouble Keeping Your Mind On The Lord in The Holy Place and Holy of Holies
- While listening to either the Father, the Son, or the Holy Spirit it is important to focus on His Voice!

Again you can pray using any of the "Be" techniques (as follows):

- Holy Spirit, I ask You to pray to my Lord in Heaven, quicken me, cause me to hear and know the Lord's Voice or My Heavenly Father's Voice
- Say the Name of Jesus: "Jesus", "Jesus", "Jesus", though if you arein a room of people speak under your breath because it might distract the other people in the room.
- Holy Spirit, I ask You to pray to my Lord in Heaven, to quicken me back to where I was with the Lord Jesus Christ, cause me to hear His Voice, not a strange voice. Speaking in Tongues may manifest itself here and would be entirely appropriate.
- Holy Spirit, I ask You to pray to my Lord in Heaven, to quicken me back to where I was with My Heavenly Father and cause me to hear His Voice, not a strange voice. Speaking in Tongues may manifest itself here and would be entirely appropriate.

Then be quiet and listen. He will speak.

Usually while I am in either the Holy Place or the Holy of Holies, the Lord will purify me in His Light. His Light will wash over me. Changes are being made in us as we yield and turn ourselves over to Him. We are being made more like Him. Do not even concern yourself with what is going on or happening during that process, just know it is for the better, His and ours. Just simply trust Him!

"Moving on" In The Holy of Holies

As the time with the Lord draws to an end you realize you have been in a special place where you were "closed in" with Him. In fact, this actually happened when He drew you into the Holy of Holies. You may have even felt engulfed about with a void or nothingness. What happened is that you were pulled or separated into His Most Holy Presence! All other things were also being blocked out for you, so you could have a strong one-on-one intimate relationship and time with Him. You have to realize how very important you are to Him and how much He incredibly loves you! It is to be an uninterrupted, intimate time together, giving full attention to Him, as He does with you! Yes, you are extremely important to Him and I am sure He wants us to value that time with Him to the same degree or measure. All our focus is to be devoid of self and all other existence except Him during this time, this only leaves hearing and knowing Him. He knows we need that because of the way we are. God knows best for each of us!

Through more trips into the Holy of Holies, He will take you into deeper levels of being still before Him, deeper times of exchange, and a deeper getting to know Him. Your entire mind, spirit, and body will be affected. You will **never** be the same! It is so incredibly wonderful, that you will desire and covet that time you spend with Him. Nothing else will satisfy like being "in" Him! We have to learn to be patient with ourselves! Wait! Call upon the Name of the Lord! You are a work in progress and you can't do this yourself! We need to see that we need Him. We are His Tabernacle, His building, being built up in a Holy Way, in Him.

Leaving the Holy of Holies

Usually there is silence and the Lord says, "Go" or "go upstairs to be with your spouse, daughter, and/or son." I respond with, "Lord did You say go?" I am implying to the Lord I don't want to leave His Presence. His response is usually "Yes" or "Go." I must obey! (*Matthew 7:21*) He will say to me at that time, "I love you son." I respond in love with, "I love You Lord/Daddy/GOD/Heavenly Father. So I turn and start to leave and He usually says again,I really like it when He does this again, "I love you!" I respond and probably with tears flowing, "I love You Lord!"

I thank Him for being with me no matter where I am and I say my last "I love You" to Him. I leave the room shutting the door, knowing He is with me! I usually have a little problem walking or I have a little disorientation due to being extremely saturated in His Peace from head to toe! I sometimes can hardly even think a thought (all laboring of the mind has ceased!) Do not be eager to jump back into the things of the world. Hug, or love on the spouse and kids. Just RELAX! Even reading the Word may not be God's will for you at that moment. I truly believe He wants us to enjoy the "REST" and "Soak" in it! Enjoy the journey. Dwell on things that are good and pure, and from above

WHY PRAY?

Praying to our Heavenly Father, in the Name of Jesus Christ, using God's Holy Word, the scriptures, in prayer is the most powerful thing we can do for ourselves and others. The heart of prayer is the will of our Heavenly Father. Part of that will is simply coming to Him. He desires us, as His dear children to know Him. He desires your love, your attention, your fellowship, more than just being related to Him through Jesus, He also desires a time of communion, an intimate time of personal exchange and involvement, and finally a release of His will and manifest Presence in the earth through prayer. As you pray for your needs and the needs of others, you are actually becoming a prayer warrior, an intercessor, just as Jesus was and is today for each of us. Jesus is constantly interceding for us to our Heavenly Father. It is written that Jesus was sent to destroy the works of the devil, *1 John 3:8.* We are to do the same. We have the power and authority through Jesus Christ. All we have to do is live in the promise of the Word of God and to use His precious Name. The most powerful weapons we have are the Name of Jesus Christ and God's Holy Word against Satan and his foul wicked demons. No power of darkness can stand against the Word of God in the Name of Jesus Christ, and through the Blood of Jesus Christ.

The importance of confessing our sins and worshipping God, according to the Word of God:

- *"If I regard iniquity in my heart, the Lord will not hear me" Psalms 66:18.*
- *"We know that God does not listen to sinners: but if anyone is God-fearing and a worshipper of Him and does His will, He listens to him" John 9:31.*
- Prayerlessness is a sin according to *1 Sam. 12:23.*

THE LORD'S PRINCIPLE OF PRAYER

I suppose all new Christians begin their walk with many questions, and of course a lot of advice from those who might have prayed with them when they received Jesus as Savior. Several pieces of advice that are always given, and of course, good advice it is, starts with; "Be sure to read your Bible and of course don't forget to pray". The first of these is not so hard if you can read, but the second can most often lead to the hard question, how do I pray? I think, as I look back, that was one of my questions when I was saved some 34 years ago now, and I did not have a clue, but I learned a real good way to start was reading the Bible daily, and also truly learning the word of God.

Now turn to *Matthew 6.* Here we find Jesus, with His disciples on the mount, just after He taught them the beatitudes, speaking to them concerning prayer and in *verses 7 - 13:*

> *"And when you pray, do not heap up phrases (multiply words, repeating the same ones over and over) as the Gentiles do, for they think they will be heard for their much speaking. Do not be like them, for your Father knows what you need before you ask Him. Pray then in this way: `Our*

Father Who art in heaven, Hallowed be Thy Name, Thy Kingdom come,
Thy will be done. On earth as it is in heaven, Give us this day our daily
bread, And forgive us our debts, as we also have forgiven our debtors.
And do not lead us into temptation, But deliver us from evil, For thine is
the kingdom, And the power, and the glory, Forever, Amen"

This is a truly beautiful teaching of the Lord, as of course all were and are, but it is not a prayer as we think of prayer. Jesus did not say, when you pray, pray this prayer, rather He said, "Pray then in this way". He gave them the principle, a pattern to follow as they went to the Lord with their petitions and requests. I, for one, still have many questions to ask, but I am also learning that the Holy Spirit is a most willing teacher and never fails to give the answer that I need, so I always go to Him first and wait.

The first word, "Our" reveals a new dimension in our lives. We are no longer a solo act, doing our own thing, but we are now in a community, a fellowship that includes many brothers and sisters in the Lord. We may not always be in their company, but we are always members of the same body and as such, no longer alone. We are addressing the Father of us all. Now we progress to the second word, "Father", which tells us that we are part of a very large family that is seeking to communicate with the One God and Father who is reaching out to us. He is the One you are opening your heart to; the One who has tender ears to hear His children calling out to Him.

"Who art in heaven" This is a given knowledge, of where your petition is being heard. He Who sits in the heavens *Psalms. 2:4a*, is He Who resides in His kingdom and sits upon His throne. He is also the One who has sent His Son to redeem us and we are now not our own, but we are His property *1 Corinthians 6:19 & 20*. He rules and reigns over the universe from His eternally divine position.

"Hallowed be Thy Name", now you are really at the part that could be labeled worship, which we all should move into as we go into prayer, We are calling on the Almighty God and we are first acknowledging His holiness 'hallowed'; What an awesome thought. When Moses met Him at the burning bush, the hallowed ground, he asked Him, Who should I tell them is sending me? God spoke and said that he should tell them that I AM is sending you. Paul wrote of Jesus in *Philippians* that God had highly exalted Him and had given Him a Name that is higher than any other, that at the Name of Jesus every knee must bow and every tongue confess that Jesus Christ is Lord to the glory of God. As we go back into the Old Testament we find many of the compound Names of God:

- Jehovah Nissi - Strength
- Jehovah Rohi - Shepherd
- Jehovah Shalom - Peace
- Jehovah Rapha - Healer
- Jehovah Jireh - Provider
- Jehovah Tsidkenu - Righteousness
- Jehovah Makaddesh - Sanctification

There are many others that your study will reveal, but Names to the Hebrew man or woman of that day revealed the character of God. His character is much broader, but that is to be found in further study. But in Jesus, all these character virtues are present, because He was born the Godhead incarnate. In the Amplified Bible, in *John 14, 15, & 16* you will find bracketed behind the phrase, "In My Name" the words [presenting all that I AM]. He is the fullness of the Godhead and so as you use His Name in prayer you are calling on and expressing all that God is. *Read Acts 4:12*.

"Thy Kingdom come..." You have entered, through your born again experience, the kingdom of God. It is the dimension that embodies the way God does things. You are to call into this earth realm, by prayer to God, His kingdom answer to every need. Jesus said that it should be in the earth the same as it is in heaven. What you are in reality asking, is that the Father not only send the kingdom of God to the earth, but send the revelation into our hearts as well, so that we can alter our lives' thinking accordingly, now add the rest of the verse;

"Thy will be done ... in the earth as it is in heaven". How is it in heaven? It's liberty in Christ Jesus, free of illness and affliction, free of lack and poverty, and free of all oppression and the strength of the Almighty expressed through your weakness as was Paul's, in *2 Corinthians 12* where God said that His strength and power are made perfect and show themselves most effective in our weakness. The Supernatural expressing Himself in the natural. Remember, that His word is His will, so study to show yourselves approved *2 Timothy 2:15*, and your prayer life will take on the power of His answers. Find in the Word, scriptures that apply to your requests and pray those scriptures as prayer. There are several verses in the Old Testament that address this powerfully.

Jeremiah 23:29 "Is not my Word like fire that consumes all that cannot endure the test? Says the Lord, and like a hammer that breaks in pieces the rock [of most stubborn resistance]?"

"Put Me in remembrance [remind Me of your merits]: *let us plead and argue together. Set forth your case, that you may be justified* (proved right)." [Your case in the courts of heaven is His word] *Isaiah 43:26* -- Now read and add to this *1 John 5:14 & 15*.

"Give us this day our daily bread" Here you are addressing Jehovah Jireh, God our Provider, asking Him to provide your daily bread. Yesterday has passed and you have today to rejoice and be glad in and He will supply all your needs according to His riches in glory by Christ Jesus. He declared this in *Philippians 4:19,* and nothing escapes His sight and heart, for your 'needs' can cover much ground, and not just your financial needs. Jehovah Jireh literally means, God Who sees ahead. He knew your daily needs ahead of all time, since before time was, and He made advance provision for all of them. In prayer, you are traveling a course that will cause you to intersect His supply for you. In the trek through the wilderness, when Manna fell from heaven, they were only allowed to take just what the day would demand for their well being. More taken would only spoil, except on the weekend when they could get an extra portion, to meet every need until the Sabbath passed. This is a marvelous avenue to build faith and trust on and God is faithful to the promises in His word. He is our provider and is to be trusted completely.

"Forgive us our debts as we have also forgiven our debtors" There is a great measure of God's will in this portion 'Forgiveness'. One of the most important words to be grasped in this is "as". When we do not have any forgiveness in our hearts, we are basically saying; judge me as I am judging the one that I have an aught against. We have amplified the "as". When you go just a little further in *Mark 11:24 & 25*, you will find Jesus, discussing this with His disciples, and relating it to prayer, *"For this reason I am telling you, whatever you ask for in prayer, believe* (trust and be confident) *that it is granted to you and you will get it. And whenever you stand praying, if you have anything against anyone, forgive him and let it drop* (leave it, let it go), *in order that your Father Who is in heaven may also forgive you your [own] failings and shortcomings and let them drop."*

Here you can see how much emphasis the Father puts on our forgiving others in order to have our prayers be effective. Forgiveness is one of the conditions of answered, believing prayer and is an important condition that the Father places on receiving an answer. Forgiveness and answers are tied together. God's love is to be the radiant virtue of the righteous and His word in *1 Corinthians 13:7b* declares that love believes the best in every person and as such forgiveness is the way of life for the Christian. There is a verse in *James 5:16c* that makes a tremendous statement; *"...The earnest* (heartfelt, continued) *prayer of a righteous man makes tremendous power available* [dynamic in its working]."

One of the key virtues displayed in the righteous man's life is walking in the attitude of forgiveness as His Father has forgiven him. God's love is shed abroad in our hearts by the Holy Spirit. *(Romans 5:5)*

"And lead us not into temptation" Here we need to see the word that the Greeks used for the word 'temptation' properly translated makes this a more palatable request. The word is 'peirasmos' and means trials with a beneficial purpose. The way this verse reads when this translation is used is, 'lead us not into a hard trial or testing'. Again we look at the book of *James 1:13* we read; *"Let no one say when he is tempted, I am tempted from God; for God is incapable of being tempted by [what is] evil and He Himself tempts no one (with evil)."*

Jesus was saying, don't pray yourself into a hard spot, your Father is loving and will not be a part of that. He wants only that which is beneficial for you and that might occur in testing and usually does, but not because you pray for it, it just comes as a part of life's journey and it comes daily, but the Holy Spirit is always there to strengthen you, for He is the strengthener. Spiritual testing is always a growing experience, and mature growth is a most desperate need in the body of Christ, *John 14:26* AMP. Just for the record, look at *Psalms 119:67, 71 & 75*: *"I know, O Lord, that Your judgments are right and righteous, and that in faithfulness You have afflicted me."* [Afflicted here is tried, proven]

"...but deliver us from the evil one" I won't go too far with this one except to say this; The Bible never gives any doubt that there is a power of evil in this world. Some translations have had this to read, 'deliver us from evil' and that is not complete. It should always read, "deliver us from the evil one". The Bible does not teach that evil is some sort of principle that is an abstract, but rather it is a very active personal power, an enemy, an adversary called the devil who opposes God and all He stands for. It is from that power of destruction, that Jesus has us to pray for deliverance. We do know that in *1 John 4:4* there is a powerful statement in our behalf and it declares; *"Little children, you are of God* [you belong to Him] *and have already defeated and overcome them* [the agents of the anti-Christ], *because He Who lives in you is greater* [mightier] *than he who is in the world."*

The agents of anti-Christ here are the powers of evil and He has already disarmed them and triumphed over them and made a public display of them, read *Galatians 2:15.*

"For Yours is the kingdom and the power and the glory forever. Amen" All glory to God, Who is able to answer all prayer, prayed in the right manner and context. Prayer is to be a simple conversation with the God of all creation. He is your creator and the lover of your soul and He does not know how to hurt and He is more desirous and willing to answer than you are to pray. Look to Him, seek His face and not His hand and He will meet you at the intersection of any need you have and any desire your heart longs for. Sit down and talk to Him, He is so easy to know and He desires that you know Him well.

There is nothing on earth or in heaven, for time or eternity, that God's Son did not secure for us. By prayer God gives us the vast and matchless inheritance which is ours by virtue of His Son. God is glorified and Christ is honored by large asking. (E. M. Bounds)

Always remember, we are heirs of God, joint heirs with Christ Jesus. Remember though, all we have been sharing is not a prayer, but rather it is the "Lord's Own Principle" for praying, it is a rich pattern to follow. The scriptures that you have seen in this that are now written are those that you should look up, study, and get into your heart. Invest in some good books on prayer. The following are just a few:

- Destined for the Throne by Paul E. Billheimer
- Prayer [Understanding the Purpose of...] by Myles Munroe
- The Names of God by Nathan Stone
- Prayer: Life's Limitless Reach by Jack Taylor
- Beyond the Veil by Alice Smith
- Prison To Praise by Merlin Carrothers

DIFFERENCE BETWEEN JOHN 14:14 AND JOHN 16:23

When praying according to *John 14:14*, you are asking Jesus, in the Name of Jesus Christ, to do something for you; as an example: to forgive your sins to forgive sins of a loved one to destroy curses to destroy evil strongholds to protect your child, etc. When praying according to *John 16:23*, you are asking your Heavenly Father to give you something in Jesus Christ's Name; for an example: to give you total deliverance; to give to you total peace, to give your child salvation, to give you financial freedom, etc. You are either asking Jesus to do something for you or asking God to give you something; the importance is to pray to God; mirroring the scripture that applies to what you are asking; stating to God that Your Word says this; *John 14:14*, do – or - *John 16:23,* give; and I am standing on Your Word to do/give unto me _____ .

HINDRANCES CAN BLOCK YOU FROM RECEIVING YOUR DELIVERANCE

By definition a hindrance is generally anything that impedes, obstructs, stops or retards progress. Anything that blocks or inhibits you or me from receiving what is rightfully ours through the Word and by the Blood of Jesus can be considered a hindrance. A hindrance can also be defined as any legal, biblical ground the enemy has over you. Examples of some hindrances are: sin, an unforgiving heart, disbelief, curses, pride, fear, embarrassment, lack of desire, lack of knowledge, passivity, occultism, and ungodly soul ties.

BIBLICAL GROUNDS FOR SICKNESS, DISEASE, DEMONS, ETC.

Most of us do not like to use the word "legal" as in "legalism" after how the Pharisees and Sadducees of the New Testament treated Jesus. We do not want to be associated with them or their "religious" ways or "religion", both of which were "traditions of man" and not God's ways. They did not have a relationship with the Lord!

In this case, the word legal gives way to the rights "possessed" by being within the law and therefore rightfully protected or something right fully belongs to you. This can also cause us to be legally or lawfully separated or cut off from something that we could have a right to. In this case we have cut ourselves off from something we have a right to. The Word of God is the deciding factor. Demons through our sins can obtain legal, biblical grounds to kill, steal, and destroy, we do it to ourselves. If demons have a right to remain, if we have given them any type of legal ground, there will always be a fight because they want you under them in one way or another. They will try to make you feel that things are hopeless, why even care! Those are total lies and tricks of the enemy. The Word of God came to Job, an Old Testament saint, and it tells us that his captivity (a state of being a prisoner to something.) was turned. So there is hope! This hope is through the precious Blood sacrifice of our Lord and Savior Jesus Christ.

We are here to help you kick out the demons, take back what is rightfully yours that you have been robbed of, and walk in a victorious life in Jesus! Our Heavenly Father wants us to realize as His daughters and sons that we all can have healing, forgiveness, restored relationships, and walk in a glorious relationship with Him, here on His Earth. He has promised this to us, His dear children through Jesus Christ, in His Word. It is time to take back what is rightfully ours through Christ, in prayer! We should never be given over to the whims of any devil due to ignorance. We are not going to sit down and give up. We are not going to take that as a child of God and just perish. I am a child of the Most High God, Creator of Heaven and Earth and we, His children through Jesus Christ, have been given authority and power over the enemy (*Luke 10:19*). I choose to obey and have a life that is victorious in Christ. I am an over comer in Jesus! Thank you Lord for giving me and helping me to live a life that is Victorious in Jesus Christ and to help my brothers and sisters to walk in that Light too! Amen. (So be it!)

PRAYER MAKES THE DIFFERENCE

Prayer brings the unseen, the Kingdom of God, on the scene, or into our lives where we and other people need it, so God's Kingdom is seen (manifest and/or experienced). We are here to be a part of and not a hindrance to the Kingdom of God, but to set the captives free, this is the acceptable year of the Lord! We need no longer live below what is rightfully ours in Christ and neither should His children! In *1 Samuel 1:23* David clearly states that it would be a sin not to pray for Israel. In *James chapter 5* we are told to pray for one another. Let us not go forth sinning in this way in ignorance, not praying for our brothers and sisters in Christ, anymore!

ASKING FOR HIS WISDOM

The Word of God is very clear on asking for Wisdom. Wisdom, true wisdom comes from God. Jesus is as wisdom as declared in His Word in *1st Corinthians 1: 30*, "But of Him you are in Christ Jesus, who became for us wisdom from God — and righteousness and sanctification and redemption — God's Word to us says to ask for [His] wisdom!

> *If any of you lacks wisdom, let him ask of God, who gives to all liberally and without reproach, and it will be given to him. But let him ask in faith, with no doubting, for he who doubts is like a wave of the sea driven and tossed by the wind. For let not that man suppose that he will receive anything from the Lord; he is a double-minded man, unstable in all his ways. James 1:5-8*

So go boldly to the throne of grace through the precious Blood of Jesus Christ and ask for wisdom, call, cry out for wisdom and His promise to us is that our Heavenly Father will give it to you!

PHYSICAL HEALING

Miracles of Healing are not of the old as some confess because God's Word says "I am the same yesterday, today and tomorrow." *"The work that I do you will do; you shall do even greater works than Me"*, according to *John 14:12*. It does take faith though, faith of a mustard seed. Confess God's Word with authority over your body two times a day, it will increase your faith, and according to *Isaiah 55:11*, God's Words (the following scriptures) will not return to Him void. We are to return His Word to Him by giving it voice!!! *"So shall my word be that goes forth out of My mouth: it shall not return to me void (without producing any effects, useless), but it shall accomplish that which I please and purpose, and it shall prosper in the thing in which I sent it." Isaiah 55:11. "I create the fruit of the lips; Peace, peace to him that is far off, and to him that is near, saith the Lord; and I will heal him, according to Isaiah 57:19.*

PRAYING AGAINST THE ROOT CAUSE, NOT THE SYMPTOM

We all have a heart to see the sick healed and the afflicted made whole. It is, after all, God's will to heal and that was accomplished by the stripes that Jesus bore for each of us. We love to quote or hear quoted verses from the word of God that give us encouragement and build our faith, and one of those has something to say that sometimes we pass over, so let me share a thought on it with you, and I quote from *Psalm 103:1-3*;

As God did for us in deliverance from sin, He has also done for us in physical healing and we are to believe and receive just as much for that wholeness (healing) in Him, in each of our lives!

Bless the Lord, O my soul; and all that is within me, bless His holy name!

Bless the Lord, O my soul, and forget not all His benefits:

Who forgives all your iniquities,

Who heals all your diseases.

He was wounded for our transgressions,

He was bruised for our iniquities;

The chastisement for our peace was upon Him,

And by His stripes we are healed. Isaiah 53:5 NKJV

He daily loads us with benefits... (Psalms 68:19b, NKJ)

Born again, and filled with the Spirit, most of us have no trouble believing the miracle of salvation in our hearts, but the same God Who saved you, also sent the word and healed you, yet so often we are troubled believing the truth presented here. We are finding that often, when called on to pray for someone, the Lord leads us to pray in the Spirit for a moment before offering a prayer for healing. I believe that the reason is, that we need to understand that some sickness is the result of another problem, and the Lord will often reveal the root cause of the problem and as we pray for that root, the symptom leaves and does not reoccur. We have scripture that would lend itself to this in *Romans 8:26*. For an example of a root, it has been said that diabetes, many times can be caused or activated by emotional shock, such as a sudden death in the family, injury, financial lost, anything that jars us emotionally.

Lets read the following scriptures as one statement and be blessed by how much God loves us and made Word provision for our problems, regardless what they may be or how difficult they may seem to resolve.

In the beginning, was the Word, and the Word was with God, and the Word was God. Forever, O Lord, Your word is settled in heaven, Your *faithfulness endures to all generations. He (God) sent His word and healed them, and delivered them from their destructions. So shall My word be that goes forth from My mouth; It shall not return to Me void, But it shall accomplish what I please, And it shall prosper in the thing for which I sent it. And He (the Word) prayed in John 17:4 .I have glorified You on the earth. I have completed the work, which You sent Me to do. And on the cross, the Word cried out, `It is finished'. And the God has already said, `I am alert and active, watching over My word to perform it'.*

John 1:1, Psalm 119:89, Psalm 107:20, Isaiah 55:11, John 17:4, John 19:30, Jer. 1:12

PUTTING THE WORD OF GOD INTO ACTION

Finally, as referred to in Job 22:27-28, "You shall also decide and decree a thing, and it shall be established for you; and the light of God's favor shall shine upon your ways."

First, we need to get the mind of the Spirit, don't just do a scattershot prayer. The Word of God says in *Jude 20, "building yourself up, on your most holy faith, praying in the Holy Spirit."* The Holy Spirit reveals to us the very Word we "decide to pray", which will give us what we want, Victory in Jesus!

Second, we decree the Word as applies to the problem through prayer.

IMPORTANCE OF FORGIVENESS & REPENTANCE FOR JUDGING

"For if you forgive men when they sin against you, your Heavenly Father will also forgive you. But if you do not forgive men their sins, your Heavenly Father will not forgive your sins." Matthew 6:14-15.

"Our Father in heaven, hallowed be Your Name, your kingdom come, your will be done on earth as it is in heaven. Give us today our daily bread. Forgive us our debts, as we also have forgiven our debtors." Matthew 6:9-13

We, being sinners, had a huge, accumulated debt. Then we accepted Jesus as our Lord and Savior, saying, "Heavenly Father, will you please have mercy on me and forgive my sins?" And He said, "My son, my daughter, step up into the grace and mercy of the Lord Jesus Christ. My Son took your place, your debt is paid." Sweet forgiveness, it was just as though we had never sinned; completely covered by the Blood of the Lamb. Jesus died instead of us and paid off every debt we ever owed. God then says, *"Now, if you want to live in this place where you receive My full forgiveness, you must be forgiving. You cannot ask for mercy for yourself and justice for others who wronged you."*

Matthew 5:23, 24 tells us that when we come and bring our gifts before the Lord, and there we remember that we have something against our brother, we should first go and be reconciled with him and then return and offer our gifts. Then we have clean hearts.

Jesus tells us about the Pharisee and the publican (tax collector). The Pharisee said, "Thank you, Lord that I am not like the other man. I fast and pray and I give thanks. I do all these good things for you." The publican came in abject humility and prayed, "Lord, be merciful to me a sinner." not comparing himself to anyone else, just admitting how guilty he was, *Luke 18:10-14*. The Lord said the man that came in humility went away justified, but the self-righteous one did not.

Some people have had unbelievable tragedies happen in their lives. They realize they were victims. They don't understand that their own recurring problems have anything to do with their sins of judging. The only way out of your prison is forgiveness, and then repentance for judging.

When we are the sinner, and the Holy Spirit reminds us of it, we want mercy, but when we are sinned against, we often cry out for justice and become bitter. If Satan can get us demanding justice, then he will be legally entitled to bring into our lives all the reaping and punishment we deserve. That is what gives Satan power and legal rights. Yet Jesus, whom the greatest crime of all was committed against, didn't say, *"Father, get these murderers and give them what they deserve."* Jesus said, *"Father, forgive them for they know not what they do." Luke 23:34.*

One of the most dangerous attitudes in the world today is that the person who wronged us must pay. Bitterness and resentment are like toxic thorns in your soul, sapping your mental processes, thought life, will, motivation and joy of life. If you cannot forgive, you are a prisoner of your own strongholds. You are bound by unforgiveness, pain, and destructive patterns of thinking. Forgiveness is a deliberate act of the will to pardon another individual or self whether you like it or not. We receive forgiveness in the same manner that we forgive others. You can work out the torments of forgiveness with God alone or God and the other person. (*Make a list of every person and situation that caused you hurt.)

FINANCES

Throughout the Bible, we see that God has a lot to say about finances. God wanted to be involved with Abraham's finances, and He wants to be involved in yours. Fundamental principles of Abraham's prosperity:

"And Abram was very rich in cattle, in silver, and in gold." Gen. 13:2

"He listened to, and obeyed God." Gen. 12:1-4

"He honored God, who prospered him." Gen. 12:7

"He was generous, and avoided strife." Gen. 13:5-9

"He was compassionate toward others." Gen. 18:24-33

If you want God to be involved in your finances and prosper you, you must honor these basic principles. You cannot be greedy and truly prosper. There is nothing wrong with wanting to have abundance for yourself and your family, but giving to God and being generous to others is part of the spiritual law.

Solomon understood the principles of prosperity. He was one of the richest men who ever lived. His proverbs reveal many truths regarding finances.

> *"Honor the Lord with thy substance, and with the first fruits of all thine increase: so thy barns be filled with plenty, and thy presses shall burst forth with new wine." Proverbs 3:9-10*

> *"He who gives to the poor will not want, but he who hides his eyes [from their want] will have many a curse." Proverbs 28:27 AMP*

But in order to have true riches, the motive of your heart must be pure, to bless others and establish God's covenant.

> *"And beware lest you say in your [mind and] heart, my power and the might of my hand have gotten me this wealth. But you shall earnestly remember the Lord your God, for it is He Who gives you power to get wealth that He may establish His covenant which He swore to your fathers, as it is this day." Deuteronomy 8:17-18 AMP*

God does indeed want to be involved in our finances. Most Christians who are defeated in their finances are defeated because they believe and confess the words of the enemy, and those words hold them in bondage. What we believe and speak affects the natural world, including our finances. God has given us His Word so that we can understand these spiritual laws. When you work with these laws, they work for you. When you work against God's spiritual laws, they work against you.

When you speak negatively about your financial situation, you have what you say and believe. Here is a very important spiritual law: You can have what you say. With your words you can choose life or death, poverty or riches, sickness or health. You may tithe 10%, work hard, and pray for prosperity every day, but if your words are negative and contrary to God's Word, you could stay in debt, struggling to make ends meet.

Words are powerful, but God's Word is full of creative power. When you agree with what God has said about you, speaking His Word, your circumstances will begin to change and line up with His Will for your life.

CONFIRMATION BY TWO OR THREE WITNESSES

In *2 Corinthians 13:1b* there exists a very important prayer principle about confirming to us when we have heard God's Voice. The verse reads, *"By the mouth of two or three witnesses every word shall be established."* This works in the natural on establishing a testimony over certain matters and you will find out that it works the same in the spiritual. We have learned that the Lord is consistent and does not tell one person one thing and then tell another person something else. For example, "Lord, did you tell brother Joe that we are to go to his friend and lay hands on him?" If I pray or you pray and get a "No" and you have made sure you are clean of sin, demonic spirits, no evil spirits in the room, you have tested the spirits, that your mind is not deceiving you, then let your friend Joe know that you heard the Lord tell you know "No." Something is going on. Maybe, it is a no, not now. Maybe it's a no, it is not necessary. Maybe Joe has an evil spirit in HIS presence and is not hearing properly. Maybe Joe has it in his emotions or head, "well it has to be God's will!" Let the Word from the Lord to You be established by the mouth of two or three witnesses! Something is going on, seek God, He will reveal it to you!

CURSES

The Word of God says that a curse without a cause cannot settle on a righteous person. Sin opens the door for a curse to settle on a person. Generational curses are curses in which a parent or ancestral parent that we are in direct lineage of, has sinned and opened a door for it to be passed on from one generation to the next. Usually there is some type of display or manifestation in the natural realm, indicating what the curse is, through a person's behavior. No matter how pronounced the manifestation is, it needs to be dealt with through repentance. A curse without a cause cannot settle on a righteous person or a person free of sin. Curses are clearly spoken of in the Bible and just because the Word tells us Jesus became a curse on a tree for us does not mean we can't still get a curse actively working in our lives. We either get curses through our sin or when we get into sin, a curse spoken of by others gets attached to us after we sin, actively affecting us. We need to repent immediately! These things really do affect our thoughts and the thought processes of our mind more than we tend to realize! With generational curses, we also repent for our own sins. No matter the sin, and no matter the type of curse, we need to ask the Lord to take it. Then we are appropriating and applying what Jesus did for us by going to the cross and becoming a curse for us.

POWER OF YOUR SPOKEN WORD

We can speak words about ourselves and others containing curses and spiritual death without realizing what we are doing.

> *"death and life are in the power of the tongue" Proverbs 18:21 AMP*

> *"for the tongue can kill or nourish life." Proverbs 18:21 NLT*

We need to practice the Words of God, speaking in love, with patience and kindness in every sentence. "Love endures long and is patient and kind; love never is envious nor boils over with jealousy or haughtily. It is not conceited (arrogant and inflated with pride); it is not rude (unmannerly) and does not act unbecomingly, Love (God's love in us) does not insist on its own rights or its own way, for it is not self-seeking; it is not touchy or fretful or resentful; it takes no account of the evil done to it (it pays no attention to a suffered wrong). It does not rejoice at injustice and unrighteousness, but rejoices when right and truth prevail. Loves bears up under anything and everything that comes, is ever ready to believe the best of every person, its hopes are fadeless under all circumstances, and it endures everything (without weakening). Love never fails (never fades out or becomes obsolete or comes to an end)". *1 Corinthians 13:4-8.*

When our own words align with the Words of God we have a special connection to God. Our words truly have the power of life and death. Loose the power and effects of any word curses you have spoken upon yourself and others, whether unbeknownst or in anger. Repent of having spoken evil words, remembering that to repent means to turn away from ever speaking such evil words again. If you have spoken negative words about your children, your finances, your health, your spouse, your life or your relationship with God – get on your knees alone and bind these to the Will of God and loose the power and effects of any wrong words you have spoken. The following prayer also will bind and loose the power and effects of any wrong words spoken about you or to you.

Prayers

DAILY PRAYER

(Pray Out Loud)

Heavenly Father, I come to You now in the Name of my Lord and Savior Christ Jesus. (Note - if two or more praying: Heavenly Father, _____ and I come to You in one accord in the Name of Christ Jesus of Nazareth according to Matthew 18:19). Holy Spirit, I/We pray that You will quicken me/us to hear my/our Heavenly Father's Voice and lead me/us in prayer. Holy Spirit, I/We ask you to reveal to me/us any un-confessed sins I/We have in my/our heart at any time. Heavenly Father, I/We bow and worship before You. I/We come to You with praise and with thanksgiving. I/We come to You in humility, in fear, and in trembling and seeking truth. I/We come to You in gratitude, in love, and through the precious Blood of Your Son Jesus Christ of Nazareth. **Amen**

PRAYER OF SPIRITUAL DOORS

Heavenly Father, I come to You now in the Name of my Lord and Savior Christ Jesus. Heavenly Father, I ask that You shut any doors that need to be shut and open any doors that need to be opened in the spiritual and natural realms of my life in Jesus' Holy Name. Heavenly Father, I plead the Blood of Jesus over those doorways and ask that the enemy be rendered powerless and harmless so they cannot come back through those doorways ever again to my home, property, automobile, work place, business, finances, ministry, my spouse, spouse's work place, our children, their schools, their work places, our friends and loved ones in Jesus Christ's Holy Name I pray with thanksgiving. **Amen.**

PRAYER FOR THE RELEASE OF RESENTMENT & BITTERNESS

Heavenly Father, I come to You now in the Name of my Lord and Savior Christ Jesus. Father, help me to let go of all bitterness and resentment. You are the One Who binds up and heals the broken-hearted. I receive Your anointing that breaks and destroys every yoke of bondage. I receive healing by faith according to Your Word, *Isaiah 53:5, "and with His stripes we are healed"*. Thank You for sending me Your Holy Spirit, I acknowledge the Holy Spirit as my wonderful Counselor! Thank You for helping me work out my salvation with fear and trembling, for it is You, Father, Who works in me to will and to act according to Your good purpose.

In the Name of Jesus, I choose to forgive those who have wronged me. I choose to live a life of forgiveness because You have forgiven me. I repent of all resentments, bitterness, rage, anger, brawling, and slander, along with every form of malice. I desire to be kind and compassionate to others, forgiving them, just as in Christ You forgave me. With the help of the Holy Spirit, I make every effort to live in peace with all men and to be holy, for I know that without holiness no one will see You. I will watch and pray that I will not enter into temptation or cause others to stumble. Thank You, Heavenly Father, that You watch over Your Word to perform it and that whom the Son has set free is free indeed. I declare that I have overcome resentment and bitterness by the Blood of the Lord Jesus Christ and by the Word of my testimony. **Amen**

PRAYER FOR THE HELP OF THE LORD

We are not moved by what we see, hear, smell, touch or taste. We are not moved by reason. We are only moved by Your Spirit and Your Word and we know Your Voice, and we hear Your Voice and we refuse to follow strangers according to *John 10:27*. Our seed is mighty upon the earth according to *Psalms 112:2*. Lord Jesus, I ask you to expand my territories; to fill me and increase me in the Holy Spirit and anointing with power. I ask You to lead me in paths of righteousness for Your Name's Sake. I Bless You, Praise You, Worship You, and commit all that I am to You, that Your perfect will be done through me. I ask that You help me to cease from my own labors. I do so by faith. I ask that You cause me to enter Your Rest now, in Jesus' Name and I receive that. I ask You to release my warring and ministering angels to minister and war on my behalf. I ask you to fill this, Your temple; with as much Shikinah Glory as possible. Help me to bear the cross You have prepared for me and help those in my family. I ask that the Holy Spirit speak to my heart through Your Word. I ask that You prepare me with reverence and worship, and with humility through Your Holy Spirit. I ask that You take out of me, add to me or do to me; anything You want. I ask that the Word I read would be engrafted into me and become part of me; spirit, mind, will and emotions. I declare by Your power; You are helping and causing me to be bold, dauntless, fearless, confident, intrepid, valiant, steadfast, faithful, true and loyal for Your Name's Sake. I ask You to deliver me where I am blind, wretched, naked, and poor. I ask for your help. I ask You to help me not be the accuser of the brethren but to teach others in gentleness, to be a help in season, to edify, to exhort and comfort others. I ask for Love and Grace for others and Grace from You Lord. I ask for help that Your Love and Grace in me; flow and be administered to others by Your Spirit in me, to manifest Your Presence in and through me. I release all things into Your hands and commit myself unto You, trusting You. I ask for help, that You give me the Word that You want me to give to others. Lord forgive me and help me to follow Your direction. I ask that You would send those that would receive the gift of salvation to me, that I may witness to them. Let them ask and receive, Father! I ask that You give me a clear mind and thoughts toward You, clear will toward You, and clear of all emotional clutter. (This is all about You. Hearing You is easier than thinking!) I ask that You cause me to hear You louder and clearer, and rest in You. I ask You to release Your love, joy, peace, patience, kindness, goodness, faithfulness, gentleness, with long-suffering, and self-control to flow over and in and throughout my life. I ask You Father for a clear, sharp, and healthy mind and body in You. Heavenly Father, I ask for Your perfect Will being worked out through my life and the lives of those that my life touch; as You direct me. I ask You for eyes to see, ears to hear, and a heart to comprehend and receive what the Holy Spirit has to say. I ask to speak and to do Your perfect will in this life; for You, for me, and for my family. I ask You to guard me and my family with many angels and that they manifest as needed. I ask You to make me alert, awake, sharp and attentive in Your thoughts and ways. I ask that I may prosper in what I put my hands to do for You. I ask you to renew my youth like the eagles. I ask for a heart like Yours and growth and maturity to walk in it to the fullest with You; in Jesus' Name. Amen! Holy Spirit have Your way with all of me, in Jesus' Name. Amen! Heavenly Father, I declare Your faithfulness to the heavens and Your loving kindness and tender mercies anew every morning. **Amen**

DAILY PRAYER FOR A CHILD

Heavenly Father, I pray that you will forgive me and every member of my family and all of my friends for anything we have done wrong. Lord help me to forgive anyone who may have hurt me and help anyone that I may have hurt or upset to forgive me. Lord, help me to love others and do what you want me to do. Please come into my heart Lord, and wash away my sins.

Lord, help my family to be happy and love one another and not be sad or mad at each other. Dear Lord, please take care of my loved ones and protect and love them as they care for me. I thank you for this wonderful day. Please show my family how much You love them and that you will always be there for them. Teach us to always come to you in prayer. Lord, I pray that every member of my family and all of my friends will accept You into their hearts so that they will go to heaven.

Lord Jesus, heal the sick so they will live a long, happy and healthy life. Lord, keep every member of my family, principals, teachers, friends, classmates, and pets safe from any harm or evil. Help me Lord to get good grades in school. Lord Jesus, I pray you protect the President, the leaders of our country and state, and their families. Lord, keep our pastors, firemen, policemen, ambulance drivers, emergency workers and all the soldiers, safe as they do their jobs. I pray for the poor and hungry. Send people to help them and give them a place to sleep, and if they are sick please make them well and feel better.

Lord I ask you to visit the sick in the hospitals and prisons, please heal them, and tell them about Your Son, Jesus Christ. Lord Jesus, I ask you to bless everyone that I have prayed for today and send Your mighty angels to protect all of us. Please help us to know you better, Lord Jesus, and have more of you Lord, in our hearts. I pray Lord, that you will be with everyone that I have prayed for today so they will be able to know and love You the way I love You. In Jesus Name I pray. **Amen**

PRAYER FOR THOSE WHO BLESS THE POOR

Heavenly Father, I come to You in the Name of Your Son, Jesus Christ according to *Psalm 41*. Heavenly Father, I pray that You will deliver me and each person that I pray for that remembers and blesses the poor. I pray that You will deliver each of us in our times of trouble. I pray Heavenly Father, that You will protect each of us and keep us alive because we remember and bless the poor. I pray that we will be called blessed upon the earth and that you will not deliver us into the will of our enemies. I ask You Heavenly Father to sustain each of us on our sick bed and in our illnesses and restore us to health. Oh Lord be gracious to us and heal our souls because we consider the poor and the helpless. Heavenly Father, I ask You to do this because of Your promises to us in *Psalms 41*. I ask for and receive these things in the Name of our Lord and Savior Jesus Christ of Nazareth according to *John 14:14*. **Amen**

PRAYER FOR THE FORGIVENESS OF SIN

Heavenly Father, I pray for myself (and for _____, _____, _____, and _____). I ask You to forgive me for all of my sins, iniquities, trespasses, transgressions, sins of commission, sins of omission, unknown sins or hidden sins according to *Psalms 19:12* and specifically any sins of doubt, unbelief, distrust, not abiding in You Lord Jesus and not letting Your Word abide in each of us at all times. Forgive us any strife, bitterness and anger. Forgive us for having other gods before you, making or buying images, bowing down or serving images. For taking your Name in vain, for not observing and keeping Holy the Sabbath Day, for not honoring our fathers and mothers, murder, adultery, stealing, bearing false witness, coveting our neighbor's spouse, house, land, donkeys, or anything else that is our neighbors, for not loving you with all of our heart, strength, mind, soul, love, and obedience, for not loving our neighbor as ourselves, for not loving ourselves, for entering into unrighteous agreements, not granting forgiveness, etc, etc, etc. [Please see "Sin List" on page 181 and ask God's forgiveness for any other sins that may apply to you]. Heavenly Father, I ask You to forgive me and each person that I pray for; for all my sins, iniquities, trespasses, and transgressions and to cover each of our sins, transgressions, iniquities, and trespasses with the Blood of the Lord Jesus Christ.

Heavenly Father, I repent for all my sins. I ask You to cleanse each of us of all unrighteousness according to *1 John 1:9*. I ask You to do this according to *John 14:14* in the Name of the Lord Christ Jesus of Nazareth. Heavenly Father I receive my forgiveness now. To God be the Glory. **Amen**

PRAYER FOR THE FORGIVENESS OF OTHERS I

Heavenly Father I forgive _____ for anything he/she has ever said or done to me or my family and I bless _____ in the Name of Jesus Christ of Nazareth. I ask You Lord to forgive and bless _____ in the Name of the Lord Jesus Christ of Nazareth. Lord Jesus show him/her Your mercy and loving-kindness, teach _____ as You have done with me. To God be the glory according to *John 14:14*. **Amen**.

PRAYER FOR THE FORGIVENESS OF OTHERS II

Jesus, I come to You now, in Your precious Name, and I ask You to forgive _____, for any unforgiveness they have in their heart toward me or others. I ask You to bless them and forgive them for this unforgiveness, in the Name of Jesus Christ of Nazareth, according to *John 14:13-14*

PRAYERS FOR THE BREAKING OF CURSES

Lord Jesus, I ask You to break and destroy any curses, ungodly soul ties, unholy alliances or any unrighteous agreements that I have entered into. Destroy any side effects, effects, residual effects, influences or stings of any curses that have been put on me, placed on me, declared over me, decreed over me, anyone that I have prayed for today, including our children, our grandchildren, our marriages, our homes, our cars, our trucks, our offices, our properties, our buildings, our businesses, our ministries, and our finances. I ask You to do this in the Name of Jesus Christ of Nazareth according to *John 14:14*. I ask You to destroy any witchcraft prayers, charismatic witchcraft prayers, psychic prayers, ungodly soul-ish prayers, side effects, effects, residual effects, influences, or stings of any witchcraft prayers or charismatic witchcraft prayers or psychic prayers, ungodly soul-ish prayers about me, over, or about anyone that I have prayed for today, including our children, our grandchildren, our marriages, our homes, our cars, our trucks, our offices, our properties, our buildings, our businesses, our ministries, our finances, our pets. I ask You to destroy them now in the Name of Jesus Christ of Nazareth according to *John 14:14*. I ask You to destroy any false prophecies that have been prophesied over me, or about me anyone that I have prayed for today, including our children, our grandchildren, our marriages, our homes, our cars, our trucks, our offices, our properties, our buildings, our businesses, our ministries, our finances. I ask You to destroy them now in the Name of Jesus Christ of Nazareth according to *John 14:14*. Lord Jesus, I ask You to destroy any hexes, vexes, witchcraft spells, voodoo spells, satanic spells, incantations, chains, fetters, snares, traps, effects, side effects, or residual effects, darts, arrows, stings, claws, spears, darkness, evil imprints, false memories, wrong mind sets, trauma, shock, any unrighteous instruments of the enemy that have attempted to penetrate me, any lies of the enemy, false memories, evil imprints, impressions, wrong thoughts and mind sets, that have been spoken into me, over me, anyone that I have prayed for today, including our children, our grandchildren, our marriages, our homes, our cars, our trucks, our offices, our properties, our buildings, our businesses, our ministries, our finances. I ask You to destroy them now in the Name of Jesus Christ of Nazareth according to *John 14:14*. Lord Jesus, I ask You to destroy any words, declarations, decrees, effects, side effects, stings and influences that have been spoken into me or over me, or into anyone or over anyone that I have prayed for today by ourselves or others that do not conform to Your will or Your destiny for our lives or the way You want us to believe and think and do. I apply the Blood of Jesus Christ of Nazareth, His Blood Covenant, *Psalms 91*, and Your healing virtue over me, into me, my spirit, mind, will, desires, emotions, ego, imaginations, anyone I prayed for today.

In the Name of the Lord Jesus Christ of Nazareth, I ask You Lord Jesus to destroy any assignments or plans that Satan or our spiritual enemies or physical enemies have against me, anyone that I have prayed for today, against our children, our grandchildren, our marriages, our homes, our cars, our trucks, our offices, our properties, our finances, our buildings, our businesses, our ministries, etc. I ask You to destroy them now in the Name of Jesus Christ of Nazareth according to *John 14:14*. To God be the Glory. **Amen**

In the Name of the Lord Jesus Christ of Nazareth, I ask You Lord Jesus to pull down and cast aside every demonic stronghold that is in my mind or that are in the minds of anyone that I have prayed for today. I ask You to pull down every vain imagination in me and in everyone that I pray for today and cast them aside in the Name of the Lord Christ Jesus. Lord Jesus, I ask You to pull down every high thought in me and in everyone that I have prayed for today; that exalts itself against the knowledge of God and cast them aside in the Name of the Lord Jesus Christ of Nazareth and to bring every thought captive in each of us to the obedience of Christ Jesus according to *2 Corinthians 10:3-6*.

Lord Christ Jesus, I ask You to pull down, cast aside and destroy any demonic strongholds that are over or in me, or over or in anyone that I have prayed for today; over our homes, cars, trucks, offices, property, buildings, businesses, ministries, marriages, finances. I ask You to destroy them now according to *John 14:14* in the Name of the Lord Jesus Christ of Nazareth. To God be the Glory. **Amen**

In the Name of my Lord and Savior Jesus Christ, I command my mind, desires, will, emotions, ego, imaginations, and thoughts, to come now to the obedience of Christ in me. Lord Jesus I ask You to destroy and remove all vain imaginations, demonic strongholds, and any deception that is in my thoughts and mind, and cast them aside in the Name of Jesus Christ. I ask You to wash my mind clean with the Precious Blood of Jesus Christ of Nazareth and enable me to stay in Your Presence all day long, according to *John 14:14*, to God be the glory! **Amen**

Lord Jesus, Your Word says that Your anointing destroys all yokes of bondage (*Isaiah 10:27*) so I ask You now to cause Your anointing to break and destroy any yokes of bondages along with all of their works, roots, fruits, tentacles and links that are in my life, the lives of anyone that I have prayed for today according to *John 14:14*, in the Name of the Lord Jesus Christ. **Amen**

PRAYER FOR BINDING AND BANISH DEMONIC SPIRITS

Heavenly Father, according to *Matthew 16 and 18*, I thank you that whatsoever I shall bind on earth shall be bound in heaven and whatsoever I loose on earth shall be loosed in heaven. KJV

In the Name of the Lord Jesus Christ of Nazareth, I bind all of Satan's evil, wicked, demon, lying and tormenting spirits and strongmen along with all evil principalities, powers and rulers of wickedness in high places; including all their works, roots, fruits, tentacles and links including any spirits and strongmen of doubt, unbelief, leviathan, pride, anger, rage, strife, deception, self-deception, confusion, self-confusion, divination, Jezebel, python, accusation, familiar spirits, delusion, self-delusion, and unforgiving heart, witchcraft, and willful sins: ____, ____, and ____. [Please look at the "Demon List" on page 183 and banish any foul spirits that you feel may apply to you.] I bind and banish all these demonic spirits and strongmen from me, from everyone that I have prayed for today, from every organ in our bodies, from every cell in our bodies, from every gland, muscle, ligament and bone in our bodies, from our homes, properties, marriages, cars, trucks, businesses, ministries, objects, work places, finances, and pets. I banish them to where Jesus sends them and I bind them and command them to stay there; in the Name of Jesus Christ of Nazareth. I place the Blood of the Lord Christ Jesus between us.

Heavenly Father, it is written in *Psalms 91*, and *Matthew 6*, and many other places of Your Word that You are my Deliverer and I ask that You give me, and everyone that I prayed for today: total deliverance, total freedom, total liberty, and total salvation from all evil, wicked, demon, lying, perverse, unclean, foul, demonic spirits, strongmen, and their messengers, and from all sicknesses, diseases, infirmities, afflictions, infections, viruses, inflammations, disorders of any kind in every cell in our bodies, in every gland in our bodies, in every organ in our bodies, abnormal cells, radical cells, abnormal growths, radical growths, cancers, tumors, spasms, lesions, or cysts in any parts of our bodies. Heavenly Father, I ask You to give our homes, cars, trucks, offices, businesses, finances, ministries, properties and pets: total deliverance and liberty and freedom from all evil, wicked, lying, perverse and unclean spirits in the Name of Jesus Christ. I thank You for giving me this deliverance, freedom, liberty and salvation from all these things in the Name of the Lord Jesus Christ of Nazareth. Heavenly Father, I ask You to give me and each person I pray for today divine healing, divine health, and the manifestation of every miracle and every healing that you have ever given me according to *John 16:23*. May these deliverances be used to glorify You, Heavenly Father.

In the Name of the Lord Jesus Christ of Nazareth, I command our minds, wills, and emotions to submit to the obedience of Christ in me. To God be the Glory. **Amen**

PRAYER TO APPLY THE BLOOD OF JESUS

Heavenly Father, I bow and worship and praise before You and I apply the Blood of Jesus Christ over myself, each person that I have prayed for today; from the tops of our heads to the soles of our feet. I apply the Blood of Jesus over each of us, over the airways that surround us, over us and under us, over telephone lines, over our homes, properties, offices, cars, trucks, businesses, finances, marriages, ministries, cell phone frequencies, and I ask You to render powerless and harmless and nullify the power, destroy the power, cancel the power of any evil spirit, demonic spirit, demonic strongman, messenger of Satan and witchcraft prayer that tries to come into our presence, our homes, everything in our homes, our pets, our properties, our cars, our trucks, everything in our cars and trucks, our marriages, our finances, our ministries, our telephone lines, our telephone frequencies in the Name of Jesus Christ of Nazareth.

Lord Jesus Christ, I ask You to wash and cleanse my mind with Your Precious Blood. Give me clarity of thought; give me a sound and sober mind, in Jesus Christ Holy Name; according to *John 14:14*. To God be the Glory. **Amen**

PRAYER TO BE FILLED WITH THE HOLY SPIRIT

Heavenly Father, I ask You to fill each of us with Your precious Holy Spirit. I ask You to fill each of us with all of the fruits of Your Holy Spirit including Your love, Your joy, Your peace, Your gentleness, Your goodness, Your meekness, Your faithfulness and Your self-control. Heavenly Father, in Christ Jesus' Holy Name I ask You to fill me, everyone I prayed for today with Your Holy Ghost anointing and power, cover us with Your presence, Your anointing, Your power; in the Name of Jesus Christ of Nazareth and I ask You Lord Jesus to heal me and fill me with Your Holy Spirit and power, cover us with Your anointing and presence, and to fill me and seal me with Your peace, character, and nature. I ask You to do all these things in the Name of the Lord Jesus Christ of Nazareth according to *John 14:14*. To God be the Glory. **Amen**

BINDING THE ENEMIES EYES AND EARS PRAYER

In the Name of the Lord Jesus Christ of Nazareth, I bind all of Satan's evil, wicked, demon, lying, unclean, perverse tormenting spirits and strongmen and messengers, their eyes blind, their ears deaf to our prayers, conversations and actions unless we speak directly to them in the Name of the Lord Christ Jesus. I bind them and command them not to manifest in my presence, the presence of anyone that I will be around today, the presence of anyone that I have prayed for today; or in the presence of our homes, cars, trucks, offices, properties, buildings, businesses, ministries, marriages, finances.

Heavenly Father, I ask that You shut any doors that need to be shut and open any doors that need to be opened in the spiritual and natural realms of our lives in Jesus' Holy Name. Heavenly Father, I apply the Blood of Jesus over those doorways and ask that the enemy be rendered powerless and harmless so they cannot come back through those doorways ever again to our homes, properties, cars, trucks, work places, businesses, finances, minds, ministries, our spouses, spouse's work places, our children, their schools, their work places, our friends and loved ones in Jesus Christ's Holy Name. To God be the Glory. **Amen**

PRAYER TO WEAR THE FULL ARMOR OF GOD

Heavenly Father, I give thanks for Your mighty armor which You have provided for us. I put on us the full armor of God: the Helmet of Salvation; the Breastplate of Righteousness; the Girdle of Truth; the Sandals of Peace; the Shield of Faith which protects us from all fiery darts of the enemy; and I pick up the Sword of the Spirit, the Word of God, that I choose to use against all the forces of evil in our lives. I ask You Lord according to *John 14:13 & 14*, to be our Guard and a Shield about us. Take us into the cleft of the Rock and underneath Your Mighty Wings according to *Psalms 91*. I put Your Armor on us and live and pray in complete dependence upon You, and pray in the Spirit at all times and on all occasions, *Ephesians 6:10-18*. Blessed Heavenly Father. To God be the Glory. **Amen**

PRAYERS FOR THE PROTECTION OF THE ANGELS

According to *John 14:14*, I ask You Lord Jesus to loose Your angels in great abundance in my presence, the presence of everyone that I have prayed for today and into our homes, cars, trucks, lands, properties, buildings, and work places to protect us, guard us and to force out, drive out, and cleanse out all evil, wicked demon and tormenting spirits from our presence, and our homes, cars, trucks, lands, properties, animals, and work places and send them to where You want to send them in Christ Jesus' Holy Name. To God be the Glory. **Amen**

Lord Jesus, I ask you to put a hedge of protection around our minds and around each of us to protect us from the enemy. I ask You to do this according *John 14:14*. **Amen**

PSALMS 91 PRAYER OF PROTECTION

Heavenly Father, I pray for myself everyone that I prayed for today. I pray for all members of congress and of the armed forces of our nation, all of our intercessors, teachers, pastors, friends, enemies, neighbors, doctors, dentists, all people of Israel, everyone we go to church with, and all of Your workers.

Heavenly Father, I ask You to let us dwell in the secret place of the most High and abide under the shadow of the Almighty. I ask You to let us say that You are our Lord, our refuge, our fortress and our God in whom we can trust. I ask You to deliver us from the snare of the fowler, and from the deadly pestilence. I ask You to cover each of us with Your feathers and let us walk under Your wings to take refuge. I ask You to let Your faithfulness and truth be our shield and armor. I ask You to let us not be afraid of the terror by night; nor for the arrow that flies by day; nor for the deadly pestilence that walks in darkness nor for the destruction that wastes at noonday. I ask You to cause a thousand to fall at our side, and ten thousand at our right hand and not to let any come near us. I ask You to give Your angels charge over us to keep us in all Your ways and let Your angel's hands lift us up, so we do not even dash our foot against a stone or be hurt in any way. I ask You to let us tread upon the lion and serpent and to let us trample the young lion and the serpent under our feet. I ask You Heavenly Father, to answer us when we call upon You, be with us in trouble, deliver us, honor us and satisfy us with a long life and show us Your salvation.

Heavenly Father, I thank You that these things are written in *Psalms 91*. I am thankful that our Lord Christ Jesus spoiled all principalities and powers and made a show of them openly and triumphed over them in Himself. I claim all that victory for our lives. I reject all the insinuations, accusations, and temptations of Satan. I affirm that the Word of God is true and we choose to live in obedience to You Lord Jesus and in fellowship with You. Open our eyes and show us the areas of our lives that do not please You. Work in us to cleanse us from all ground that would give Satan a foothold against us. We do in every way stand in all that it means to be your adopted child and we welcome all the ministry of Your Holy Spirit.

Heavenly Father, I pray that now and through our lives, You would strengthen and enlighten us, show us the way Satan and his demonic spirits are trying to hinder, tempt, lie, and distort the truth in our lives. Enable us to be the kind of person that will please you. Enable us to be aggressive in prayer and faith. Enable us to be aggressive mentally, to think about and practice Your word, and to give You, Your rightful place in our lives.

Heavenly Father, I place all of my cares, all of my anxieties, all of my worries and all of my concerns once and for all on You, because I know that You love me and watch over me according to *1 Peter 5:7*. I pray for the peace of Jerusalem and may all those prosper who love You. *Psalms 122:6*. I pray that You will establish Jerusalem and make her a praise in the earth. *Isaiah 62:7*. To God be the Glory. Amen!

DEMONS CAN FOLLOW UNAWARE

It has been my experience to come away from going on a Prison Ministry, to a hospital and other various places and not feel right when I came back. What I found out was that evil spirits though they might not get on you, they follow at a distance. On one of those occurrences someone had the sense to pray about anything that might be evil to force and drive them back where they came from. My nights of sleep were better and there was less turmoil in the office and home that week. Remember that anywhere people congregate, like malls, gas stations, grocery stores, apparel stores, etc., that demons will be. Some of these demons are sent out due to wrong prayers or on assignment against you and me. Amen

PRAYER AGAINST DEMONS THAT FOLLOW

Heavenly Father, I come to You in Jesus Christ's Holy Name. I ask You Lord Jesus Christ according to *John 14:13 & 14*, that any evil spirits that are following me and/or _____, _____, and _____ that you would force and drive those evil spirits into the Abyss and any of their replacements, destroy their assignments and attacks against me, and _____, _____, and _____, force and drive those evil spirits far from our houses, cars, lands, properties, vehicles, animals, and work places, and do not let them return anywhere near us in Jesus Name we pray. **Amen**

UNRIGHTEOUS AGREEMENTS

I was at work one day when I was hit with sharp pains in my head. I prayed and had others pray and the pain temporarily went away. Soon to my surprise the sharp shooting pains returned. I was leaving work and they hit hard. I called Brother Jim, who prayed in the Spirit to get to the root of it. He said the attack was coming from unrighteous agreements. I believe unrighteous agreements are agreements in prayer formed between two people, two evil spirits, or the combination there of. Jim and I prayed in agreement against the unrighteous agreement and the pain ceased immediately. You will also want to pray against any side effects and stings of these prayers too.

PRAYER TO DESTROY UNRIGHTEOUS AGREEMENTS

Heavenly Father, I come to You in Jesus Christ's Holy Name. I ask You Lord Jesus Christ according to *John 14:13 & 14*, that You destroy the unrighteous agreement that is coming against me that has been prayed, is being prayed, or will be prayed throughout the rest of this day and into tomorrow afternoon, along with its effects, side effects, and stings. I ask You Lord to destroy all demonic hordes that have been sent forth from those prayers and cast them into the Abyss, along with any pain, darkness, darts, arrows, stings, claws, spears, lies, evil imprints, impressions, false memories, wrong mindsets, throughout the rest of this day into tomorrow afternoon. **Amen**

DEUTERONOMY 28 PRAYER OF BLESSING

Heavenly Father, I ask You to bless us when we come in. I ask You to bless us when we go out. I ask You to bless us in the city. I ask You to bless us in the country. I ask You to bless our fruits. I ask You to bless our seed. I ask You to bless our land. I ask You to bless our store house. I ask You to bless and prosper everything we touch. I ask You to cause our enemies to come at us in one direction but to flee from us in seven directions because greater are You who is in us than he that is in the world. To God be the Glory. **Amen**

NUMBERS 6:23-26 PRAYER OF BLESSING

Heavenly Father, in Christ Jesus' Holy Name; I thank You for Your Word in *Numbers 6:23-26*. Heavenly Father, I pray that You will bless us and that You will keep us. I pray that You will make Your face shine upon us and be gracious to us. I pray that You will lift up Your countenance upon us and give us peace. Lord Jesus, I thank You for blessing us.

Lord Jesus, I ask You destroy false memories, lies of the enemy, unrighteous agreements, bad attitudes, bad thoughts, ungodly negative impressions, and imprints according to *John 14:14*. I ask You to cleanse our minds with the Blood of the Lord Christ Jesus of all thoughts and preconceived ideas that do not conform to Your will and destiny for our lives and the way You want us to believe and think. Lord Jesus, I ask You to prevent our minds from deceiving us in any way.

Lord Jesus, I ask you to do all of these things according to *John 14:14*; and Heavenly Father I ask You to give us these things according to *John 16:23*. In the Name of the Lord Jesus Christ of Nazareth, I pray with thanksgiving. To God be the Glory. **Amen**

DAILY PRAYER TO COMMIT YOUR LIFE TO THE LORD

I renew and give my total allegiance to You, Lord Jesus Christ, Father God and Holy Spirit, fresh and anew, today and for the rest of my life, to do Your work, to do Your will and obey You at all times. I give my life, and all that is in it, as a living sacrifice, unto You which is my reasonable service, that first and foremost, all that I am would be a glory, honor, and praise unto You, Heavenly Father, Son, and Holy Spirit, in Jesus Christ's Holy Name. I commit my life and all that is in it, to You, to do Your Good Works, and to have and be in Your Total Desire, Will, and Presence, that I will, I am, and I will be, transformed into Your total likeness in Jesus Christ's Holy Name. Come Lord Jesus Christ take Your rightful place in my life, I give it to You, for eternity and I ask You Lord, to bind all that I am to all that you are, in Jesus Christ's Holy Name. **Amen**

PRAYER FOR GOD'S PRESENCE TO BE WITH YOU

Heavenly Father, I come to You now in the Name of my Lord and Savior Christ Jesus. Holy Spirit I pray that You will quicken me to hear my Heavenly Father's Voice and lead me in prayer. Heavenly Father, I bow and worship before You. I come to You with praise and with thanksgiving. I come to You in humility, in fear, in trembling and seeking the truth. I come to You in gratitude, in love, and through the precious Blood of Your Son Jesus Christ of Nazareth.

Heavenly Father God, I thank You that Your Word says that when I pray to You that You will hear me according to *Job 22:27 & 28*. Your word says that in every place I go where Your Name is remembered, You will come to me and bless me according to Your word in *Exodus 20:24*, and Your presence will go with me wherever I go and You will give me rest according to *Exodus 33:14*.

Heavenly Father, I pray that You will continually guide me and satisfy my desires in scorched places, give strength to my bones and I will be like a watered garden and like a spring of water, whose waters do not fail, according to your Word. *Isaiah 58:11*. I pray in the Name of my Lord and Savior Jesus Christ of Nazareth that You would destroy the power of all demonic spirits that are coming against me, _____ and _____, our homes, properties, automobiles, business, finances, ministries. That You would encamp Your angels and chariots of fire all around me, according to *2 Kings 6:17 & 18*. I declare these things in the Name of the Lord Jesus Christ of Nazareth and I thank You that they will be established for us. **Amen**

PRAYER FOR CLARITY

Heavenly Father, I ask you to give me and each person I have prayed for today clarity of vision, clarity of sight, clarity of thought, clarity of mind, clarity of knowing, and hearing Your Voice according to *John 16:23*. **Amen**

PRAYER FOR MIND CLEANSING

Heavenly Father, I come to You now in the Name of my Lord and Savior Christ Jesus. Lord we ask You according to *John 14: 13 & 14*, to wash over our minds with the Blood of Jesus and cleanse out all darkness and all thoughts that are contrary to Your will and destiny for our lives. I ask You Lord Jesus to shut any doors that need to be shut whether spiritual or natural, and to open any doors that need to be opened whether spiritual or natural in my life. **Amen**

PRAYERS OF BLESSING

Heavenly Father, I come to You now in the Name of my Lord and Savior Christ Jesus. I ask You to give me divine healing now in every area of my life, spirit, mind, will, emotions and physical being in accordance with Your Divine Plan and Order for my life. I receive Your Divine Healing, Wholeness and Newness of life, in the Name of Jesus Christ. Lord, I ask You to expand in me Your territories. Lord I ask for and receive beauty for ashes, the oil of joy for mourning, the garment of praise for the spirit of heaviness: for I am a tree of righteousness, the planting of the Lord, that You may be glorified, in Jesus' Name. Thy will be done on earth as it is in Heaven, Father, I pray with thanksgiving in Jesus' Name. **Amen**

Heavenly Father, I ask you to give me and every person I prayed for today, according to *John 16:23*, the manifestation of every miracle and every healing You have given to me and the manifestation of divine healing and divine health in my body **Amen!**

Heavenly Father, I come to You now in the Name of my Lord and Savior Christ Jesus. Lord Jesus Christ, I ask You, according to *John 14:13 & 14*, to cover me with Your anointing, glory, and tangible Presence, give me a fresh new release and flow in my inner man with rivers of living waters springing up forth abundantly with Life abundant, fill me to over-flowing with Your favor, compassion and love, Your wisdom and understanding. Anoint me to hear Your Voice, not that of a stranger; cause me to clearly discern Your Voice over that of a strange voice. Give me Your eyes to see spiritually, and a heart to understand and be led by Your Holy Spirit, clearly, help me to be bold, confident and be obedient, to do Your will. Fill me with Your gifts, anointing, and blessings and all else You have for me. I ask You to anoint me, pour out Your anointing on me (you may apply the anointing oil to the forehead now if available). I receive Your Anointing in the Name of the Father, the Son, and the Holy Spirit.

Lord Jesus Christ, I ask You, according to *John 14:13 & 14*, to do all these things and let Your love so brightly shine through me into others and as an act of worship to You, in Jesus' Name. **Amen**

LUKE 21:36 PRAYER OF WATCHFULNESS

Heavenly Father, I come to You now in the Name of my Lord and Savior Christ Jesus and I pray for myself and each person I prayed for today. I pray that each of us may be counted worthy to escape all things that will come to pass, and that I may stand before the Son of man.

Heavenly Father, I thank You for keeping me watchful and praying at all times, I thank You letting us be counted worthy to escape all things that will come to pass. I thank You for letting me stand before the Son of Man, Jesus Christ. In Jesus Christ's Holy Name I pray. **Amen**

1 THESSALONIANS 5:23-24 PRAYER OF SANCTITY

Heavenly Father, I come to You now in the Name of my Lord and Savior Christ Jesus. I pray for myself and everyone that I prayed for today and I ask that You, the God of peace Himself will sanctify us completely; and that our whole spirit, soul, and body will be preserved blameless at the coming of our Lord and Savior Jesus Christ. I ask You Heavenly Father Who is called Faithful to do it. **Amen**

ISAIAH 40:31 PRAYER TO RENEW STRENGTH

Heavenly Father, I come to You now in the Name of my Lord and Savior Christ Jesus. I pray for myself and everyone that I prayed for today and I ask that You will renew our strength, the ones that wait upon You: that we shall mount up with wings like eagles, they we will run and not be weary we will walk and not faint.

Heavenly Father, I thank You that You will renew our strength, the ones that wait upon You: that we shall mount up with wings like eagles, they we will run and not be weary we will walk and not faint. In the Name of Jesus Christ of Nazareth I pray. **Amen**

EPHESIANS 1:17-23 PRAYER FOR THE SPIRIT OF WISDOM

Heavenly Father, I pray according to Your Word in *Ephesians 1:17-23*, that You will give each of us a spirit of wisdom and revelation in the knowledge of Christ Jesus. I pray that the eyes of our understanding will be enlightened so we may know what is the hope of the calling of Christ Jesus and the riches of the glory of Christ Jesus' inheritance in the saints, and what is the exceeding greatness of Your power towards us who believe, according to the working of Your mighty power which You used to raise Christ Jesus from the dead and seated Him at Your right hand in heavenly places, far above all principality and power and might and dominion, and every name that is named, not only in this age but also in the age which is to come. Heavenly Father, I thank You that You put all things under the feet of Christ Jesus, and gave Him to be head over all things to the church, which is His body, the fullness of Him who fills all in all. To God be the Glory.

Heavenly Father, open my eyes that I may see how great You are and how complete Your provision is for me. I thank You that the victory the Lord Christ Jesus won for me on the Cross and in His resurrection has been given to me and I am seated with the Lord Christ Jesus in the heavenlies.

Heavenly Father, by faith and in dependence upon You; I put off the fleshly works of the old man and stand unto all the victory of the crucifixion where the Lord Christ Jesus provided cleansing from the old nature. I put on myself the new man and I stand into all the victory of the resurrection and the provisions that Christ Jesus has made for me. I put off all forms of selfishness and put on myself the new nature with its love. I put off all forms of fear and put on the new nature with its courage. I put off all forms of lust and put on the new nature with its righteousness, purity, and honesty. I am trusting You to show each of us how to accomplish this in our daily lives. In every way we stand into the victory of the ascension and glorification of the Lord Christ Jesus, whereby all principalities and powers were made subject to Christ Jesus. I claim our place in Christ as victorious with Him over all the enemies of our souls. Holy Spirit, I pray that You would fill us. Come into our lives, breakdown every idol and cast out every foe and continually lead us in prayer.

I am thankful Heavenly Father for the expression of Your will for our daily lives that You have shown us in Your Word. By the power of the Lord Christ Jesus; I claim all the will and destiny of God for each of us. I am thankful that You have blessed us with all spiritual blessings in heavenly places in Christ Jesus. I am thankful that You have begotten us unto a living hope by the resurrection of Christ Jesus from the dead. I am thankful that You have made provision for us so that we can be filled with the Spirit of God with love, joy, peace, with longsuffering, gentleness and goodness, with meekness, faithfulness and self-control in our lives. I recognize that it is Your will for us and I therefore reject and resist all the efforts of Satan and his wicked spirits to rob us of the will of God. Lord Jesus, I ask You to put a hedge of protection around our minds to protect us from the enemy of all accusations, distortions, insinuations and lies. I claim the fullness of the will of God for our lives.

In the Name of the Lord Christ Jesus, I completely surrender myself to You Heavenly Father, as a living sacrifice. I choose not to be conformed to this world. I choose to be transformed by the renewing of our minds and I pray that You would show us Your will and enable us to walk in Your will. In the Name of the Lord Jesus Christ of Nazareth, I bind our wills to the will of God, I bind our minds to the mind of Christ. To God be the Glory. **Amen**

EPHESIANS 3:16-21 PRAYER FOR INNER STRENGTH

Heavenly Father, I pray according to Ephesians 3:16-21, I ask You to grant each of us, myself, _____, and _____ according to the riches of Christ Jesus' glory, I ask You to strengthen our inner man with might through Christ Jesus, that through faith, Christ may dwell in our hearts; that we are rooted and grounded in love, and we may be able to comprehend with all the saints what is the width and length and depth and height of Christ' love – to know the love of Christ; that we may be filled with all the fullness of You, Heavenly Father. I thank You that Christ Jesus is able to do exceedingly abundantly above all that we ask or think according to the power that works in us, to Him be the glory in the church by Christ Jesus to all generations, forever and ever. **Amen**

PRAYERS OF SPIRITUAL WARFARE FROM THE PSALMS

PSALMS 35

Heavenly Father, I come to You now in the Name of my Lord and Savior Christ Jesus. Heavenly Father, I pray for myself and everyone that I prayed for today and I ask that You will plead my cause, O LORD, with them that strive with me. I ask You to fight against them that fight against me. Lord, I ask that You take hold of shield and buckler, and stand up for my help. I ask You to draw out the spear, and stop them that persecute me: I ask You to say unto my soul, I am your salvation. I ask that they be confounded and put to shame that seek after my souls: let them be turned back and brought to confusion that devises my hurt. Let them be as chaff before the wind: and let the angel of the LORD chase them. Let their way be dark and slippery: and let the angel of the LORD persecute them. For without cause have they hid for me their net in a pit, which without cause they have dug for our souls. I ask that destruction come upon him at unawares; and let this net that he hath hid; catch himself: into that very destruction let him fall. I ask that my souls shall be joyful in the LORD. I ask that we shall rejoice in our salvation. I ask that all of my bones shall say, LORD, who is like unto thee, which delivers the poor from him that is too strong for him. **Amen**

PSALMS 61

Heavenly Father, I come to You now in the Name of my Lord and Savior Christ Jesus. I pray for myself and everyone that I prayed for today and I ask that You will hear my cry, O God; attend unto my prayers. From the end of the earth will I cry unto thee, when my hearts are overwhelmed; lead me to the rock that is higher than me. For thou hast been a shelter for me and a strong tower from the enemy. I ask that I can abide in thy tabernacle for ever: I ask that I can trust in the shelter of thy wings. For thou, O God, I ask that You hear my vows: You hast given me the heritage of those that fear Your Name. I ask that You will prolong the king's life: and his years as many generations. I ask that he shall abide before God forever: prepare mercy and truth, which may preserve him. So will I sing praise unto Your Name forever, that I may daily perform my vows.

Heavenly Father, I thank You that You will hear my cry and attend unto my prayers. I thank You that from the end of the earth will I cry unto thee, when our hearts are overwhelmed; I thank You for leading us to the rock that is higher than me. I thank You for being a shelter for me, and a strong tower from the enemy. I thank You for me abiding in thy tabernacle for ever: that I trust in the cover of thy wings. O God, I thank You that You hear my vows: I thank You for giving me the heritage of those that fear Your Name. I thank You that You will prolong the king's life and his years as many generations. I thank You that he shall abide before God for ever. Thank You for preparing mercy and truth; that will preserve me. I thank You that I sing praise unto Your Name forever, that I daily perform my vows. In the Name of Jesus Christ of Nazareth I pray. **Amen**

PSALMS 64

Heavenly Father, I come to You now in the Name of my Lord and Savior Christ Jesus. Heavenly Father, I pray for myself and everyone that I prayed for today. I ask You to hear my voice in my meditation and preserve my life from fear of the enemy. God, I ask You to hide me from the secret counsel of the wicked; from the rebellion of the workers of iniquity: Who whet their tongue like a sword, and bend their bows to shoot their arrows, even bitter words: That they may shoot in secret at the perfect: suddenly they shoot at him, and do fear not. They encourage themselves in an evil matter: they commune of laying snares privately; they say, Who shall see them? They search out iniquities: they accomplish a diligent search: both the inward thought of every one of them, and the heart, is deep. But God shall shoot at them with an arrow; suddenly shall they be wounded. So they shall make their own tongue to fall upon themselves: all that see them shall fall away. All men shall fear, and shall declare the work of God; for they shall wisely consider His doing. The righteous shall be glad in the LORD, and shall trust in him; and all the upright in heart shall glory. **Amen**

PSALMS 32

Heavenly Father, I come to You now in the Name of my Lord and Savior Christ Jesus. Heavenly Father, I pray for myself and everyone that I prayed for today and I ask You to bless me. I ask You to forgive my transgression and cover my sin. I ask that I are blessed as to the man unto whom the LORD imputeth not iniquity and in whose spirit there is no guile. When I kept silence, my bones waxed old through my groaning all the day long. For day and night thy hand was heavy upon me: my moisture is turned into the drought of summer. Selah. I acknowledged my sin unto thee, and my iniquity I have not hid. I ask that I may confess our transgressions unto the LORD; and I ask that You may forgive the iniquity of my sin. Selah. For this shall every one that is godly pray unto thee in a time when thou mayest be found: surely in the floods of great waters they shall not come nigh unto him. I ask that You are my hiding place; thou shalt preserve me from trouble; You shalt compass me about with songs of deliverance. Selah. I ask that You will instruct me and teach me in the way which I shalt go: I ask that You will guide me with Your eye. I ask that I will not be as the horse, or as the mule, which have no understanding: whose mouth must be held in with bit and bridle, lest they come near unto You. Many sorrows shall be to the wicked: but he that trusteth in the LORD, mercy shall compass us about. I ask that I be glad in the LORD, and rejoice, and be righteous: and I may shout for joy, and be upright in heart.

Heavenly Father, I thank You that I are blessed and my transgression is forgiven, that my sin is covered. That I are blessed as to the man unto whom the LORD imputeth not iniquity and in whose spirit there is no guile. When I kept silence, our bones waxed old through my groaning all the day long. For day and night thy hand was heavy upon me:

my moisture is turned into the drought of summer. Selah. I thank You that we acknowledged my sin unto thee, and my iniquity I have not hid. I thank You that I may confess my transgressions unto the LORD; and I thank you that You may forgive the iniquity of my sin. Selah. I thank You that I shall, everyone that is godly, pray unto thee in a time when thou mayest be found: surely in the floods of great waters they shall not come nigh unto him. I thank You that You are my hiding place; thou shalt preserve me from trouble; You shalt compass me about with songs of deliverance. Selah. I thank You that You will instruct me and teach me in the way which I shalt go: I thank You that You will guide me with Your eye. I thank You that I will not be as the horse, or as the mule, which have no understanding: whose mouth must be held in with bit and bridle, lest they come near unto You. Many sorrows shall be to the wicked: but he that trusteth in the LORD, mercy shall compass me about. I ask that I be glad in the LORD, and rejoice, and be righteous: and I may shout for joy, and be upright in heart. In the Name of Jesus Christ of Nazareth I pray. **Amen**

PSALMS 51

Heavenly Father have mercy on me according to Your tender mercy and Your steadfast love. Blot out my transgressions. Wash me thoroughly and repeatedly from my iniquity and guilt and cleanse me and make me pure from my sin. I am conscious O'Lord of my transgressions and I acknowledge them. My sin is ever before me. I have sinned against You and only You O'Lord. I have sinned and done that which is evil in Your sight. You are justified in Your sentence and faultless judgment of me O'Lord. Heavenly Father I know that I was (were) brought forth in a state of iniquity; my mother was sinful who conceived me and I too am sinful. I know, O'Lord, that You desire truth in my inner being; make me therefore to know wisdom in my inmost heart. Purify me O'Lord with Your anointing and cleanse me and I will be white as snow, free of sin. Heavenly Father, help me to hear Your joy and gladness and be satisfied; let the bones You have broken rejoice once again and be completely healed. O'Lord have mercy on me and hide Your face from my sins and blot out all my guilt and iniquities. Create in me a clean heart; O'Lord, and renew a right; persevering and steadfast spirit in me. O'Lord cast not me from Your presence and do not take Your Holy Spirit from me. Restore unto me O'Lord, the joy of Your salvation and uphold me with You free Spirit. I will teach transgressors Your Ways O'Lord and sinners shall be converted and then return to You. Heavenly Father deliver me from this guiltiness and death. You are the Lord of my salvation and I will sing aloud Your righteousness. O'Lord open my lips and my mouth shall bring forth Your praise. I pray O'Lord that You will delight in my sacrifice of my broken spirit; my broken and contrite heart and I humble myself in complete repentance before You. In Jesus Name I pray. **Amen**

PSALM 67

We know Lord that all my happiness comes from Your mercy; so I pray that You Lord, be merciful to me. I ask You, Lord, to continue to cause Your face to shine upon me. Pardon me from all my sins. God, I need your grace and blessings. Everything that I have, everything that I need, comes from you and you alone. Most of all, I need you. I need to know you. I need to have the light of your face shine on me, so Father, show grace to me. Bless me abundantly. But also help me to remember that you give your blessings not just for me alone, but that I might be a blessing for others. You show me your ways that I might humbly teach your way to others. You save my life now and for eternity that I might give my life for the salvation of others. Father, help me to not look so intently on gifts you have given me than I no longer seek your face. Help me to not cling to my blessings so tightly that I can't open my hands to give to others or even to receive more from you. Help me not to fear that if I give, you won't be able to replenish what I lack. Help me to trust your sufficiency, your abundance even, and that whatever is for your glory is ultimately for my good–no matter what the initial cost. In Jesus Name We Pray. **Amen**

JABEZ PRAYER

Lord Jesus, I call on the God of Israel saying "Oh, that You would bless me indeed, and enlarge my territory, that Your hand would be with me, and that Your hand would be with me, and that You would keep me from evil, that I may not cause pain!" Father God, I ask You to grant me what I have requested the way You did for Jabez, according to *1 Chronicles 4:9-10.* **Amen**

BIND MIND TO THE WILL OF GOD

Heavenly Father, I come to You now in the Name of my Lord and Savior Christ Jesus. I bind my mind to the will of God, I bind _____'s mind to the will of God in the Name of Jesus Christ of Nazareth. **Amen**

ROMANS 12 PRAYER FOR GRACE & PATIENCE IN TRIBULATION

Heavenly Father, we thank You Lord for the mercies by which You allow us to present our bodies as living sacrifice, holy and acceptable, which is our spiritual service of worship to You.

Dear Lord, it is not our will to be conformed to this world, but to be transformed by the renewing of our minds, that we may prove good, acceptable, and perfect to what Your will is. By grace given to us, show us how to not esteem ourselves more or less important to the body of Christ than another. Thank You Lord for the spiritual gifts that have been given to us that we may prophesy in proportion to our faith and to teach according to Your precious Word and to exhort and to give liberally and lead with diligence and show mercy with cheerfulness.

Lord, show us how our love can be without hypocrisy. Teach us to abhor what is evil and cling to what is good. Teach us to be kind and affectionate to one another in honor and give preference to one another not lagging in diligence to be fervent in spirit to serve You Lord. Dear Father, we rejoice in hope, we are patient through tribulation, and we shall continue in distributing to the needs of the saints and be truly given to hospitality.

We will bless those who curse and persecute us. We will rejoice with those who rejoice, and weep with those who weep. We will be of the same mind toward one another and not set our minds on high things but associate ourselves with the humble. We will not be wise in our own opinions and we will not repay anyone evil for evil for Your Word says to repay evil with good. We will not give place to wrath but will wait on the Lord for vengeance is Yours, therefore, we will live peacefully with all people and be overcomers through Christ. Lord we will offer drink to a thirsty enemy and food to one that is hungry that we may abide in Your Word forever, because we love You Heavenly Father, in Christ Jesus Holy Name we pray, with thanksgiving. **Amen**

HEARING GOD'S VOICE PRAYER

Heavenly Father, I come to You now in the Name of my Lord and Savior Christ Jesus. It is written in Your Word according to *John chapter 10* that Your sheep know Your Voice. Heavenly Father, I am one of Your sheep. I ask You Heavenly Father, to teach me to hear Your Voice distinctly and clearly. I ask You increase Your anointing on me to clearly hear and know Your Voice and not that of a stranger, I ask You to do this in the Name of Jesus Christ of Nazareth. Give me the ability Heavenly Father to hear Your Voice, I ask this according to *John 16:23* in the Name of Jesus Christ of Nazareth. **Amen**

TESTING THE SPIRITS

Heavenly Father, it is written in Your Word in *1 John 4:1 & 2* that we should not believe every spirit but test the spirits to determine whether the spirits are of God. By this I will know the Spirit of God: for every spirit that confesses that Jesus Christ has come in the flesh is of God. Heavenly Father if You told me, "_____", confess, "Jesus Christ has come in the flesh." **Amen**

***Explanation: If you believe the Lord has told you something, the Word tells you to test the spirits. If the Lord does not tell you that "Jesus Christ has come in the flesh", then you have not heard the Spirit of God.

REMOVE ANY DECEPTION

Heavenly Father, I come to You through the Precious Blood of my Lord and Savior Jesus Christ, I ask You to destroy and remove any deception in my mind in Jesus Christ's Holy Name, **Amen**

TRAVELING MERCIES PRAYER

Heavenly Father, I come to You now in the Name of my Lord and Savior Christ Jesus. Holy Spirit I pray that You will quicken me to hear my Heavenly Father's Voice and lead me in prayer. Heavenly Father, I bow and worship before You. I come to You with praise and with thanksgiving. I come to You in humility, in fear, and in trembling. I come to You in gratitude, in love, and through the precious Blood of Your Son Jesus Christ of Nazareth.

Heavenly Father, I ask You to give me and every person I prayed for today traveling mercies and to deliver us safely to our destinations. I ask You to deliver us safely to our destinations. I ask You to loose Your angels to go before us and to protect us and to force all darkness and all destructive forces away from us. If Your angels have to manifest themselves to protect us, please let them do so. **Amen**

THE PRAYER FOR JUDGES

Heavenly Father, I ask You to forgive Judge _____ for all of his/her sins, iniquities, trespasses, transgressions, sins of commission, sins of omission and any unknown sins according to *Psalms 19:12.*

According to Your Word in *Matthew 16:19*, I have been given the Keys to Your Kingdom of Heaven and whatever I bind and loose on earth shall be bound and loosed in heaven. So I ask You to loose Your angels in great abundance into Judge _____'s presence, the presence of his/her courtrooms, into their rooms, their chambers, halls, restrooms, and work areas.

Now I bind, in the Name of Jesus Christ, all of Satan's evil wicked demons, lying and tormenting spirits and strongmen along with all their works, roots, fruits, tentacles and links; along with all evil principalities, powers, and rulers of wickedness in high places and command them not to manifest and transfer into Judge _____'s presence. I bind and command them not to manifest themselves or transfer themselves onto anybody's presence in Judge _____'s courtroom.

Heavenly Father, it is written in *Psalms 91* and *Matthew 6* in Your Word that You are our deliverer and I ask that You give Judge _____ and every organ, every gland, every cell in his/her body - total deliverance, total freedom, total liberty and total salvation from all evil, foul, wicked, demon, lying, perverse, unclean, foul, demonic spirits, strongmen, and his/her messengers, and from all sicknesses, diseases, infirmities, afflictions, infections, viruses, inflammations, disorders of any kind in every cell in their body, in every gland in their body, in every organ in his/her body; rooms, chambers, court rooms, halls, restrooms, and work areas, and wherever they are at this time. I thank You for giving Judge _____ this deliverance, freedom, liberty and salvation from all these things in the Name of the Lord Jesus Christ of Nazareth according to *John 16:23*. May these deliverances be used to glorify You, Heavenly Father.

I apply the Blood of Jesus over, under, and around every attorney, policeman, law official, all the Court House staff and anyone else that comes into their presence, the airways that surround them, their rooms, their chambers, court rooms, halls, restrooms, and work areas, every place that Judge _____ may be; and anybody that Judge _____ comes in contact with today and everyday. I ask You to render powerless and harmless and nullify, destroy, and cancel the power of any evil spirit, demonic spirit, demonic strongman, messenger of satan that tries to come into their presence or anyone that is around Judge _____ in the Name of Jesus Christ of Nazareth.

Heavenly Father, I ask You to fill Judge _____ with Your precious Holy Spirit. I ask You to fill Judge _____ with all of Your fruits of Your Holy Spirit including Your love,

Your joy, Your peace, Your gentleness, Your goodness, Your meekness, Your faithfulness and Your self-control.

Heavenly Father, in Christ Jesus Holy Name; I ask You to fill Judge _____ with Your Holy Ghost anointing and power, cover them with Your presence, Your anointing and Your power in the Name of Jesus Christ of Nazareth.

Loose extra angels around Judge _____ and leave them there as long as Judge _____ is in the Court House, to guard and protect him/her. In Jesus Name I pray. To God be the Glory. **Amen**

PASTOR'S PRAYER

Heavenly Father, I come to You in the Name of my Lord and Savior, Jesus Christ. I come to You with praise and thanksgiving, in worship, in humbleness and through the Blood of my Lord and Savior, Jesus Christ of Nazareth. Holy Spirit I ask You to quicken me to my Heavenly Father's Voice and reveal to me all unconfessed sins I have in my heart at this time. I ask You to forgive me of any sins of ____, ____, ____ and ____, and any hidden or unknown sins according to *Psalms 19:12*. Heavenly Father, I ask you to forgive me and ____, ____, ____, & ____, and Pastor _____, the leadership, the intercessors and all of the families attending _____ Church for all of our sins and cleanse us from all unrighteousness, according to *1 John 1:9*. Your Word says in that if we confess our sins that you are faithful and just to forgive us and cleanse us of all unrighteousness. Heavenly Father Your Word says in *Matthew 6:15* that if I don't forgive others You won't forgive me, so, I forgive ____ & ____ for anything they have ever said or done to me and I bless them in the Name of Jesus Christ and I ask You to forgive them and bless them in the Name of the Lord Jesus Christ. Heavenly Father, I ask you to cover all of our sins, iniquities, trespasses and transgressions with the Blood of Jesus Christ. Lord Jesus, I ask You to destroy any ungodly prayers, witchcraft prayers, psychic prayers, or evil words, side effects, effects, and influences that have been prayed or spoken over me or anyone that I pray for today. I ask You to destroy any assignments or plans that Satan has against us, our children, grandchildren, businesses, finances, ministries, cars, homes, or properties. I ask You to cause Your anointing to break and destroy the yokes of all bondages that are over us along with all their works. Lord Jesus, I ask You to pull down and destroy and cast aside all demonic strongholds, vain imaginations, and any high thoughts in each of us that exalts itself against the knowledge of God, and to bring every thought captive in each of us to the obedience of Christ according to *2 Corinthians 10:3-6*. I thank You that no weapon formed against us shall prosper. Lord Jesus I ask You to do all these things according to *John 14:14*, to God be the glory. Heavenly Father, it is written in *Psalms 91* and *Matthew 6* and many other places that You are our Deliverer, and I ask You to give me and every person that I pray for today total deliverance, total freedom, total liberty, total salvation, from all sickness, diseases, infirmities, afflictions, infections, viruses, abnormal cells, radical cells and I ask You to give us this according to *John 16:23*. Heavenly Father, I plead the Blood of Jesus Christ over me and everybody I pray for today, our houses, cars, offices, properties, buildings, and ask You to render powerless and harmless and to destroy any demonic spirit, strongman, curses, witchcraft prayers, psychic prayers, destructive forces that try to come against us. Heavenly Father, I ask You to fill me and each person I pray for today with Your Holy Spirit and all the fruits of Your Holy Spirit. Heavenly Father, I submit my life to You and I trust You and love You, with all my heart, soul, mind and strength. I bind each of our wills to the will of God and each of our minds to the mind of Christ. Heavenly Father, I ask You to put a hedge of protection around us to protect us from the enemy. Heavenly Father, I apply the full armor of God over me and everyone I pray for today. According to Ephesians 6, Heavenly Father, help us to know and hear your Voice and to walk in righteousness. Lord Jesus I ask You to fulfill Your will and destiny for each of our lives. Heavenly Father, please help us to keep our eyes fixed and focused on our Lord Jesus Christ. Heavenly Father, I ask you to Bless me and everyone that I pray for today, guard us and protect us and let your Holy Spirit comfort us, guide us, convict us and lead us into all truth. We choose health and wholeness today in Christ Jesus and through Him we are victorious. Heavenly Father, I ask you to release your healing virtue into each of our bodies and to give each of us divine health. Heavenly Father, we ask You to give us all these things. Lord Jesus we ask You to help us walk in your perfect love, presence, and anointing that God may be glorified in Jesus Name. **Amen**

Hospital Prayer

Heavenly Father, I ask You to forgive (_____) for all of his/her sins, iniquities, trespasses, transgressions, sins of commission, sins of omission and specifically any sins of ____, ____, or ____; and any unknown sins according to *Psalms 19:12*.

According to Your Word in *Matthew 16:19*, I have been given the Keys to the Kingdom of Heaven and whatever I bind and loose on earth shall be bound and loosed in heaven. So I ask You to loose Your angels in great abundance into (_____'s) presence, the presence of every doctor, every nurse, into his/her room, the surgery unit, and recovery room. Now I bind, in the Name of Jesus Christ, all of Satan's evil wicked demons, lying and tormenting spirits and strongmen along with all their works, roots, fruits, tentacles and links; along with all evil principalities, powers, and rulers of wickedness in high places and command them not to manifest and transfer into (_____'s) presence, nor the doctors' or nurses' presence, or into (_____'s) room, surgery unit, recovery room, and every place that (_____) may be. Heavenly Father, it is written in *Psalms 91* and *Matthew 6* in Your Word that You are our Deliverer and I ask that You give (____) every organ, every gland, every cell, every bone, every muscle, every ligament, in his/her body - total deliverance, total freedom, total liberty and total salvation from all evil, wicked, demon, lying, perverse, unclean, foul, demonic spirits, strongmen, and their messengers, and from all sicknesses, diseases, destructive organisms, bacteria, MRSA, viruses, and fungi, infirmities, afflictions, infections, inflammations, abnormal cells, radical cells, abnormal growths, radical growths, all cancers, tumors, and disorders of any kind in every cell, every gland, every organ in his/her body. In his/her room and wherever they are at this time. I thank You for giving (____) this deliverance, freedom, liberty and salvation from all these things in the Name of the Lord Jesus Christ of Nazareth according to *John 16:23*. Heavenly Father, I ask You to release Your miracle virtue, Your Healing virtue into (_____) in the Name of the Lord Jesus Christ of Nazareth. Heavenly Father, I plead the Blood of Jesus Christ over (_____), from the top of his/her head to the soles of his/her feet, under and around every doctor, every nurse, all the hospital staff in his/her presence, the airways that surround him/her, the surgery unit, recovery room, every place that (_____) may be; and anybody that (_____) comes in contact with today and every day. I ask You to render powerless and harmless and nullify, destroy, and cancel the power of any evil spirit, demonic spirit, demonic strongman, messenger of Satan that tries to come into his/her presence or anyone that is around me (_____) in the Name of Jesus Christ of Nazareth. Heavenly Father, I ask You to fill (_____) with Your precious Holy Spirit. I ask You to fill (_____) with the fruits of Your Holy Spirit including Your love, Your joy, Your peace, Your gentleness, Your goodness, Your meekness, Your faithfulness and Your self-control. Heavenly Father, in Christ Jesus' Holy Name; I ask You to fill (_____) with Your Holy Ghost anointing and power, cover him/her with Your presence, Your anointing and Your power in the Name of Jesus Christ of Nazareth.

Heavenly Father, I ask you now according to *John 16:23*, in the Name of our Lord and Savior Jesus Christ of Nazareth to release your miracle virtue, your miracle anointing into (_____) in the Name of Jesus Christ of Nazareth, and ask that your miracle virtue, and miracle anointing flow through every cell, every organ, every gland, every part of (_____)'s body in the Name of Jesus Christ of Nazareth. I ask you to give divine healing and divine health, wholeness and newness of life according to *John 16:23* in the Name of the Holy Jesus Christ of Nazareth. Heavenly Father, I ask you to let the manifestation of every miracle and every healing that you have given (_____) be manifested in him/her now in the Name of Jesus Christ of Nazareth. Heavenly Father, I ask you to loose extra angels around (_____) and leave them there as long as (_____) is in the hospital, to guard and protect him/her. In Jesus' Name we pray. To God be the Glory. **Amen**

PRAYER FOR INMATES

Heavenly Father, I ask You to forgive _____, their fellow inmates, their guards, their warden, and all the staff members at _____ prison (jail) for all their sins, transgressions, iniquities and trespasses and to cleanse them of all unrighteousness in the Name of our Lord Jesus Christ.

Heavenly Father, according to Your Word in *Matthew 16 & 18*, You have given me the Keys to the Kingdom of Heaven and whatever I bind and loose on earth shall be bound and loosed in heaven. I ask You to loose Your angels in great abundance into _____'s presence; the presence of their cells, rooms, buildings, or any other areas they're in or will be in today.

I bind all of Satan's evil wicked demon, lying, tormenting, perverse, and unclean spirits that are in _____'s presence, the presence of their cells, rooms, recreational areas, work areas, and loose them from _____'s presence, and from the presence of these areas and any other areas that _____ will be in today.

Heavenly Father, it is written in *Psalms 91* and *Matthew 6*, that You are our deliverer and I ask that You give _____, every organ, every gland, every cell in their bodies, total deliverance, total freedom, total liberty, and total salvation from all evil wicked demon, lying, perverse, unclean, foul, demonic, spirits, and strongmen, and their messengers. Heavenly Father, I ask You to give _____ deliverance from all sicknesses, diseases, infirmities, afflictions, infections, viruses, inflammations, disorders of any kind in any cell, gland, organ, bone, muscle, and ligaments in their bodies, their rooms, cells, restrooms, recreation areas, work areas, visiting areas, food areas, or any area they will be in today. I thank You for giving _____ deliverance, freedom, liberty, salvation from all these things according to *John 16:23*. May these deliverances be used to Glorify our Heavenly Father in Jesus Christ of Nazareth.

Heavenly Father, I apply the Blood of Jesus Christ over _____ from the top of their head to the soles of their feet and around every guard, inmate and visitor that comes into _____'s presence, their cells, rooms, corridors, visiting areas, dining areas, recreation areas, restrooms, work areas, any place in that facility where _____ will be today.

Heavenly Father, I ask You to render harmless and nullify, destroy and cancel the power of any evil demonic spirit, demonic strongman or messenger of satan that tries to enter into the presence of _____.

Heavenly Father, I ask You to fill _____ and all other Christians that I prayed for today with your precious Holy Spirit and with all the fruits of Your Spirit including Your love, joy, peace, gentleness, goodness, meekness, faithfulness, and self control and I ask You to loose into each of them a spirit of repentance, conviction, and wisdom.

Heavenly Father, I ask You to cover _____ and all those around them with Your presence and Your glory in the Name of Jesus Christ of Nazareth. **Amen**

MALACHI 3: PRAYING GOD'S PROMISES FOR THE TITHER

Heavenly Father I come to you now in the Name of my Lord and Savior Jesus Christ and Heavenly Father as I sow my tithes according to Your Word in *Malachi 3:*, I claim the seven supernatural promises that You have given to me as a tither in. Heavenly Father I ask You to open the Windows of Heaven and to revive me because I am a tither and I have obeyed You by sowing my tithe. Heavenly Father, You have promised me through Your Word that because of my tithes you will open the windows of heaven and pour out a blessing on me and there shall not be enough room to receive it. Heavenly Father You have promised me that because of my tithe that I will be prosperous. Heavenly Father it says in Your Word, that You will rebuke the devourer for me. So I ask You Lord to rebuke the devourer for my sake because of my obedience to You in sowing my tithe. Heavenly Father Your Word says that You promise to cripple and paralyze the enemy so he will not be able to come near me. Heavenly Father I ask You not to let the enemy destroy the fruits of my ground. Heavenly Father I ask You to prevent the enemy from touching my finances, the fruits of my ground because of my obedience to paying my tithe. Heavenly Father I ask You that my vine not cast it's fruit before it's time. Heavenly Father, I ask You to prevent the enemy from touching my family. Heavenly Father I ask You to bless me with Your seven blessings of the tither. In the Name of Your Son, Jesus Christ of Nazareth, according to *John14:14*. **Amen**

PRAYER FOR A PERSON WHO HAS LOST A LOVED ONE

Heavenly Father, I thank You that we have You, Lord, to understand and sympathize and know our true hearts without us saying word. I ask you Lord to comfort _____'s weaknesses and grief over the loss of his/her_____. Therefore, I fearlessly and confidently and boldly draw near to the throne of grace; that _____ may receive mercy and find grace to help in time for every need with appropriate and well-timed help, coming just when _____ needs it.

Heavenly Father, I thank You that _____ does not sorrow, as one who has no hope, because he/she believes that Jesus died and rose again; even so his/her loved one also who sleeps in Jesus, God will bring back with Him. I ask that You comfort _____, for You said, Blessed are they that mourn: for they shall be comforted according *Matt. 5:4*).

Lord, You told us in *John 14:1-4* that in Your Father's house there are many mansions and that You have gone to prepare a place for those that love You and that You will come back and take us to where You are. Help _____him/her take comfort, Lord, in knowing that _____him/her is with You.

Jesus, You have came to heal the brokenhearted. It is in the name of Jesus that You, Lord, comfort _____ because You have loved him/her and have given him/her everlasting consolation and good hope through Your grace. Blessed be God, even the Father of our Lord Jesus Christ, the Father of mercies, and the God of all comfort; Who comforts _____ in all his/her tribulation, that he/she may be able to comfort those who are in any trouble with a comfort as only you can provide, Lord Jesus.

Heavenly Father, I thank You for appointing unto _____, who mourns, to give unto him/her beauty for ashes, the oil of joy for mourning, the garment of praise for the spirit of heaviness; that he/she might be called a tree of righteousness, the planting of the Lord, that You might be glorified. In Jesus' Name, **Amen**

PRAYER FOR A PERSON GRIEVING THE LOSS OF A LOVED ONE

Please help me in this time of loss of. I seem to be frozen with this overwhelming grief. I don't understand why my life is filled with this pain and heartache. But I turn my eyes to you as I seek to find the strength to trust in your faithfulness. You, Lord are a God of comfort and love and I ask You to help me to patiently wait on you and not despair; I will quietly wait for your salvation. My heart is crushed, but I know that you will not abandon me forever. Please show me your compassion, Lord. Help me through the pain so that I will hope in you again. I believe the promise in your Word to send me fresh mercy each day. Though I can't see past today, I trust your great love will never fail me.

Jesus, You came to heal the brokenhearted and my heart is broken today Lord, and only you can heal my sorrow over losing my I ask You, Lord to comfort me because You love me and have promised me everlasting consolation and hope through Your grace.

Blessed be God, even the Father of our Lord Jesus Christ, the Father of mercies, and the God of all comfort; Who comforts me in all my tribulations, that I may be protected from any trouble and hurt as I walk with You, Lord, through the grief of losing my _____. In Jesus Name I pray. **Amen**

COMPREHENSIVE DAILY PRAYER

Heavenly Father, I pray for myself, _____, _____, _____, and _____. I ask You to forgive us for all of our sins, iniquities, trespasses, transgressions, sins of commission, sins of omission, [Please see "Sin List" on page 181 and ask God's forgiveness for any other sins that may apply to you] and any unknown sins according to *Psalms 19:12*. Heavenly Father, I repent for all of my sins and I ask You to forgive each of us for all our sins, iniquities, trespasses and transgressions and to cover them with the Blood of the Lord Christ Jesus, and to cleanse us of all unrighteousness. I ask You to do this in the Name of the Lord Christ Jesus of Nazareth according to Your Word, *1 John 1:9*.

Heavenly Father, I pray that You will give each of us all the things that I ask according to *John 16:23* and I ask You Lord Jesus to do all things that I ask for each of us according to *John 14:14*.

I am thankful for this day; for this is the day that You have made. I will rejoice and be glad in it. I am thankful for the Blood of Jesus, knowing it cleanses us from all unrighteousness and allows us to come boldly to the throne of grace according to *Hebrews 4:16*. I am thankful for the power in the Blood of the Lord Jesus Christ of Nazareth to protect, cleanse, heal, deliver, sanctify, redeem, justify, and to make all things new.

Heavenly Father, Your Word says that whatsoever I shall bind on earth shall be bound in heaven and whatsoever I loose on earth shall be loosed in heaven according to *Matthew 16 and 18*. In the Name of the Lord Jesus Christ I bind: all evil, wicked, demon, lying, unclean, tormenting, demonic spirits and strongmen in the Name of the Lord Jesus Christ of Nazareth. I bind them in my presence and everyone I just prayed for in the Name of the Lord Jesus Christ and I banish them to where Jesus sends them and I bind them and command them to stay there in the Name of Jesus Christ of Nazareth.

I apply the Blood of Jesus Christ of Nazareth over our homes according to *Exodus 12:7*. I apply the Blood of Jesus over every door and window of our homes. I apply the Blood of Jesus over all the contents of our homes. I apply the Blood of Jesus over all who enter in and all who exits out of our homes. Thank You Lord; for our homes and the Blood of Jesus over them.

I apply the Blood of Jesus over us as witnesses for You wherever we go. A city on a hill that can not be hid. We will not hide our light under a bushel, but we will let our light shine before men and they may see our good works and glorify You Heavenly Father. We will give light to all those in our homes and our surroundings according to *Matthew 5:14-16*. Thank You Lord; for our ministries and the Blood of Jesus over them.

I apply the Blood of Jesus over our businesses and jobs. I apply the Blood of Jesus over our finances and possessions. I apply the Blood of Jesus over our bills, our checking accounts, and savings. I apply the Blood of Jesus over all of our possessions (list them) and everything we have and everything we will have. Thank You Lord; for our finances and possessions and the Blood of Jesus over them. I declare and decree that where the Blood of Jesus Christ is applied, Satan can't enter according to Hebrews 10:4-23 and I confess now that Jesus is Lord over our families, churches, finances, businesses, jobs, and possessions. Not sickness, not poverty, not death, not problems, but Jesus is Lord over our families and our lives and where the power and presence of Jesus is: sickness, poverty, problems, and death can't remain.

Heavenly Father, I am thankful for so many things. I am thankful that Your Word is true and established in heaven according *Matthew 24:35*; that Your mercy endures forever according to *Psalms 118:1*; that Your grace is sufficient for us according to *2 Corinthians 12:9*; for Your angels and for Your protection according to *Psalms 91*; for Your salvation. That our names are written in the lamb's book of life according to *Revelation 21:27*; that everyone in our households are saved according to *Acts 16:31*; for Your righteousness that is imparted to us according to *1 Corinthians 5:21*. I am thankful for Your Holy Spirit, the inward voice, the inward witness, the candle of the Lord according to *Proverbs 20:27*; that You sanctify us daily in Your Word according to *John 17:17*. Thank You for Your peace which passes all understanding according to *Philippians 4:7*. Thank You for every battle and every problem we face, knowing that the battle is an opportunity to cause our revelation knowledge parts (pebbles) to become one solid rock that the gates of hell can't prevail against us. Each and every battle is an opportunity for us to take root so we can bear fruit. We know that the trying of our faith turns into patience, causing us to form into perfect men and women, wanting nothing. Thank You that we can ask You for whatever we will and as long as we are connected to the vine, we have the petitions we ask for. Thank You for Your provisions as You supply all our needs according to Your riches in glory. Thank You for divine prosperity. Thank You for Your healing, past, present, and future as You are Jehovah Rophe. Thank You for divine health. Thank You for physical and spiritual hearing, seeing, feeling, smelling, and tasting. Thank You for the sun, moon, stars, trees, grass, air, water, plants, flowers, animals, mountains, valleys and all the other wonderful things You created for us yet we so often take for granted.

Thank You Heavenly Father for Your Holy Spirit. Thank You for being present with us always. Thank You for the gifts of the Spirit: The word of wisdom, word of knowledge, faith, gift of healing, workings of miracles, prophesy, discerning of spirits, divers kinds of tongues and the interpretation of tongues according to *1 Corinthians 12:8-10*. Thank You for the fruits of the Spirit: Love, joy, peace, long suffering, kindness, goodness, faithfulness, gentleness, and self control according to *Galatians 5:22*. Thank You for Your faithfulness. Thank You for being the Wonderful Counselor, Mighty God, Everlasting Father, Prince of Peace according to *Isaiah 9:6*; The Way, The Truth, The Life according to *John 14:6*; The Light according to *John 8:12*; The Door according to *John 10:9*; The Bread of Life according to *John 6:35*; The Good Shepherd according to *John 10:11*; The Redeemer according to Psalms *78:35*; The King of Kings and the Lord of Lords according to Rev. *19:16*.

Heavenly Father, I praise and thank You for everything You have done, for everything You are doing, and for everything You are going to do. I bless You Lord.

Heavenly Father, I know that our battle is not with flesh and blood, but against principalities, against powers, against the rulers of darkness of this age, against spiritual wickedness in high places, therefore, I put on each of us the whole armor of God, that we may be able to withstand in the evil day, and having done all to stand. We will be strong in You, Lord, and in the power of Your might according to *Ephesians 6:10-13*. We have Christ in us, the hope of glory, according to *Colossians 1:27*, so we shall prevail because the battles are not ours, but Yours Lord according to *1 Samuel 17:47*.

Heavenly Father, I now put on each of us the Breastplate of Righteousness according to *Ephesians 6:14;* and pray Your Word that we have hidden in our hearts, that we might not sin against You; because You made Christ who knew no sin to be sin for us, that we might become the righteousness of You, God, in Him. I acknowledge You God as our Jehovah Tsidkenu Your Word says it means our righteousness; and Jehovah Mekaddishkem, our sanctifier.

Heavenly Father, I realize that our own self-righteousness is as filthy rags in Your eyes according to *Isaiah 64:6*; but Your Word says if we confess our sins, You are faithful and just to forgive our sins and to cleanse us from all unrighteousness according to *1 John 1:9*. Heavenly Father, please forgive us for our sins. We want to be Your loving and obedient child. We want to be Your spotless bride, presented unto You in glorious splendor, without spot or wrinkle or any such thing according to *Ephesians 5:27*. We want to be holy and without blemish, through the washing of the water of Your Word according to *Ephesians 5:26*; and acknowledge You are our Jehovah Mekaddishkem, our sanctifier, and we want to be Your humble servant, to walk in love, forgiveness, and gentleness toward each other, showing the love of Christ as Your body according to *Ephesians 5:2*. Remind us that if we do this we will exit out from Your righteousness and enter back into our old self-righteous filthy rags. Help us to be a doer of Your Word, not just a hearer only, deceiving ourselves according to *James 1:22*, so we may act upon the revelation knowledge You gave us.

I crucify our flesh now according to *Romans 8:13*, as we die daily from self desires and live to do Your desires according to *1 Corinthians 15:31*. In the Name of Christ Jesus, I command the mind of our flesh to shut up: Don't talk to us about sin for we are dead to sin according to *Romans 6:2*; Don't talk to us about condemnation, for there is no condemnation to us because we are in Christ according *Romans 8:1*; We walk after the Spirit and not after the flesh according to *Romans 8:4*; We have been healed by the stripes of Jesus according to *Isaiah 53:5*.We have been redeemed from the curse of the law according to *Galatians 3:13*; We are blessed when we come in and blessed when we go out. We are blessed in the city and blessed in the country. Our fruits, seed, land and storehouse are blessed. Everything we touch is blessed and it prospers according to *Deuteronomy 28:3-6*. All these blessings shall come upon us and overtake us, because we obey the Voice of the Lord our God. Thank You God that you did not give us the spirit of fear, but of power, and of love, and of a sound mind according to *2 Timothy 1:7.*

Heavenly Father, Your Word says we are not to be deceived, that the unrighteous will not inherit the Kingdom of God, neither fornicators, nor idolaters, nor adulterers, nor homosexuals, nor sodomites, nor thieves, nor covetous, nor drunkards, nor revilers, nor extortionists, according to *1 Corinthians 6:9 & 10*. Your word continues to say; and such were some of us. But we were washed, but we were sanctified, but we were justified in the Name of the Lord Jesus and by the Spirit of God according to *1 Corinthians 6:11*.

Heavenly Father, I pray that our path is like the shining sun and not of darkness for Your Word says: But the path of the just is like the shining sun, that shines ever brighter unto the perfect day. The way of the wicked is like darkness; they do not know why they stumble according to *Proverbs 4:18 & 19*. Your Word is a lamp unto our feet and a light unto our path according to *Psalms 119:105*.

Lord, You have created a clean heart in us; You have renewed a right spirit within us. You have made old things passed away and all things new. You didn't cast us away from Your presence and You didn't take Your Holy Spirit away from us when we failed You for Your mercy endures forever. You restored us to the joy of Your salvation according to *Psalms 51:10-13*. Your joy is our strength according to *Nehemiah 8:10*.

Heavenly Father, I now put on each of us the Helmet of Salvation. I declare that we are spiritually minded according to *Romans 8:6* and have the mind of Christ according to *1 Corinthians 2:16*. I take off the carnal way of thinking according to *Romans 12:2*. Putting on this Helmet we no longer allow our five carnal senses to affect the way that we think. I exercise our spiritual senses, spiritual hearing, spiritual sight, spiritual touch, spiritual taste, and spiritual smell according to *Romans 8:14*. I thank You for being our God of peace; Jehovah Shalom, according to *Judges 6:24*.

Heavenly Father, I ask that You give us knowledge of Your will in all wisdom and spiritual understanding and the strength and might of You, to be involved in what you want us to be involved in, and not to be involved in the things You don't want us to be involved in according to *Colossians 1:9*. Your Word says if any man lacks wisdom, let him ask of You, and he will receive wisdom according to *James 1:5*. I ask for wisdom in every decision we have to make today. Help us to remember that our mind is a judge according to *1 Corinthians 11:31* and we are always listening to fear and faith. Fear produces substances of things not hoped for, the evidence of this world's circumstances: evidence of things we can hear, see, smell, taste, and touch. These things are temporal according to *2 Corinthians 4:18*. God did not give us a spirit of fear according to *2 Timothy 1:7*. Faith produces substances of things hoped for, the evidence of things from the Word of God ("Thus saith the Lord.."): things we cannot hear, see, smell, touch or taste according to *Hebrews 11:1*. Now these things are eternal. From both of these reports, we choose to believe the report of the Lord according to *2 Timothy 1:12*.

Heavenly Father, I ask that each of us will hear Your Voice today for our families according to *John 10:16*: That we will not be deceived in any area, that You will speak through us to our families, and that we will follow You and set a clear path for our families to follow according *to John 16:13-15*. Let the words of our mouths and the meditation of our hearts be acceptable in Your sight, for You are our strength and our redeemer according to *Psalms 19:14*. Let our mouths speak wisdom and the meditation of our hearts be of understanding according to *Psalms 19:3*. Let our speech always be with grace, seasoned with salt, that we will know how to answer every man according to *Colossians 4:6*. Give us the tongue of the learned and lead us to speak a word to him that is weary in season according to *Isaiah 50:4*. Teach us to exhort one another today, lest anyone of us be hardened through the deceitfulness of sin according to *Hebrews 3:13*. Help us to never criticize, condemn, or complain because these are destructive weapons that kill, steal, and destroy. They are weapons of the enemy according to *John 10:10*. Help us to abstain from all appearances of evil according to *1 Thessalonians 5:19-22*.

Heavenly Father, implant in our hearts: We are doers of the Word according to *James 1:22*; We are in Jesus and Jesus is in us according to *John 17:23;* We are the body of Christ according to *1 Corinthians 12:27*; We are more than conquerors through Christ Jesus according to *Romans 8:37*. We are overcomers. We overcome by the Blood of Jesus and the word of our testimony and we love not our life unto death according to *Revelation 12:11*; We are the head and not the tail according to *Deuteronomy 28:13;* We can do all things through Christ who strengthens us according to *Philippians 4:13*; As we speak Your Word, we know it won't return back to You void, but it will accomplish what it was sent to do according to *Isaiah 55:11*; If we ask anything according to Your will, You hear us, and because You hear us, we have whatsoever it is we ask for according to *1 John 5:14 & 15*.

Heavenly Father, I thank You for it is written in *Psalms 103* that we will not forget all of Your benefits. You forgave all our sins and have healed all our diseases, You redeemed our lives from destruction. You have crowned us with loving kindness and tender mercies; You satisfy our mouths with good things, so that our youth is renewed like the eagles; You are merciful and gracious, slow to anger, and plenteous in mercy; You have not dealt with us according to our iniquities; As far as the heaven is high above the earth, so great is Your mercy toward us for we fear You; As far as the east is from the west, You have thrown our sins from us.

Heavenly Father, I now girt our loins with Your Belt of Truth. We are set free from bondages and strongholds according to *II Corinthians 10:4*. We operate in discernment according to *Hebrews 5:14* that we may continue to be free. I take off all dependency of the flesh and dependency on anything in this world or this world system. We trust and depend completely on Jesus according to *Psalms 31:1*. I thank You that You are our Healer, Jehovah Rophe, and You are our Provider; Jehovah Jireh.

Heavenly Father, thank You for being our Healer, our Jehovah Rophe according to *Exodus 15:26*. I declare that You are our health, healing, and soundness in and over us. We have the healing of God, for by Your stripes, we were healed according to *I Peter 2:24*. We have spiritual healing, soulish healing, physical healing, healing in relationships for we have been redeemed from the curse of the law according to *Galatians 3:13*. We have been redeemed from sickness, poverty, and spiritual death according to *Deuteronomy 28:2-13*. We have the health of God. We have Your soundness in our spirits, souls, and bodies. We present our bodies as living sacrifices, holy and acceptable to You, which is our reasonable service. We are not conformed to this world, but we are transformed by the renewing of our minds to Your Word according to *Romans 12:1-2*. Lord, You are on our side. We fear no man according to *Psalms 118:6*. We are overcomers. We overcome all strongholds and bondages by the Blood of the Lamb, which cleanses us from all unrighteousness according to *1 John 1:9* and the word of our testimony which is Your Word that we have hidden in our hearts to keep us from returning to those strongholds according to *Psalms 119:11* and we love not our life unto death according to *Revelation 12:11*.

Heavenly Father, thank You that all of Your blessings will come on us because we hear and obey Your Voice. Thank You that: Blessed is the fruit of our bodies (our children); Blessed is the fruit of our ground (our possessions); Blessed is the fruit of our cattle (our businesses); Blessed is the increase of our kine (our prosperity); Blessed are the flocks of our sheep (those we have authority over); Blessed is our basket and our store (our finances). Lord, You have commanded blessings on us, our storehouse and in all we set our hands to. You have blessed us in the land that You gave us. You have established us as a holy people unto You as You promised us, as we keep Your commandments and walk in Your ways. We are blessed because we refuse to walk in the counsel of the ungodly, nor will we stand in the way of sinners, nor will we sit in the seat of the scornful. Our delight is in Your Word, and in Your Word do we meditate day and night. We are like a tree planted by rivers of water that bring forth its fruit in its season; our leaves shall not wither, and whatsoever we do shall prosper according to *Psalms 1:1-3*. We bring all our tithes into Your storehouse, that there may be meat in Your house, and I will prove You now that You will open the windows of heaven for us and pour out blessings that we won't have room to store it all so we will have to give most of it away. For as we have received; freely we shall give according to *Matthew 10:8*.

Lord, Your goodness and mercy shall follow us every day of our lives according to *Psalms 23:6*. In You, we will praise Your Word and put our trust according to *Psalms 16:1*. We will not fear what flesh and blood can do to us according to *Ephesians 6:12*. We know that all things work together for good because we love You and we were called according to Your purpose according to *Romans 8:28*. According to *Romans 8:31*, if You are for us; who can be against us? You are on our side; we will not fear what man can do to us, according to *Psalms 118:6*. Now Lord, I bring our requests to You according to *Philippians 4:6*: [Hereis where you would list your prayer requests.]

Heavenly Father, I now cover our feet with the preparation of the Gospel of Peace Sandals enabling us to walk in the Spirit so we won't fulfill the lust of the flesh according to *Galatians 5:16*. Thank You that the Spirit leads us and we walk in the light, as Jesus is the light according to *1 John 1:7*. As we cover our feet with this preparation, we take off vanity, pride, darkness, and ignorance according to *Colossians 3:8-10*. I thank You for being: our EVER PRESENT GOD, our JEHOVAH SHAMMAH and our SHEPHERD, JEHOVAH ROHI.

Lord, Your Spirit is upon us. You have anointed us to preach the gospel to the poor; You have sent us to bind up the broken hearted, to proclaim liberty to the captives, and the opening of the prison to them that are bound; To proclaim Your acceptable year, and Your day of vengeance; To comfort all that mourn; To appoint unto them that mourn in Zion, to give unto them beauty for ashes, the oil of joy for mourning, the garment of praise for the spirit of heaviness; that they might be called trees of righteousness, which is Your planting, that You may be glorified.

Heavenly Father, I ask that utterance be given to us, that we may open our mouths boldly to make known the mysteries of the Gospel, for which we are ambassadors in chains, that in it we may speak boldly, as we ought to speak according to *Ephesians 6:19 & 20*.

Heavenly Father, I ask that You order our steps according to *Psalms 37:23*. We acknowledge You Father, precious Jesus, and precious Holy Spirit in all our ways, according to *Proverbs 3:6*. I acknowledge You Jesus as Lord over all our ways and in everything we do, we will do it heartily according to *Colossians 3:23*, listening to Your Spirit and rejoicing as we do it for You. We have Your promise that You will direct our path according to *Proverbs 4:18*. We will not lean to our own understanding, go by what we think is good, but we will trust Your Holy Spirit with all our heart and will believe our path is directed by You according to *Proverbs 3:5 & 6*.

Heavenly Father, I speak in Jesus' Name to every person and thing in our paths, that if it would not bring glory to You God, and if it would not be in Your will for our paths to cross, then in Jesus' Name, I forbid our paths to cross until, if ever, it would be in God's will. Also, I speak in Jesus' Name and believe for every person and things in our path that would be in God's will and for God's glory for our paths to cross, I speak and believe for our paths to cross in God's right timing. I declare KINGDOM OF GOD COME, WILL OF GOD BE DONE IN EVERY STEP WE TAKE AND WITH EVERY PERSON WE MEET. Truly all things work together for good for us because we love You Lord, and we are called according to Your purpose according to *Romans 8:28*.

Heavenly Father, we do not seek after the praises of men according to *John 5:44*, nor do we seek after our own glory according to *John 7:18*, but we seek first Your kingdom; we seek after Your righteousness according to *Matthew 6:33*. Your Spirit leads us, as You are Jehovah Rohi, our shepherd according to *Psalms 23:1*. Instruct us and teach us in the way we should go. Guide us with Your eye according to *Psalms 32:8*. Holy Spirit guide us into all truth, speak to us the words that you hear from our Heavenly Father and tell us the things to come. Glorify God in us by taking the things of God and declaring it to us according to *John 16:13 & 14*. We will keep Your word, Lord, make Your home in us. Teach us all things, and help us to remember all things You have taught us according to *John 14:26*.

Heavenly Father, we want to be wise sons and daughters who gather the harvest instead of sons and daughters who causes You shame and sleeps during the harvest according to *Proverbs 10:5*. Help us to keep a right heart and a hearing ear according to *Proverbs 20:12*. Give us wisdom to use You to win Your people to Your kingdom. Lead us to them and tell us what to say that they may be saved according to *Acts 1:8*. We are not ashamed of Your Gospel for it is the power of You, God, unto salvation according to *Romans 1:16*. Give Your servants boldness to stand up for You and tell others what You have done for us according to *Acts 4:29*. Help us to make disciples for You, for where no counsel is, the people fall, but in a multitude of counselors, there is safety according to *Proverbs 11:14*. We want to be vehicles for Your Holy Spirit. Lead us into the north, south, east, and west. Help us to bring them and lead them out of darkness into Your light according to *1 Peter 2:9*. I believe You are adding to Your church daily such as should be saved according to *Acts 2:47*. We go forth to do Your will. We go into the entire world that You have called us to and preach Your gospel according to *Mark 16:15*. We go rejoicing in hope, patient in tribulation, continuing instantly in prayer, and distributing to the necessity of the saints according to *Romans 12:12-13*. We will walk worthy of our calling with all lowliness and gentleness, with longsuffering, bearing with one another in love, enduring to keep the unity of Your Spirit in the bond of peace according to *Ephesians 4:1-3*. We will not follow after signs to believe on Your Word, but rather signs will follow us because we believe on Your Word according to *Mark 16:17*.

Heavenly Father, I now put on each of us the Shield of Faith, which protects us from all fiery darts of the enemy according to *Ephesians 6*: As I put on each of us Shield of Faith, we take off all fear, mistrust, unthankfulness, unfaithfulness, and disobedience. I thank You God that You are OUR BANNER, JEHOVAH NISSI and THE GOD WHO IS MORE THAN ENOUGH, EL SHADDAI.

Heavenly Father, I come boldly to the throne of grace according to *Hebrews 4:16*, praying for all men. I ask that every man, woman, boy, and girl will come to know You as their Lord and Savior according to *1 Timothy 2:1*. Let everyone that has breath praise You according to *Psalms 150:6*.

Heavenly Father, I pray that Your Kingdom come, Your will be done over our families. I ask You to make Your Word stronger and greater than our wills. I ask You to make us hunger and thirst after Your righteousness according to *Matthew 5:6*. I stand on Your promises that [List your children's names here] will prophesy according to *Acts 2:17*. I intercede in the Spirit that our families are saved by faith. Help each of us to keep a pure heart according to *1 Peter 1:22*. Keep us in remembrance of Your promise that You will never leave us or forsake us according to *Hebrews 13:5*. I take the Shield of Faith and cover our families, and churches: For You will bless the righteous with favor and protect us; surrounding us with a shield according to *Psalms 5:12*.

Heavenly Father, I declare that we dwell in Your secret place and we abide under Your shadow, I declare that You are our refuge and our fortress, You are our habitation, therefore no demon, devil, fallen angel, principalities, rulers of darkness, power, spiritual wickedness, Satan, or those under him shall befall us, neither shall any plague, flu, virus, cancer, disease, headache, cold or poverty come near our dwellings. A thousand may fall at our side, and ten thousand at our right hand, but it will not, shall not, and cannot come near our dwellings because I now apply the Blood of Jesus to the doorpost of our hearts. You have given Your angels charge over us to keep us in all our ways, lest we dash our foot against a stone, with long life You satisfy us and show us Your salvation, because we have set our love upon You according to *Psalms 91:1-16*.

Heavenly Father, I ask that [church's name here] becomes a great soul winning church for You. I pray for Pastor _____ and ask You to bless him. Bless [church's name here] financially to have and maintain abundant provision, to fulfill Your mission for us. Help us to have Your abundance to give as we are led by Your Spirit in giving to others. Make our leaders sensitive to You and the needs of our children and our youth, making them grow mightily in the ways and things of God according to *Ephesians 4:15*, making them giants for You. Bring a great revival so we will be strong in You and in the power of Your might according to *Ephesians 6:10*. Let us recognize sin immediately and turn from it. Let us walk in love according to *Ephesians 5:2* and desire spiritual things according to *Colossians 3:2*.

Heavenly Father, I now intercede for those You have called me to intercede for. I pray the will of God be done in and over me and everyone I have prayed for today. Strengthen us today and clothe us with Your glory. Let us hear Your Voice today and teach us in Your ways. Keep each of us covered in Your Blood and heal us of every sickness and disease that the devil tries to hit us with. I cover each of us with the Shield of Faith and declare that no weapon formed against us shall prosper, but everything we put our hands to shall prosper, for we are like a tree planted by rivers water according to *Psalms 1:3*.

Heavenly Father, I now put on each of us the Sword of the Spirit, the Word of God, which we choose to use against all forces of evil. I declare that we defeat the enemy with the Word of God as the Spirit of God leads us according to *Revelation 19:11-16*. I put away murmuring, complaining, condemning and criticizing from each of us. I thank You that You are OUR AUTHORITY, JESUS and THE LORD OF HOST, JEHOVAH SABBOATH. I now take the Sword of the Spirit and use the authority that God has ordained me with according to *Luke 9:1*, for we have been given power and authority over all the devils and demons, to tread upon serpents and scorpions, and over all the power of the enemy according to *Luke 10:19*.

Heavenly Father, as we go out today, let us recognize You as Jehovah Sabaoth, we will not fear, for You have called us by name, we are Yours. When we pass through the waters, You will be with us, and through the rivers, they will not overtake us. When we walk through the fire, we will not be burned, neither will the flame kindle upon us according to *Isaiah 43:1-2*. We will not be dismayed, for You are our God according to *Isaiah 41:10*. We will wait upon You Lord and You will renew our strength. We will mount up with wings as eagles. We will run and not be weary. We will walk and not faint according to *Isaiah 40:31*. We will not be afraid or dismayed by reason of the great multitude. The battle is not ours but Yours according to *II Chronicles 20:15*. You are on our side; therefore we will fear no man according to *Psalms 118:6*. When the enemy comes in like a flood, Your Spirit will lift up a standard against him according to *Isaiah 59:19*. You did not give us a spirit of fear, but of power, and of love, and of a sound mind according to *2 Timothy 1:7*. Greater is Jesus in us than any demon, devil, fallen angel, evil force, power, principality, and rulers of darkness, spiritual wickedness, Satan, and those under him. Greater is Jesus in us than the devil is in the world according to *I John 4:4*. Greater is Jesus in us than all our circumstances and all our reasoning. Therefore, we follow You Jesus. We cry out to You Holy, Holy, Holy, Lord God Almighty, who was, who is, and who is to come according to *Revelation 4:8*. You have created all things and for Your pleasure and by Your will, which is Your Word, they are and were created and continue to exist. You are worthy to receive glory, honor, and power according to *Revelation 4:11*. To You belongs the kingdom, and the power, and the glory forever according to *Matthew 6:13*. **Amen**

PRAYER TO BIND & BANISH STRONGMEN (GENERAL)

Heavenly Father, I come to You now in the Name of my Lord and Savior Christ Jesus. Holy Spirit I pray that You will quicken me to hear my Heavenly Father's Voice and to lead me in prayer. Heavenly Father, I bow and worship before You. I come to You with praise and with thanksgiving. I come to You in humility, in fear, in trembling and seeking truth. I come to You in gratitude, in love, and through the precious Blood of Your Son Jesus Christ of Nazareth.

Strongman called spirit of rejection, spirit of anti-christ, spirit of error, spirit of seducing spirit, spirit of bondage, spirit of death, spirit of divination, spirit of dumb and deaf, spirit of familiar spirit, spirit of fear, spirit of pride, spirit of Leviathan, spirit of heaviness, spirit of infirmity, spirit of jealousy, spirit of lying, spirit of perverse spirit, and spirit of whoredoms; I rebuke you and bind you in the Name of the Lord Jesus Christ, along with all of your works, roots, fruits, tentacles, links, that are in my presence, the presence of anybody I have prayed for today, every organ, every cell, every gland, every muscle, every ligament, every bone in our bodies, our houses, cars, trucks, buildings, properties, and pets, and I banish you to go where Jesus Christ sends you. I apply the Blood of Jesus Christ over myself, each person I prayed for today, our houses, cars, properties, offices, work places, and pets as our protection.

Lord Jesus Christ, we ask You to destroy any familiar spirit that has allowed any of these demonic strongmen into our presence. In the Name of the Lord Jesus Christ according to *John 14:14*.

I declare in the Name of Jesus Christ that all of your works, roots, fruits, tentacles, and links are now dead works in our lives. I declare that your power over us is broken. Heavenly Father, I ask you in the Name of Jesus to break all generational and word curses that we have placed on ourselves or by others in the Name of Jesus.

Heavenly Father, I ask You to loose into each of us: the Spirit of Adoption *Romans 8:15*, the Spirit of Truth *1 John 4:6 & Psalms 51:10*, the Holy Spirit of Truth *John 16:13*, the Spirit of Resurrection Life and Life more Abundantly *John 11:25, John 10:10b*, the Holy Spirit and His Gifts *1 Corinthians 12:9-12*.

Heavenly Father, I ask You to fill each of us with Your precious Holy Spirit. I ask You to fill each of us with all of the fruits of Your Holy Spirit including Your love, Your joy, Your peace, Your gentleness, Your goodness, Your meekness, Your faithfulness and Your self-control. Heavenly Father, in Christ Jesus' Holy Name I ask You to fill me, everyone I prayed for today with Your Holy Ghost anointing and power, cover us with Your presence, Your anointing, Your power; in the Name of Jesus Christ of Nazareth.

Heavenly Father, I bow and worship and praise before You and I apply the Blood of Jesus Christ over myself, each person that I have prayed for today; from the tops of our heads to the soles of our feet. I apply the Blood of Jesus over the airways that surround us, over telephone lines, over our homes, properties, offices, cars, trucks, businesses, finances, marriages, ministries, cell phone frequencies. I apply the precious Blood of Christ Jesus as our protection and I ask You to render powerless and harmless and nullify the power, destroy the power, cancel the power of any evil spirit, demonic spirit, demonic strongman, messenger of Satan that tries to come into our presence, everything in our homes, our pets, our properties, everything in our cars and trucks, our marriages, our finances, our ministries, our telephone lines, our cell phone frequencies. In the Name of Jesus Christ of Nazareth. **Amen**

PRAYERS TO BIND & BANISH STRONGMEN (SPECIFIC)

SPIRIT OF REJECTION

Genesis 3:6-13 "Strongman called Spirit of Rejection, I bind you in the Name of Jesus Christ along with all of your works, roots, fruits, tentacles, links and spirits that are in my life _____, _____, _____, _____, and the lives of everybody I have prayed for today, along with all of your fruits and spirits of:

- Rejection by Others
- Rejection of Others
- Self-Rejection
- Rejection of God
- Fear of Rejection

And I cast you out of me, _____, _____, _____, and everybody I have prayed for today along with all of your works, roots, fruits, tentacles, links and spirits, and I banish you from us and I force you into outer darkness in the Name of Jesus Christ.

I bind you in the Name of Jesus Christ and declare that all of your works, roots, fruits, tentacles, links, and spirits, are dead works in my life _____, _____, _____, _____, and the lives of everybody I have prayed for today, in Jesus Christ' Name, and I bind you and banish you from me, everybody I prayed for today and I command you to go wherever Jesus Christ sends you and command you not to come back into our presence again. I ask You, Heavenly Father, to loose into me and each person I prayed for today the Spirit of Adoption according to *Romans 8:15*. **Amen**

- Bind & Banish the Spirit of Rejection
- Loose the Spirit of Adoption
- *Romans 8:15*

SPIRIT OF ANTI CHRIST

1 John 4:3 "Strongman called Spirit of Anti-Christ, I bind you in the Name of Jesus Christ along with all of your works, roots, fruits, tentacles, links and spirits that are in my life _____, _____, _____, _____, and the lives of everybody I have prayed for today, along with all of your fruits and spirits of:

- Deny the Deity of Christ *1 John 4:3; 2 John 7*
- Deny the Atoning Blood of Jesus *1 John 4:3*
- Go Against Christ & His Teachings *2 Thessalonians 2:4; 1 John 4:3*
- Humanism 2 Thessalonians 2:3.7
- Worldly Speech & Actions *1 John 4:5*
- Teacher of Heresies *1 John 2:18, 19*
- Anti-Christian *Revelation 13.7*
- Deceiver 2 Thessalonians 2:4; 2 John 7
- Lawlessness/Rebellion *2Thessalonians2:3-12*

And I cast you out of me, _____, _____, _____, and everybody I have prayed for today along with all of your works, roots, fruits, tentacles, links and spirits, and I banish you from us and I force you into outer darkness in the Name of Jesus Christ.

I bind you in the Name of Jesus Christ and declare that all of your works, roots, fruits, tentacles, links, and spirits, are dead works in my life _____, _____, _____, _____, and the lives of everybody I have prayed for to-day, in Jesus Christ' Name, and I bind you and I banish you to go wherever Jesus Christ sends you and command you not to come back into our presence again. I ask You, Heavenly Father, to loose into me and each person I prayed for today the Spirit of Truth according to *1 John 4:6*. **Amen**

- Bind and Banish the Spirit of Anti-Christ
- Loose the Spirit of Truth
- *1 John 4:6*

SPIRIT OF ERROR

1 John 4:6 "Strongman called Spirit of Error, I bind you in the Name of Jesus Christ along with all of your works, roots, fruits, tentacles, links and spirits that are in my life _____, _____, _____, _____, and the lives of every-body I have prayed for today, along with all of your fruits and spirits of:

- Resistance to Biblical Truths
- Spiritual Hindrances to Prayer, Bible Study, Listening to Sermons & Moving in the Gifts of The Holy Spirit. *Proverbs 14:33 1 John 4:6 2 Peter 3:16,17*
- Reprobate Mind
- Deceit
- Foolish Talking
- Unsubmissive Proverbs 29:1; 1 John 4:6
- Mental Confusion

- Fears
- Physical Illnesses & Pains
- Depression
- Dullness of Comprehension
- False Doctrines 1 Timothy 6:20, 21; 2 Timothy 4:3 Titus 3:10 1 John 4:1-6
- Unteachable Proverbs 10:17; 12:1; 13:18;15:10,12,32; 2 Timothy 4:1-4; 1 John 4:6
- Profanity
- Servant of Corruption *2 Peter 2:19*
- Defensive/Argumentative
- Having a Form of Godliness
- Variance
- Contentions *James 3:16*
- Uncleanness
- New Age Movement 2 Thessalonians; 2 Peter 2:10

And I cast you out of me _____, _____, _____, and everyone I have prayed for today along with all of your works, roots, fruits, tentacles, links and spirits, and I send you from us and I force you into outer darkness in the Name of Jesus Christ.

I bind you in the Name of Jesus Christ and declare that all of your works, roots, fruits, tentacles, links, and spirits, are dead works in my life _____, _____, _____, _____, and everyone I have prayed for today in Jesus Christ' Name, and I bind you and banish you from me, everyone I have prayed for today and I banish you to go wherever Jesus Christ sends you and command you not to come back into our presence again. I ask You, Heavenly Father, to loose into me and into each person I have prayed for today the Spirit of Truth according to *1 John 4:6* and *Psalm 51:10*. **Amen**

- Bind and Banish the Spirit of Error
- Loose the Spirit of Truth
- *1 John 4:6; Psalm 51:10*

SEDUCING SPIRITS

1 Timothy 4:1 "Strongman called Seducing Spirits, I bind you in the Name of Jesus Christ along with all of your works, roots, fruits, tentacles, links and spirits that are in my life _____, _____, _____, _____, and the lives of everybody I have prayed for today, along with all of your fruits and spirits of:

- Hypocritical Lies I Timothy 4:1l; Proverbs 12:22

- Seared Conscience 1 Timothy 4:1; James 1:14
- Attractions/Fascination to False Prophets, Signs & Wonders Mark 13:22
- Deception Romans 7:11; 2 Timothy 3:13; Deuteronomy 13:6-8; 2 Thessalonians 2:10
- Confusion
- Wander From The Truth; 2 Timothy 3:13
- Fascination to Evil Ways, Objects or Persons Proverbs 12:26
- Seducers – Enticers 1 Timothy 4:1; 2 Timothy 3:13; Proverbs 1:10
- Controlling spirit (Jezebel) 1 John 2:18-26

And I cast you out of me _____, _____, _____, and everybody I have prayed for today along with all of your works, roots, fruits, tentacles, links and spirits, and I banish you from us and I force you into outer darkness in the Name of Jesus Christ.

I bind you in the Name of Jesus Christ and declare that all of your works, roots, fruits, tentacles, links, and spirits, are dead works in my life _____, _____, _____, _____, and the lives of everybody I have prayed for today, in Jesus Christ' Name, and I bind you and send you from me, everybody I have prayed for today and I command you to go wherever Jesus Christ sends you and command you not to come back into our presence again. I ask You, Heavenly Father, to loose into me and each person I prayed for today the Holy Spirit of Truth according to *John 16:13*. **Amen**

- Bind and Banish the Seducing Spirits
- Loose the Holy Spirit of Truth
- *John 16:13*

SPIRIT OF BONDAGE

Romans 8:15 "Strongman called Spirit of Bondage, I bind you in the Name of Jesus Christ along with all of your works, roots, fruits, tentacles, links and spirits that are in my life _____, _____, _____, _____, and the lives of everybody I have prayed for today, along with all of your fruits and spirits of:

- Fears Romans 8:15
- Addictions to Drugs, Alcohol, Cigarettes, Sleep, Sex Food, Pornography, etc.
- Fear of Death/Dying *Hebrews 2:14,15*
- Captivity to Satan *2 Peter 2:19*
- Compulsive Sin Proverbs 5:22; John 8:34

- Servant of Corruption Luke 8:26-29; John 8:34; Acts 8:23; Romans 6:16, 7:23
- Bondage to Sin *2 Timothy 2:26*

And I cast you out of me _____, _____, _____, and everybody I have prayed for today along with all of your works, roots, fruits, tentacles, links and spirits, and I banish you from us and I force you into outer darkness in the Name of Jesus Christ.

I bind you in the Name of Jesus Christ and declare that all of your works, roots, fruits, tentacles, links, and spirits, are dead works in my life _____, _____, _____, _____, and the lives of everybody I have prayed for today, in Jesus Christ' Name, and I bind you and banish you from me, everybody I have prayed for today and I command you to go wherever Jesus Christ sends you and command you not to come back into our presence again. I ask You, Heavenly Father, to loose into me and each person I have prayed for today Liberty and the Spirit of Adoption according to *Romans 8:15*. Amen

- Bind and Banish the Spirit of Bondage
- Loose the Spirits of Liberty and Adoption
- *Romans 8:15*

SPIRIT OF DEATH

1 Corinthians 15:26 "Strongman called Spirit of Death, I bind you in the Name of Jesus Christ along with all of your works, roots, fruits, tentacles, links and spirits that are in my life _____, _____, _____, _____, and lives of everybody I have prayed for today, along with all of your fruits and spirits of:

- Murder *Genesis 4:8*
- Suicide
- Accidents
- Fear of Death/Dying
- Anger That Leads to Death
- Near Death Experiences
- Miscarriages
- Abortion *Exodus 20:13; 21:22-25*
- Barrenness

And I cast you out of me _____, _____, _____, and everybody I have prayed for today along with all of your works, roots, fruits, tentacles, links and spirits, and I banish you from us and I force you into outer darkness in the Name of Jesus Christ.

I bind you in the Name of Jesus Christ and declare that all of your works, roots, fruits, tentacles, links, and spirits, are dead works in my life _____,
_____, _____, _____, and the lives of everybody I have prayed for today, in Jesus Christ' Name, and I bind you and banish you from me, everybody I have prayed for today and I command you to go wherever Jesus Christ sends you and command you not to come back into our presence again. I ask You, Heavenly Father, to loose into me and each person I have prayed for today the Resurrection Life and Life More Abundantly according to *John 11:25; John 10:10b*. **Amen**

- Bind and Banish the Spirit of Death
- Loose the Spirits of Resurrection Life and Life More Abundantly
- *John 11:25; John 10:10b*

SPIRIT OF DIVINATION

Acts 16:16-6 "Strongman called Spirit of Divination, I bind you in the Name of Jesus Christ along with all of your works, roots, fruits, tentacles, links and spirits that are in my life _____, _____, _____, _____, and the lives of everybody I have prayed for today, along with all of your fruits and spirits of:

- Fortuneteller-Soothsayer Micah *5:12; Isaiah 2:6*
- Stargazer-zodiac, Horoscopes, Astrology *Isaiah 47:13; Leviticus 19:26; Jeremiah 10:2*
- Warlock-Witch, Sorcerer *Exodus 22:18*
- Hypnotist-Enchanter *Deuteronomy 18:11; Isaiah 19:3*
- Rebellion *1 Samuel 15:23*
- Manipulation & Control
- Water Witching- Divination; *Hosea 4:12*
- Drugs (Pharmakos) *Galatians 5:20; Revelation 9:21; 18:23; 21:8; 22:15*
- Astral Projecting, Levitation, Seances, Dungeons & Dragons
- Magic; *Exodus 7:11; 8:7; 9:11*
- Tarot Cards, Ouija Boards,
- Palm Reading, Crystal Balls

And I cast you out of me, _____, _____, _____, and everybody I have prayed for today along with all of your works, roots, fruits, tentacles, links and spirits, and I banish you from us and I force you into outer darkness in the Name of Jesus Christ.

I bind you in the Name of Jesus Christ and declare that all of your works, roots, fruits, tentacles, links, and spirits, are dead works in my life _____,
_____, _____, _____, and the lives of everybody I have prayed for today, in Jesus Christ' Name, and I bind you and loose you from me, every-

body I have prayed for today and I command you to go wherever Jesus Christ sends you and command you not to come back into our presence again. I ask You, Heavenly Father, to loose into me and each person I have prayed for today the Holy Spirit and His Gifts according to *1 Corinthians 2:9-12*. **Amen**

- Bind the Spirit of Divination
- Loose the Holy Spirit and His Gifts
- *1 Corinthians 12:9-12*

DUMB AND DEAF SPIRIT

Mark 9:17-29 "Strongman called Dumb & Deaf Spirit, I bind you in the Name of Jesus Christ along with all of your works, roots, fruits, tentacles, links and spirits that are in my life _____, _____, _____, _____, and the lives of everybody I have prayed for today, along with all of your fruits and spirits of:

- Dumb-Mute *Mark 9:25; Matthew 9:32,33; 12:22; 15:30,31; Luke 11:14; Isaiah 35:5,6*
- Crying *Mark 9:26*
- Drown *Mark 9:22*
- Tearing *Mark 9:18, 20, 26*
- Mental Illness *Matthew 17:15; Mark 5:5; 9:17*
- Blindness *Matthew 12:22*
- Suicidal *Mark 9:22*
- Foaming at The Mouth *Mark 9:39; Luke 9:39*
- Ear Problems *Mark 9:25, 26*
- Seizures/Epilepsy *Mark 9:18, 20, 26*
- Burn Mark 9:22
- Gnashing of Teeth *Mark 9:39*
- Pining Away, Prostration *Mark 9:18, 26*
- Madness/Insanity, Senility
- Schizophrenia, Paranoia
- Self-Mutilation

And I cast you out of me _____, _____, _____, and everybody I have prayed for today along with all of your works, roots, fruits, tentacles, links and spirits, and I banish you from us and I force you into outer darkness in the Name of Jesus Christ.

I bind you in the Name of Jesus Christ and declare that all of your works, roots, fruits, tentacles, links, and spirits, are dead works in my life _____, _____, _____, _____, and the lives of everybody I have prayed for today, in Jesus Christ' Name, and I bind you and banish you from me, everybody I have prayed for today and I command you to go wherever Jesus Christ sends you and command you not to come back into our presence again. I ask You, Heavenly Father, to loose into me and each person I have prayed for today the Resurrection Life and Gifts of Healing according to *Romans 8:11* and *1 Corinthians 12:9-12*. **Amen**

- Bind the Dumb and Deaf Spirit
- Loose the Spirit of Resurrection Life and Gifts of Healing
- *Romans 8:11; 1 Corinthians 12:9-12*

FAMILIAR SPIRIT

Leviticus 19:31 "Strongman called Familiar Spirit, I bind you in the Name of Jesus Christ along with all of your works, roots, fruits, tentacles, links and spirits that are in my life _____, _____, _____, _____, and the lives of everybody I have prayed for today, along with all of your fruits and spirits of:

- Necromancer *Deuteronomy 18:11; 1 Chronicles 10:13*
- ESP, Mind Readers, TM
- Psychics
- Medium *1 Samuel 28*
- Yoga *Jeremiah 29:8*
- Peeping & Muttering *Isaiah 8:19; 29:4; 59:3*
- Spiritist *1 Samuel 28*
- Clairvoyant 1 Samuel 28:7, 8
- Apathy
- Passive Mind-Dreamers *Jeremiah 23:16, 25, 32; 27:9, 10*
- Drugs (Pharmakos) *Revelation 9:21; 18:23; 21:8; 22:15*
- False Prophecies *Isaiah 8:19, 29:4*

And I cast you out of me _____, _____, _____, and everybody I have prayed for today along with all of your works, roots, fruits, tentacles, links and spirits, and I banish you from us and I force you into outer darkness in the Name of Jesus Christ.

I bind you in the Name of Jesus Christ and declare that all of your works, roots, fruits, tentacles, links, and spirits, are dead works in my life _____, _____, _____, _____, and the lives of everybody I have prayed for today, in Jesus Christ' Name, and I bind you and banish you from me, everybody I have prayed for today and I command you to go wherever Jesus Christ sends you and command you not to come back into our presence again. I ask, Heavenly Father, to loose into me and each person I have prayed for today the Holy Spirit and All of His Gifts according to *1 Corinthians 12:9-12*. **Amen**

- Bind the Familiar Spirit

- Loose the Holy Spirit and All Of His Gifts
- *1 Corinthians 12:9-12*

SPIRIT OF FEAR

2 Timothy 1:7 "Strongman called Spirit of Fear, I bind you in the Name of Jesus Christ along with all of your works, roots, fruits, tentacles, links and spirits that are in my life _____, _____, _____, _____, and the lives of everybody I have prayed for today, along with all of your fruits and spirits of:

- Fears/Phobias *Isaiah 13:7, 8; 2 Timothy 1:7*
- Heart Attacks Psalm *55:4; Luke 21:26; John 14:27; 14:1*
- Torment/Horror *Psalm 55:5; 1 John 4:18*
- Fear of Satan & His Demons
- Nightmares/Terrors *Psalm 91:5, 6; Isaiah 54:14*
- Fear of Persecution/Confrontation
- Fear of Rejection
- Fear of Saying No
- Fear of Man *Proverbs 29:25; Jeremiah 1:8; 17-19; Ezekiel 2:6,7; 3:9*
- Fear of Death/Dying; *Psalm 45:4; Hebrews 2:14, 15*
- Panic Attacks
- Anxiety/Stress *1 Peter 5:7*
- Fear of Mental Imbalance & Incompetence
- Untrusting/Doubt *Matthew 8:26; Revelation 21:8*
- Fear of Criticism
- Fear of Failing, Suspicion & Distrust
- Fear of Being an Introvert
- Fear That Brings Mental
- Confusion & a Double Mind
- Physical Illnesses & Pains

And I cast you out of me _____, _____, _____, and everybody I have prayed for today along with all of your works, roots, fruits, tentacles, links and spirits, and I banish you from us and I force you into outer darkness in the Name of Jesus Christ.

I bind you in the Name of Jesus Christ and declare that all of your works, roots, fruits, tentacles, links, and spirits, are dead works in my life _____, _____, _____, _____, and the lives of everybody I have prayed for today, in Jesus Christ' Name, and I bind you and banish you from me, everybody I have prayed for today and I command you to go wherever Jesus Christ sends you and command you not to come back into our presence again. I ask You, Heavenly Father, to loose into me and each person I have prayed for today the Power, Love and A Sound Mind according to *2 Timothy 1:7* **Amen**

- Bind the Spirit of Fear
- Loose the spirits of Power, Love and Sound Mind
- *2 Timothy 1:7*

SPIRIT OF PRIDE

Proverbs 16:18 "Strongman called Spirit of Haughtiness, I bind you in the Name of Jesus Christ along with all of your works, roots, fruits, tentacles, links and spirits that are in my life _____, _____, _____, _____, and the lives of everybody I have prayed for today, along with all of your fruits and spirits of:

- Arrogant-Smug 2 Samuel 22:8; Jeremiah 48:29; Isaiah 2:11,17; 5:15
- Pride *Proverbs 6:16,17; 16:18,19; 28:25; Isaiah 16:6*
- Idleness *Ezekiel 16:49, 50*
- Scornful *Proverbs 1:22; 3:34; 21:24; 24:9; 29:8*
- Strife *Proverbs 28:25*
- Obstinate/Stubborn *Proverbs 29:1; Daniel 5:20*
- Contentious *Proverbs 13:10*
- Self-Deception *Jeremiah 49:16; Obadiah 1:3*
- Self-Righteous *Luke 18:11,12*
- Rejection of God *Psalm 10:4; Jeremiah 43:2*
- Critical, Fault Finding
- Rebellion *1 Samuel 15:23; Proverbs 29:1*
- Contempt, Mocking
- Judgmental
- Interrupting spirit
- Haughtiness

And I cast you out of me _____, _____, _____, and everybody I have prayed for today along with all of your works, roots, fruits, tentacles, links and spirits, and I banish you from us and I force you into outer darkness in the Name of Jesus Christ.

I bind you in the Name of Jesus Christ and declare that all of your works, roots, fruits, tentacles, links, and spirits, are dead works in my life _____, _____, _____, _____, and the lives of everybody I have prayed for today, in Jesus Christ' Name, and I bind you and banish you from me, everybody I have prayed for today and I command you to go wherever Jesus Christ sends you and command you not to come back into our presence again. I ask You, Heavenly Fa-

91

ther, to loose into me and each person I have prayed for today A Humble and Contrite Spirit according to *Proverbs 16, 19* and *Romans 1:4*. **Amen**

- Bind the Spirit of Haughtiness
- Loose a Humble and Contrite Spirit
- *Proverbs 16:19; Romans 1:4*

SPIRIT OF HEAVINESS

Isaiah 61:3 "Strongman called Spirit of Heaviness, I bind you in the Name of Jesus Christ along with all of your works, roots, fruits, tentacles, links and spirits that are in my life _____, _____, _____, _____, and the lives of everybody I have prayed for today, along with all of your fruits and spirits of:

- Excessive Mourning *Isaiah 61:3; Luke 4:18*
- Sorrow/Grief *Nehemiah 2:2; Proverbs 15:13*
- Insomnia *Jeremiah 2:2*
- Broken-Heart *Psalm 69:20; Proverbs 12:18; 15:3, 13; 18:14; Luke 4:18*
- Self-Pity *Psalm 69:20*
- Rejection
- Depression *Isaiah 61:3*
- Despair-Dejection
- Hopelessness *2 Corinthians 1:8, 9*
- Withdrawing/Pouting
- Excessive Fatigue & Weariness
- Suicidal Thoughts *Mark 9*
- Inner Hurts/Torn Spirit *Luke 4:18; Proverbs 18:14; 26:22*
- Heaviness *Isaiah 61:3*
- Escape/Indifference;
- Root of Bitterness
- Sadness/Abandonment.
- Loneliness
- Suppressed Emotions
- Physical Illnesses & Pains

And I cast you out of me _____, _____, _____, and everybody I have prayed for today along with all of your works, roots, fruits, tentacles, links and spirits, and I banish you from us and I force you into outer darkness in the Name of Jesus Christ.

I bind you in the Name of Jesus Christ and declare that all of your works, roots, fruits, tentacles, links, and spirits, are dead works in my life _____, _____, _____, _____, and the lives of everybody I have prayed for today, in Jesus Christ' Name, and I bind you and banish you form me, everybody I have prayed for today and I command you to go wherever Jesus Christ sends you and command you not to come back into our presence again. Heavenly Father, I loose into me and each person I the Comforter, Garment of Praise, The Oil of Joy according to John 15:26; Isaiah 61:3. Amen

- Bind the Spirit of Heaviness
- Loose the Comforter, Garment of Praise, The Oil of Joy
- *John 15:26; Isaiah 61:3*

SPIRIT OF INFIRMITY

Luke 13:11-13 "Strongman called Spirit of Infirmity, I bind you in the Name of Jesus Christ along with all of your works, roots, fruits, tentacles, links and spirits that are in my life _____, _____, _____, _____, and the lives of everybody I have prayed for today, along with all of your fruits and spirits of:

- Bent Body/Spine *Luke 13:11*
- Impotent/Frail/Lame John 5:5; Acts 3:2; Acts 4:9
- Migraine Headaches
- Asthma/Hay Fever/Allergies *John 5:5*
- Arthritis *John 5:5*
- Weakness *Luke 13:11; John 5:5*
- Oppression *Acts 10:38*
- Fevers
- Physical Illnesses & Pains
- Lingering Disorders *Luke 13:11; John 5:5*
- Cancer *Luke 13:11; John 5:4*

And I cast you out of me _____, _____, _____, and everybody I have prayed for today along with all of your works, roots, fruits, tentacles, links and spirits, and I banish you from us and I force you into outer darkness in the Name of Jesus Christ.

I bind you in the Name of Jesus Christ and declare that all of your works, roots, fruits, tentacles, links, and spirits, are dead works in my life _____, _____, _____, _____, and the lives of everybody I have prayed for today, in Jesus Christ' Name, and I bind you and banish you from me, everybody I have prayed for today and I command you to go wherever Jesus Christ sends you and command you not to come back into our presence again. I ask You, Heavenly Father, to loose into me and each person I have prayed for today the Spirit of Life and His Gifts of Healing according to *Romans 8:2* and *1 Corinthians 12:9* **Amen**

- Bind the Spirit of Infirmity
- Loose the Spirit of Life and His Gifts of Healing
- *Romans 8:2; 1 Corinthians 12:9-12*

SPIRIT OF JEALOUSY

Numbers 5:14 "Strongman called Spirit of Jealousy, I bind you in the Name of Jesus Christ along with all of your works, roots, fruits, tentacles, links and spirits that are in my life _____, _____, _____, _____, and the lives of everybody I have prayed for today, along with all of your fruits and spirits of:

- Murder *Genesis 4:8*
- Revenge/Spite *Proverbs 6:34; Proverbs 14:16, 17*
- Anger/Rage *Genesis 4:5, 6; Proverbs 6:34; 14:29 22:24, 25; 29:22, 23*
- Jealousy *Numbers 5:14, 30*
- Cruelty *Song of Solomon 8:6; Proverbs 27:4*
- Strife *Proverbs 10:12*
- Hatred *Genesis 37:3, 4, 8; 1 Thessalonians 4:8*
- Extreme Competition *Genesis 4:4, 5*
- Bitterness, Resentment
- Contention *Proverbs 13:10*
- Spirit That Causes Divisions/Divorce *Galatians 5:19*
- Envy *Proverbs 14:30*
- Prejudice/Bigotry
- Violence/Retaliation
- Suspicion/Distrust
- Unforgiveness

And I cast you out of me _____, _____, _____, and everybody I have prayed for today along with all of your works, roots, fruits, tentacles, links and spirits, and I banish you from us and I force you into outer darkness in the Name of Jesus Christ.

I bind you in the Name of Jesus Christ and declare that all of your works, roots, fruits, tentacles, links, and spirits, are dead works in my life _____, _____, _____, _____, and the lives of everybody I have prayed for today, in Jesus Christ' Name, and I bind you and banish you from me, everybody I have prayed for today and I command you to go wherever Jesus Christ sends you and command you not to come back into our presence again. I ask You, Heavenly Father, to loose into me and each person I have prayed for today the Love of God according to *1 Corinthians 13* and *Ephesians 5:2*. **Amen**

- Bind the Spirit of Jealousy
- Loose Love of God
- *1 Corinthians 13; Ephesians 5:2*

LYING SPIRIT

2 Chronicles 18:22 "Strongman called Lying Spirit I bind you in the Name of Jesus Christ along with all of your works, roots, fruits, tentacles, links and spirits that are in my life _____, _____, _____, _____, and the lives of everybody I have prayed for today, along with all of your fruits and spirits of:

- Strong Deception *2 Thessalonians 2:9-13*
- Flattery *Psalms 78:36; Proverbs 20:19; 26:28; 29:5*
- Superstitions *1 Timothy 4:7*
- Profanity
- Religious Bondages *Galatians 5:1*
- False Prophecy *Jeremiah 23:16-17; 27:9, 10; Matthew 7:15*
- Accusations *Revelation 12:10; Psalms 21:18*
- Slander *Proverbs 6:16-19*
- Gossip *1 Timothy 6:20; 2 Timothy 2:16*
- Homosexuality *Romans 1:27*
- Lies *2 Chronicles 18:22; Proverbs 6:16:19*
- False Teachers *2 Peter*
- Driving Zeal
- Guilt/Shame, Condemnation
- Extortion
- Exaggeration
- Foolish Talking

And I cast you out of me _____, _____, _____, and everybody I have prayed for today along with all of your works, roots, fruits, tentacles, links and spirits, and I banish you from us and I force you into outer darkness in the Name of Jesus Christ.

I bind you in the Name of Jesus Christ and declare that all of your works, roots, fruits, tentacles, links, and spirits, are dead works in my life _____, _____, _____, _____, and the lives of everybody I prayed for today, in Jesus Christ' Name, and I bind you and banish you from me, everybody I prayed for today and I command you to go wherever Jesus Christ sends you and command you not to come back into our presence again. I ask You, Heavenly Father, to loose into me and each person I have prayed for today the Spirit of Truth according to *John 14:17, 16:13, 26.* **Amen**

- Bind the Lying Spirit
- Loose the Spirit of Truth
- *John 14:17; 16:13, 26*

PERVERSE SPIRIT

Isaiah 19:14 "Strongman called Perverse Spirit, I bind you in the Name of Jesus Christ along with all of your works, roots, fruits, tentacles, links and spirits that are in my life _____, _____, _____, _____, and the lives of everybody I have prayed for today, along with all of your fruits and spirits of:

- Evil Actions *Proverbs 17:20, 23*
- Broken Spirit *Proverbs 15:14*
- Atheist *Proverbs 14:2; Romans 1:30*
- Abortion *Exodus 20:13; 21, 22, 25*
- Child Abuse, Incest, Rape
- Molestation, Pedophilia
- Filthy Mind *Proverbs 2:12; 23:33*
- Doctrinal Error *Isaiah 19:14; Romans 1:22, 23; 2 Timothy 3:7, 8*
- Sex Perversions; *Romans 1:17-322; 2 Timothy 3:2*
- Foolish *Proverbs 1:2; 19:1*
- Twisting the Word of God *Acts 13:10; 2 Peter 2:14*
- Incubus/Succubus
- Frigidity, Prostitution,
- Bestiality, Sodomy, Oral Sex,
- Homosexuality, Lesbianism,
- Masturbation, Exhibitionist
- Contentions *Philippians 2:14-16; 1 Timothy 6:4, 5; Titus 3:10, 11*
- Lust & Pornography
- Unholy spirit, Ungodliness,
- Heresies
- Chronic Worrier *Proverbs 19:33*
- Sadism-Masochism

And I cast you out of me _____, _____, _____, and everybody I have prayed for today along with all of your works, roots, fruits, tentacles, links and spirits, and I banish you from us and I force you into outer darkness in the Name of Jesus Christ.

I bind you in the Name of Jesus Christ and declare that all of your works, roots, fruits, tentacles, links, and spirits, are dead works in my life _____,

_____, _____, _____, and the lives of everybody I have prayed for today, in Jesus Christ' Name, and I bind you and banish you from me, everybody I have prayed for today and I command you to go wherever Jesus Christ sends you and command you not to come back into our presence again. I ask You, Heavenly Father, to loose into me and each person I have prayed for today God's Spirit of Pureness and Holiness according to *Zechariah 12:10* and *Hebrews 10:29*. **Amen**

- Bind the Perverse Spirit
- Loose God's Spirit of Pureness and Holiness
- *Zechariah 12:10; Hebrews 10:29*

SPIRIT OF WHOREDOMS

Hosea 5:4 "Strongman called Spirit of Whoredoms, I bind you in the Name of Jesus Christ along with all of your works, roots, fruits, tentacles, links and spirits that are in my life _____, _____, _____, _____, and the lives of everyone I have prayed for today, along with all of your fruits and spirits of:

- Unfaithfulness/Adultery *Ezekiel 16:15, 28; Proverbs 5:1-4; Galatians 5:19*
- Spirit, Soul or Body Prostitution *Ezekiel 16:15, 28; Deuteronomy 23:17, 18*
- Chronic Dissatisfaction *Ezekiel 16:28*
- Idolatry *Judges 2:17; Ezekiel 1:6; Leviticus 17:7*
- Love of Money *Proverbs 15:27; 1 Timothy 6:7-14*
- Excessive Appetite
- Gluttony *Corinthians 6:13-16; Philippians 3:19*
- Fornication *Hosea 4:13-19*
- Worldliness *James 4:4*
- Stealing
- Break All Soul Ties *Genesis 2:24; 1 Corinthians 6:16*
- Rock & Country Music

And I cast you out of me _____, _____, _____, and everybody I have prayed for today along with all of your works, roots, fruits, tentacles, links and spirits, and I banish you from us and I force you into outer darkness in the Name of Jesus Christ.

I bind you in the Name of Jesus Christ and declare that all of your works, roots, fruits, tentacles, links, and spirits, are dead works in my life _____, _____, _____, _____, and the lives of everybody I have prayed for today, in Jesus Christ' Name, and I bind you and banish you from me, everybody I have prayed for today and I command you to go wherever Jesus Christ sends you and command you not to come back into our presence again. I ask You, Heavenly Father, to loose into me and each person I have prayed for today the Spirit of God, a Pure Spirit according to *Ephesians 3:16*. Amen

- Bind the Spirit of Whoredoms
- Loose the Spirits of God and Purity
- *Ephesians 3:16*

PRAYER OF SPIRITUAL WARFARE

Heavenly Father, I come to You now in the Name of my Lord and Savior Christ Jesus. (Note - if two or more praying; Heavenly Father, _____ and I come to You in one accord in the Name of Christ Jesus of Nazareth. We come two or more in agreement touching heaven and earth and You said it will be done, so, according to *Matthew 18:19*, we ask You to do the following in the Name of Jesus Christ of Nazareth.)

Heavenly Father, I pray for _____, _____, _____, and _____ and ask You to forgive me for all of our sins, iniquities, trespasses, transgressions, sins of commission, sins of omission and specifically any sins of: _____, _____, _____ and any unknown sins according to *Psalms 19:12*. Cover them with the Blood of the Lord Christ Jesus, and cleanse me of all unrighteousness according to Your Word, *1 John 1:9* and *John 14:14*, in Christ Jesus' Holy Name, I ask you to do this.

Heavenly Father, I thank You that no weapon formed against us shall prosper. I thank You that every tongue and every word that rises against me in judgment; You shall condemn. I thank You Heavenly Father that this is the heritage of the servants of the Lord, and our righteousness is from You according to *Isaiah 54:17*.

> *Heavenly Father, I thank You that it is written "For the weapons of our warfare are not carnal, but mighty through God to the pulling down of strongholds; Casting down imaginations, and every high thing that exalteth itself against the knowledge of God, and bringing into captivity every thought to the obedience of Christ" 2Corinthians 10:4-5.*

Heavenly Father, in the Name of Christ Jesus, I pull down every demonic stronghold [name them if you know them - doubt, confusion, etc.] that I have in my mind or in the minds of anyone that I have prayed for today. I pull down and cast them aside in the Name of the Lord Christ Jesus. I pull down every vain imagination in me and every vain imagination in everyone that I have prayed for today. I pull them down and cast them aside in the Name of the Lord Christ Jesus. I pull down every high thought in me and every high thought in everyone that I have prayed for today that exalts itself against the knowledge of God. I pull them down and cast them aside in the Name of the Lord Jesus Christ of Nazareth and I bring every thought captive in each of us to the obedience of Christ Jesus according to *1 Corinthians 10:3-6*. Lord Jesus; I thank You that *"the yoke will be destroyed because of the anointing oil,"* according to *Isaiah 10:27*. Heavenly Father, I ask You now to cause Your anointing to break and destroy any yokes of bondage including _____, [name them if you know them-example: fear, doubt, lust, drug abuse, sexual impurity, etc.]; along with all of their works, roots, fruits, tentacles and links that are in my life, and the lives of anyone that I have prayed for today.

Heavenly Father, I ask You to give us deliverance and freedom from all these bondages in the Name of Christ Jesus according to *John 16:23*.

Heavenly Father, I ask You according to *John 14:14*, to loose Your angels in great abundance in my presence, the presence of everyone that I have prayed for today and into our homes, cars, trucks, lands, properties, buildings, and work places, in great abundance, to protect us, guard us and to force out, drive out, and cleanse out all evil, wicked demon and tormenting spirits from our presence, and our homes, cars, trucks, lands, properties, animals, and work places and send them to where Christ Jesus sends them, in Christ Jesus' Holy Name.

Heavenly Father, I pray *Psalms 35:1-6* over myself, _____, and _____. "Plead our cause, O Lord, with them that strive with us, fight against those that fight against us. Take hold of shield and buckler and stand up for our help! Also draw out the spear and stop those who pursue us. Say to our souls, 'I am your salvation.' Let those be put to shame and brought to dishonor who seek after our lives. Let those be turned back and brought to confusion who plot our hurt. Let them be chaff before the wind, and let the angels of the Lord chase them. Let their way be dark and slippery. Let the angels of the Lord pursue them. For without cause they have hidden their net for me in a pit, which they have dug without cause for my life. Let destruction come upon him unexpectedly, and let his net that he has hidden catch himself; into that very destruction let him fall" *Psalms 35:1-8.*

Heavenly Father, Hear my cry, O God; Attend to my prayer. From the end of the earth I will cry unto You, when my heart is overwhelmed; Lead me to the rock that is higher than I. For You have been a shelter for me, A strong tower from the enemy. I will abide in Your tabernacle forever; I will trust in the shelter of Your wings. For You, O God, have heard my vows; You have given me the heritage of those who fear Your Name. I ask You to let me abide with You forever and prepare mercy and truth, which may preserve me. So we will sing praise to Your Name forever, that I may daily perform my vows according to *Psalms 61*.

Heavenly Father, hear my voice, O God, in my meditation; Preserve my life from fear of the enemy. Hide me from the secret plots of the wicked, from the rebellion of the workers of iniquity, who sharpen their tongue like a sword, and bend their bows to shoot their arrows – bitter words at me. I ask You, Heavenly Father to shoot at them with an arrow; suddenly wound them and make them stumble over their own tongue; all who see them shall flee away, all men shall fear, and shall declare the work of God; for they will wisely consider Your doing. The righteous shall be glad in the Lord, and trust in Him. And all the upright in heart shall glory according to *Psalms 64*.

Heavenly Father, in You, O Lord, I put my trust; Let me never be ashamed; Deliver me in Your righteousness. Bow down Your ear to me, deliver me speedily; Be my rock of refuge, a fortress of defense to save me. For You are my rock and my fortress; Therefore, for Your Name's sake, lead me and guide me. Pull me out of the net that they have secretly laid for me. For You are my strength. Into Your hand I commit my spirit; redeem me, O Lord God of truth. I have hated those who regard useless idols; but I trust in You, Heavenly Father. I will be glad and rejoice in Your mercy, for You have considered my trouble; You have known my soul in adversities, and You have not shut me up into the hand of the enemy; You have set my feet in a wide place. Have mercy on me, O Lord, for I am in trouble according to *Psalms 31:1-9*.

Heavenly Father, we thank You that it is written in *Psalms 32*; Blessed is he whose transgression is forgiven, whose sin is covered. Blessed is the man to whom the Lord does not impute iniquity, and in whose spirit there is no deceit. I have acknowledged my sin to You, and my iniquity I have not hidden. I said, "I will confess my transgressions to the Lord," and You forgave the iniquity of my sin. For this cause everyone who is godly shall pray to You in a time when You may be found; surely in a flood of great waters they shall not come near me. You are my hiding place; You shall preserve me from trouble; You shall surround me with songs of deliverance. I thank You for instructing and teaching me in the way I should go and guiding me with Your eyes according to *Psalms 32:1-8*.

Heavenly Father, I thank You *"For when the enemy shall come in, like a flood Your Holy Spirit will lift up a standard against him"* Isaiah 59:19.

Heavenly Father, I ask You to nullify, dismantle, cancel and stop all works of darkness which are designed to hinder, prevent, deny, or delay Your original plans and purposes for our lives according to *Daniel 7:25*. Lord Christ Jesus, thank You for redeeming us from the curse according to *Galatians 3:13 "Christ has redeemed us from the curse of the law, having become a curse for us"*.

Heavenly Father, thank you for saving me and all members of our household according to *Acts 16:31* "Believe on the Lord Jesus Christ, and you will be saved, you and your household."

HEDGE OF PROTECTION PRAYER

Heavenly Father, I ask You to execute divine judgment against satanic/demonic activities and help us war in the spirit of Elijah and Jehu according to *1 Kings 18:1-46, 9-10:2*. In the Name of the Lord Jesus Christ of Nazareth, I bind all of Satan's evil, wicked, demon, lying and tormenting spirits and strongmen along with all their works, roots, fruits, tentacles, and links of: _____, _____ [say what applies - examples: addictions, bad language, conniving, discouragements, fears, lusts, insomnia, pride, stress, willful sins, withdrawal, worries] all spirits and strongmen of all mental, physical, and emotional illness, sickness, diseases, disorders, death, premature death, infirmities, afflictions, inflammations, viruses, infections, abnormal cells, radical cells, lesions, cysts, pains, shock, trauma, spasms, cramps, abnormal growths, radical growths, in or on any parts of our bodies, including our eyes, ears, nose, mouth, throat, back, bones, muscles, ligaments, tissues, blood, blood vessels, arteries, colons, intestines, stomach, prostate, thyroid, brain, liver, heart, lungs, cardiovascular disorders and diseases, reproductive disorders and diseases, thyroid disorders and diseases, blood pressure disorders and diseases, throat disorders and diseases, breast disorders and diseases, neurological disorders and diseases, lymphatic disorders and diseases, chemical imbalances, hormone imbalances, allergies of any kind, senility, forgetfulness, paranoia, schizophrenia, all spirits of arthritis, crippling arthritis, acute arthritis, sinusitis, acute sinusitis, performance spirits, all spirits of disorders and diseases, hypoglycemia of all forms, degenerative diseases of all kinds, and all cancers, all tumors, and all mind diseases and disorders. I bind and banish all these demonic spirits and strongmen from me, from everyone that I have prayed for today, along with all evil principalities, powers, and rulers of wickedness in high places, from every organ in our bodies, from every cell in our bodies, from every gland in our bodies, from our homes, properties, marriages, cars, trucks, businesses, ministries, objects, work places, finances, etc., and I command them to go where Jesus sends them and I bind them and command them to stay there in the Name of Jesus Christ of Nazareth. I place the Blood of the Lord Christ Jesus between us.

Heavenly Father, I ask You to destroy all demonic covenants, contracts, chains, fetters, bondages, proclivities and captivities that are contrary to, oppose, or hinder Your Will and destiny for our lives. I ask that You liberate me from generational, satanic, and/or demonic alliances, allegiances, soul ties, spirits of inheritances and curses. Free us from any and all influences passed down from one generation to another; biologically, socially, emotionally, psychologically, spiritually, or any other channel unknown to me, but known to You. I resist every spirit that acts as a gatekeeper or doorkeeper to my soul, and renounce any further conscious or unconscious alliance, association, allegiance, or covenant. I open us to divine deliverance. Heavenly Father, have Your way now! Perfect those things concerning us. I ask these things in the Name of the Lord Jesus Christ according to *John 12:14*. Lord Jesus, I ask You to destroy all ill spoken words, all ill wishes, all enchantments, all spells, hexes, curses, all witchcraft prayers, psychic prayers, witchcraft spells, voodoo spells, satanic spells, and every idle word spoken contrary to God's original plans and purposes. Lord Jesus, I ask that You destroy the curses associated with these utterances and decree and declare that: they shall not stand; they shall not come to pass; they shall not take root; and their violent verbal dealings are returned to them double-fold according to *Isaiah 54:17*.

Heavenly Father, I ask You to place a hedge of protection around me. It hides me from the enemy, familiar spirits, any and all demon spirits, making it difficult, if not impossible for them to effectively track or trace me in the realm of the spirit. There shall be no perforations or penetrations to these hedges of protection according to *Job 1:7-10, Psalms 91:1-16, Exodus 12:13*, and *Zechariah 2:5*.

Heavenly Father, I ask You to place our names on the hearts of all prayer warriors, intercessors, and prophetic watchmen who will pray for me. I ask You to let them not cease or come down from their watchtowers until their assignments have been completed. Heavenly Father, I ask that they will conduct their intercessory assignments under the direction of the Holy Spirit and Christ Jesus who is my chief intercessor according to *Jeremiah 27:18, Ezekiel 3:17*, and *John 16:13*.

Heavenly Father, I declare that our times and seasons are in the hands of the Lord and they shall not be altered or adjusted by anyone or anything. We function under Your anointing and You give us the divine ability to accurately discern our times and seasons according to *1 Chronicles 12.32, Psalms 31:15, Ecclesiastes 3:1-8, and Daniel 2:21-22.*

Heavenly Father, I declare that from this day forward we will operate according to Your divine timetable/calendar. I declare that Your agenda is my agenda. We are not our own, we have been bought with a price. I therefore submit to You alone. I bind our minds to the mind of Christ. I bind our wills to the Will of God. I declare that *"I come: in the volume of the book it is written of me"* according to *Psalms 40:7, 139:16, 1 Corinthians 7:23*, and *James 4:7.*

Lord Jesus, I bring all my burdens and lay them at the foot of Your cross, especially the burdens of _____, _____, _____, and _____. I ask You to manage all areas of our lives. I totally rely on You, Christ Jesus, to take care of us, our families, our health, and our finances. Heavenly Father, I ask that Your Will be done in our lives. Heavenly Father, I declare *"that at the Name of Jesus every knee should bow, of things in heaven, and things in the earth, and things under the earth; And that every tongue should confess that Jesus Christ is Lord, to the glory of You, God the Father"* according to *Philippians 2:10-11.*

Heavenly Father, I ask You to prohibit the accuser of the brethren from operating or influencing the soul or mind of anyone who comes into contact with us according to *Revelation 12:10.* I declare that divine favor, grace, honor, and well-wishes now replace any and all negative feelings, perceptions, and thoughts concerning us, our families, our work, and our ministries which we are called to accomplish. I declare that nobility and greatness is our portion according to *Genesis 12:1-3* and *Psalms 5:12.*

Heavenly Father, You have called us to do great works for You. I ask You to release all finances and all resources that belong to us. I ask You to release everything prepared for us before the foundation of the world that pertains to our lives, our ministries, our calling. We shall not, we will not be denied! We shall not, and we will not accept substitutes. In the Name of Christ Jesus, I declare that every resource necessary for me to fulfill God's original plans and purposes comes to us without delay according to *2 Peter 1-3.*

Almighty God, In the Name of Christ Jesus grant unto us, according to Your riches in glory, Your tender mercies and immeasurable favor, the treasures of darkness and hidden riches of secret places according to *Isaiah 45:1-3.* I declare that the Cyrus anointing flows unhindered and uncontaminated in our lives according to *Isaiah 60:10-17*, and *Philippians 4:19.* Lift up your heads, oh ye gates; and be lifted up forever, you abiding doors that the King of Glory, the Lord strong and mighty, the Lord of Hosts, may come in according to *Psalms 24:7-10.* Therefore, we will not and cannot be denied of what rightfully belongs to us!

Heavenly Father, I declare that the laws that govern this prayer and all spiritual warfare strategies and tactics, are binding by the Word, the Blood, and by the Holy Spirit according to *1 John 5:7-8.*

Heavenly Father, I thank You that it is written in Isaiah 53:5 "But He was wounded for our transgressions, He was bruised for our iniquities: the chastisement of our peace was upon Him: and with His stripes we are healed." I thank You for healing us.

Heavenly Father, I praise You and thank You for strengthening the bars of my gates; for blessing my children, and making peace in my borders according to *Psalms 147:12-14*.

Heavenly Father, I place upon us: the armor of light; and the Lord Jesus Christ according to *Romans 13:12, 14*. Heavenly Father, in Jesus' Holy Name, I place upon us the belt of truth, the breastplate of righteousness, the gospel of peace sandals, the shield of faith to quench the fiery darts of the enemy, the helmet of salvation, the sword of the Spirit, which is the Word of God according to *Ephesians 6:13-17*.

Heavenly Father, if You have made a decision to take us home before the next rapture, I ask You to give us an extension of our lives according to *John 16:23*, as You did for Hezekiah according to *Isaiah 38:1-5*, or until Jesus comes to get us in the next rapture.

Heavenly Father, I declare that "we are a chosen generation, a royal priesthood, a holy nation, a peculiar people: that we shall show forth the praises of Christ Jesus who has called us out of darkness into His marvelous light" according to 1 Peter 2:9.

Heavenly Father, I thank You for Your promise: "I will make you a great nation; I will bless you and make your name great; and you shall be a blessing. I will bless those who bless you, and I will curse him who curses you; and in you all the families of the earth shall be blessed." according to Genesis 12:2-3.

Heavenly Father, I pray that You, almighty God, will bless us, and make us fruitful and multiply us. That we may be an assembly of peoples; and give us the blessing of Abraham, to us and our descendants with us, that we may inherit the land in which we are a stranger, which God gave to Abraham according to *Genesis 28:3-4*.

Heavenly Father, I pray that You would bless us indeed, and enlarge our territory, and that Your hand will be with us, and that You would keep us from evil, that we may cause no pain! Heavenly Father, I thank You for granting us this request according to *1 Chronicles 4:10*.

Heavenly Father, I ask You to bless us when we come in. I ask You to bless us when we go out. I ask You to bless us in the city. I ask You to bless us in the country. I ask You to bless our fruits. I ask You to bless our seed. I ask You to bless our land. I ask You to bless our storehouse. I ask You to bless and prosper everything we touch. I ask You to cause our enemies to come in one direction but to flee in seven directions because greater is You, Who is in us, than he that is in the world.

Heavenly Father, I thank You for Your blessings and I pray them over me and everyone we have prayed for today according to Psalms 115:14-16. "He will bless us that fear the Lord, both small and great. The Lord shall increase us more and more, us and our children. We are blessed of the Lord which made heaven and earth. The heavens, even the heavens, are the Lord's: but the earth hath He given to the children of men." Heavenly

Father, thank You for continually increasing our anointing, our love for one another other, our health, and our finances.

Heavenly Father, in Christ Jesus' Holy Name I thank You for Your Word in *Numbers 6:23-26*. Heavenly Father, I pray that You will bless me, everyone that I have prayed for today and that You will keep us. I pray that You will make Your face shine upon me, and be gracious to us. I pray that You will lift up Your countenance upon me and give us peace. Heavenly Father, thank You for blessing us! Heavenly Father, I thank You for releasing Your angels to fulfill the blessings we speak. *"Bless the Lord, ye His angels, that excel in strength, that do His commandments, hearkening unto the Voice of His Word."* according to *Psalms 103:20*.

Bless the Lord! Bless the Lord, oh my soul, and all that is within me, bless His Holy Name. Bless the Lord, oh my soul, and forget not all of His benefits, who forgives all my iniquities; who heals all my diseases, Who redeems my life from destruction, Who crowns me with loving kindness and tender mercies, Who gives me good things to eat, so that my youth is renewed like the eagle's, and has pity on me and I thank You that the angels harkens to the Voice of Your Word according to *Psalms 103:1-3, 13, 20.*

Blessed are You, Lord God of Israel, our Father, forever and ever. Yours, O Lord, is the greatness, the power and the glory, the victory and the majesty; for all that is in heaven and in earth is Yours; Yours is the kingdom, O Lord, and You are exalted as head over all. Both riches and honor come from You, and You reign over all. In Your hand is power and might; In Your hand it is to make great and to give strength to all, according to *1 Chronicles 29:10-12*

Lord Jesus, I ask you to do all of these things according to *John 14:14*; and Heavenly Father, I ask You to give us these things according to *John 16:23*. In the Name of the Lord Jesus Christ of Nazareth, I pray with thanksgiving. **Amen**

COMMUNION PRAYER

Heavenly Father, I come to You now in the Name of my Lord and Savior Christ Jesus. I thank You that we can enter in communion at this time. We thank You that Your Word says in *1 Corinthians 11:27*, that *"Whoever shall eat of the Bread of Life and drink of the Cup of the Lord, in an unworthy manner shall be guilty of the Body and the Blood of Jesus Christ."* Your Word says let every man examine himself, so let each of us examine ourselves now [pause here for a moment of silence and look inside yourself].

Heavenly Father, I ask You to forgive me, _____, and _____, of our sins, transgressions, iniquities, and our trespasses, cover each of us with the Blood of Jesus Christ and cleanse us each of all unrighteousness. Heavenly Father, I thank You that we are now able to enter into communion with You at this time. I thank You that the Lord Jesus Christ went to the cross for us, that Jesus took my sins, my transgressions, our iniquities, and our trespasses to the cross with Him. I thank You that we can take this piece of bread (body) in remembrance of Jesus.

We thank You Lord Jesus that Your body was broken for our sins, our transgressions, our iniquities, and our trespasses. Lord Jesus, we love You. We remember Your suffering, and how You were beaten and marred, spit upon, whipped and crucified for each of us. Your body was broken so that our body may be healed. I thank You that with Your stripes we are healed in the Name of the Lord Jesus. Dear Jesus, thank You for loving us, touching us, and healing us. We thank You that You took the bread and broke it and said take, eat, this is my body which was broken for you and partake in faith in the Name of Jesus. Dear Jesus, we now take this piece of bread (your body) in remembrance of You in faith.

Your Word says in *1 Corinthians*, that after supper, Jesus took the cup and said this to His disciples: *"This is the Blood of the new testament shed for you."* We thank You Lord Jesus that You shed Your Blood for us, that Your Blood is our atonement. It justifies us, sanctifies us, redeems us and cleanses and washes away all our sins, all of our iniquities, all of our transgressions, all of our trespasses and Your Blood heals us in the Name of Jesus. I now take this in remembrance of You. In the Name of Jesus Christ of Nazareth, we pray with thanksgiving. **Amen**

DESTROYING GENERATIONAL CURSES

Heavenly Father, I come to You now in the Name of my Lord and Savior Christ Jesus. I believe that You are the Son of God; that You died on the cross for my sins; that God raised You from the dead and You ascended to heaven.

Heavenly Father, I repent of any sins in my life and my ancestors' lives, going back 25 generations, that have resulted in a curse or curses. I repent of all and any sins of: not keeping Your commandments: having other gods before You; making or buying images, bowing down to or serving images; for taking the Lord my God's Name in vain; for not observing and keeping holy the Sabbath day; not honoring my father and/or mother; murder; adultery; stealing; bearing false witness; coveting a neighbor's spouse, house, land, servants, donkey, or anything that is my neighbor's; not loving You with all my heart, with all my soul, and with all my mind; not loving my neighbor as myself, or not loving myself [Please see "Sin List" on page 181 and ask God's forgiveness for any other sins that may apply to you]. I ask Your forgiveness and cleansing through the Blood of the Lord Jesus Christ according to *1 John 1:9* and *John 14:14*.

Heavenly Father, I repented of all of my sins and I thank You for forgiving me. In the Name of the Lord Jesus Christ, I now ask You to destroy all curses, generational curses that have been placed on me, my spouse, and my children, including ten generations. **Amen**

BONDAGE BREAKING PRAYER

Lord Jesus, Your Word says that Your anointing breaks and destroys all yokes of bondage so I ask You now to cause Your anointing to break and destroy any yokes of bondages; along with all their works, roots, fruits, tentacles, and links, in the Name of Jesus Christ of Nazareth [Please look at the "Demon List" on page 183 and break any bondages that you feel may apply to you.]. Heavenly Father, I ask You to give us deliverance and freedom from all these bondages in the Name of Christ Jesus according to *John 16:23*.

In the Name of the Lord Jesus Christ of Nazareth, I bind all of Satan's evil, wicked, demon, lying and tormenting spirits and strongmen, along with all their works, roots, fruits, tentacles and links of [Please look at the "Demon List" on page 183 and banish any foul spirits that you feel may apply to you.]. I bind and banish all these demonic spirits and strongmen from me, from everyone that I have prayed for today, along with all evil principalities, powers, and rulers of wickedness in high places, from every organ in our bodies, from every cell in our bodies, from every gland in our bodies, from our homes, properties, marriages, cars, trucks, businesses, ministries, objects, work places, finances... and I command them to go where Jesus sends them and I bind them and command them to stay there in the Name of Jesus Christ of Nazareth. I place the Blood of the Lord Christ Jesus between us. I claim all of our lives united together in obedient love and service to the Lord Jesus Christ. Lord, I ask you to grant us conviction of sin with Godly sorrow to repentance. I pray that we will now be set completely free from anything that now binds us.

Heavenly Father, I ask You to cause Your anointing to break and destroy every yoke of bondage in our lives. In the Name of Jesus Christ, Heavenly Father, I ask you to fill our minds with the gifts of the Spirit of God, with love, joy, peace, with longsuffering, gentleness and goodness, with meekness, faithfulness and self control. Heavenly Father, in Christ Jesus' Holy Name, I ask You to fill us with Your Holy Spirit anointing and power and cover us with Your presence.

Heavenly Father, I bow and worship and praise before You and I apply the precious Blood of the Lord Jesus Christ, from the tops of our heads to the soles of our feet. I plead the Blood of Jesus over us, over the airways that surround us, over us and under us, over telephone lines, over our homes, properties, offices, cars, trucks, marriages, businesses, finances, ministries. I plead the precious Blood of Jesus Christ and I ask You to render powerless and harmless and nullify the power, destroy the power, cancel the power of any evil spirit, demonic spirit, evil strongmen, messengers of Satan that try to come into our presence, our homes, our properties, our automobiles, our finances, our ministries... in the Name of Jesus Christ of Nazareth.

Heavenly Father, in the Name of the Lord Jesus Christ of Nazareth, I thank you for Your mighty work. Grant to me the grace, power and desire to be persistent in my intercessions for _____, and myself that You may be glorified through our deliverance. In the Name of the Lord Jesus Christ of Nazareth, I pray with thanksgiving. **Amen**

SHATTERING STRONGHOLDS ON SELF

Heavenly Father, I come to You now in the Name of my Lord and Savior Christ Jesus. I am standing on the truth of Your Word. You said You would give me the Keys to the Kingdom, that whatsoever I would bind on earth would be bound in heaven and whatsoever I would loose on earth would be loosed in heaven according to *Matthew 16 and 18*. Right now, in the Name of Jesus Christ, I bind my will to the Will of God, that I will be constantly aware of Your Will and purpose for my life. I bind myself to the truth of God that I will not be deceived by the many subtle deceptions of the world and the devil.

In the Name of Jesus Christ, I bind myself to the Blood of Jesus. I want to be constantly aware of the Blood of Christ Jesus' miracle working power to restore and heal and keep me safe. I bind my mind to the mind of Christ that I will be aware of how Jesus Christ would have me think and believe. I do not want to react out of my own human thoughts when situations arise suddenly. I want to think and act as Jesus would have me act. I bind my feet to paths of righteousness that my steps will be steady and true all day long. I bind myself to the work of the cross in my life so that I will continue to die daily to my own selfish desires and motivations and be more like Jesus. In the Name of Jesus Christ, I bind the strongman so that I may spoil his household and take back every bit of joy, peace, blessing, freedom and every material and spiritual possession that he has stolen from me. I take them back right now! I banish the strongman's influence over every part of my body, soul, and spirit. I banish, crush, smash and destroy every evil devise you may try to bring into my sphere of influence during this day.

I repent of every wrong desire, attitude and pattern of thinking I have had. Forgive me, Heavenly Father, for holding onto wrong ideas, desires, behaviors and habits according to *1 John 1:9* and *John 14:14*. I renounce and reject these things in the Name of the Lord Jesus Christ, and I banish every wrong attitude, pattern of thinking, belief, idea, desire, behavior and habit I have ever learned. I banish the strongholds around them that would keep me from being completely surrendered to the will of God for my life. I banish all doubt and confusion from myself.

I have bound my mind to the mind of Christ and I banish every wrong thought and evil imagination that will keep me from being in sweet unity with You. I bind and loose these things in the Name of Jesus Christ, who has given me the keys to do so. **Amen**

SHATTERING STRONGHOLDS ON OTHERS

Heavenly Father, I come to You now in the Name of my Lord and Savior Christ Jesus. Heavenly Father, I pray for ____, and ____. I ask You to forgive them for all of their sins, iniquities, trespasses and transgressions, and I ask you to cover their sins, iniquities, trespasses and transgressions with the Blood of the Lord Jesus Christ and cleanse them of all unrighteousness according to *John 14:14*.

Heavenly Father, by the power of Jesus Christ, I bind ____'s and ____'s body, soul and spirit to the will and purpose of God for their lives. I bind ____'s mind, will and emotions to the will of God. I bind them to the truth and to the Blood of Jesus. I bind their minds to the mind of Christ, that the very thoughts, feelings, and purposes of Christ Jesus' heart would be within their thoughts.

In the Name of Jesus Christ, I bind their feet to the paths of righteousness that their steps would be steady and sure. I bind them to the work of the cross with all its mercy, grace, love, forgiveness, and dying to self.

In the Name of the Lord Jesus Christ, I banish every old, wrong, ungodly pattern of thinking, attitude, idea, desire, belief, motivation, habit and behavior from them. I tear down, crush, smash and destroy every stronghold associated with these things. I banish any stronghold in their life that has been justifying and protecting hard feelings against anyone. I banish strongholds of unforgiveness, fear, and distrust from them.

In the Name of the Lord Jesus Christ, I banish the power and effects of deception and lies from them. I banish the confusion and blindness of the enemy from their minds that has kept them from seeing the light of the gospel of Jesus Christ. I call forth every precious word of scripture that has ever entered into their minds and hearts that it would rise up in power within them. In the Name of Jesus Christ, I banish the power and effects of any harsh or hard words, any word curses spoken to, about or by them. I banish all generational bondages and associated strongholds from them. I banish all effects and bondages from them that may have been caused by mistakes I have made. Heavenly Father, in the Name of Jesus Christ, I crush, smash, and destroy generational bondages of any kind from mistakes made at any point between generations. I destroy them right here, right now. They will not bind and curse any more members of my family.

In the Name of Jesus Christ, I bind the strongman that I may spoil his house, taking back every bit of joy, peace, blessing, freedom and every material and spiritual possession that he has stolen from me. I take back them right now! I banish the strongman's influence over every part of our body, soul, and spirit. I banish, crush, smash and destroy every evil devise the enemy may try to bring into their sphere of influence during this day.

I bind and banish these things in Christ Jesus' Holy Name. He has given me the keys and the authority to do so. **Amen**

PRAYER FOR PEACEFUL SLEEP I

Heavenly Father, I come to You now in the Name of my Lord and Savior Christ Jesus. Lord Jesus, I ask You to break and destroy any curses, side effects, effects, influences or stings of any curses that have been placed on me, anyone that I have prayed for today, our children, our grandchildren, our marriages, our homes, our cars, our trucks, our offices, our properties, our buildings, our businesses, our ministries, our finances, in the Name of Jesus Christ of Nazareth according to *John 14:14*.

Lord Jesus, I ask You to give us peaceful sleep tonight and keep us safe according to *Psalms 4:8*; and according to *Psalms 127:2*, I ask that You give us Your beloved sleep tonight. I ask You to keep Your hands on us while we sleep tonight and speak to our hearts tonight. I ask You to do this in the Name of Jesus Christ of Nazareth.

In the Name of the Lord Jesus Christ of Nazareth, I plead the Blood of Jesus Christ over us, over our sleep, over our thoughts, over everything in our rooms, over our homes, and over everything in our homes. I plead the precious Blood of Jesus Christ as our protection.

Heavenly Father, I ask You to remove from me any hurts, any turmoil's, any pains, trauma, shock, and any anguish that are deep within my soul that have been created at any time in my life that need to be removed.

Heavenly Father, I ask You to loose into each of us a Spirit of love, peace, joy, and restoration.

Heavenly Father, I ask You to camp Your angels around us, our homes, and our properties, to guard us and protect us, and to destroy any evil spirits, demonic spirits, strongmen or messengers of Satan, witchcraft or curse, that try to come against us, against our homes, or against our properties. I ask You to give us sweet sleep tonight in the Name of Jesus Christ of Nazareth.

Heavenly Father, fill us with Your Holy Ghost anointing and power, fill us with Your presence, in the Holy Name of Jesus Christ, I pray with thanksgiving. Lord Jesus, I ask you to do all of these things according to *John 14:14*; and Heavenly Father I ask You to give us these things according to *John 16:23*. In the Name of the Lord Jesus Christ of Nazareth, I pray with thanksgiving. **Amen**

PRAYER FOR PEACEFUL SLEEP II

Heavenly Father, I come to You now in the Name of my Lord and Savior Christ Jesus. Lord Jesus, I ask You to break and destroy any curses, words of deception, lies, side effects, effects, influences or stings of any curses that have been placed on me, anyone that I have prayed for today, our children, our grandchildren, our marriages, our homes, our cars, our trucks, our offices, our properties, our buildings, our businesses, our ministries, our finances... in the Name of Jesus Christ of Nazareth according to *John 14:14*.

Heavenly Father, I ask You to remove from me any hurts, any turmoil's, any pains, trauma, shock, any old hurts, old pains, and any anguishes and old anguishes, that are deep within my soul that have been created at any time in my life that need to be removed.

Heavenly Father, I ask You to empower any medication, supplement, vitamin, or herb that I, or _____ am taking to do the work that You intend it to do. I pray that You will destroy and nullify any allergic reactions and/or adverse side effects that any medication, supplement, vitamin, herb, or combinations of any of these things may cause in me, or _____.

Lord Jesus, I ask You to destroy any adverse side effects of radiation treatments and chemotherapy treatments. Lord Jesus, I ask You to destroy any adverse side effects from any organ, any cell, any gland; from my vision, sight, mind, hearing; from any part of my body, or _____'s body; and I ask You to do this according to *John 14:13-14*.

Lord Jesus, I ask You to destroy any adverse side effects of the medication of _____, _____, _____, _____, _____, _____, or any supplement or vitamin that I am taking, that is having any adverse side effects in any organ, any cell, any gland, or any part of my body.

Lord Jesus, I ask You to destroy all ill spoken words, all ill wishes, all enchantments, all spells, hexes, curses, all witchcraft prayers, acts of witchcraft, psychic prayers, ungodly soulish prayers, voodoo, witchcraft spells, voodoo spells, satanic spells, and every idle word spoken contrary to God's original plans and purposes. Lord Jesus, I ask that You destroy the curses associated with these utterances, side effects, effects, influences or stings and I decree and declare that: they shall not stand; they shall not come to pass; they shall not take root; and their violent verbal dealings are returned to them double-fold according to *Isaiah 54:17,* for each of us, in the Name of Jesus.

Heavenly Father, I thank You that no weapon formed against us shall prosper. I thank You that every tongue and every word that rises against me in judgment; You shall condemn. I thank You Heavenly Father that this is the heritage of the servants of the Lord, and our righteousness is from You according to *Isaiah 54:17, Psalms 16, Psalms 1:27.*

Heavenly Father, I ask You to place a hedge of protection around me. It hides me from the enemy, familiar spirits, any and all demon spirits, making it difficult, if not impossible for them to effectively track or trace me in the realm of the spirit. There shall be no perforations or penetrations to these hedges of protection according to *Job 1:7-10, Psalms 91:1-16, Exodus 12:13, and Zechariah 2:5.*

Heavenly Father, I ask You to camp Your angels around us, our homes, and our properties, to guard us and protect us, and to destroy any evil spirits, demonic spirits, strongmen or messengers of Satan, witchcraft, acts of witchcraft, or curse, that try to come against us, against our homes, or against our properties.

In the Name of the Lord Jesus Christ of Nazareth, I plead the Blood of Jesus Christ over us, over our sleep, over our thoughts, over everything in our rooms, over our homes, and over everything in our homes. I plead the precious Blood of Jesus Christ as our protection.

Heavenly Father, I ask You to loose into each of us a Spirit of love, peace, joy, and restoration. Lord Jesus, I ask You to give us sweet sleep tonight, give us peaceful sleep tonight and keep us safe according to *Psalms 4:8*; and according to *Psalms 127:2,* I ask that You give us Your beloved sleep tonight. I ask You to keep Your hands on us while we sleep tonight and speak to our hearts tonight. I ask You to do this in the Name of Jesus Christ of Nazareth.

Heavenly Father, fill us with Your Holy Ghost anointing and power, fill us with Your presence, in the Holy Name of Jesus Christ, I pray with thanksgiving. Lord Jesus, I ask you to do all of these things according to *John 14:14*; and Heavenly Father I ask You to give us these things according to *John 16:23*. In the Name of the Lord Jesus Christ of Nazareth, I pray with thanksgiving. **Amen**

BEDROOM BLESSING

I bless you doorway to this bedroom as the gate of security of this room
Bed, I bless you with serenity and peace

I bless you as a place of dreams and the Presence of our God
I bless you with the blessings of rest and refreshment
I bless you bed, as a gentle invitation to slumber and sleep, to regenerate
Bedroom, I bless you with quietness
I bless you to be a haven that angels watch over
I bless you as a private place, leaving all the cares of the day at the gate
I bless you as the place where we awake, fresh and alive to begin each day
I bless you as a place of beauty
I do this blessing in the Name of Jesus, Who neither slumbers nor sleeps
But gives to us, as His beloved even in our sleep

PRAYER FOR PHYSICAL HEALING I

Heavenly Father, I come to You now in the Name of my Lord and Savior Christ Jesus. Heavenly Father, according to Your Word in *John 14:14*, *"Ask anything in my Name and I shall do it."*; and according to *1 John 1:9*, *"If we confess our sins to You, You are faithful and just to forgive us and to cleanse us from all unrighteousness* (every wrong-doing)."

Heavenly Father, I ask that You would forgive me, _____, _____, and _____ of my sins, my iniquities, trespasses and transgressions, specifically sins of _____, _____, and _____, in Christ Jesus' Holy Name. Heavenly Father, I repent for all of my sins and I ask You to forgive me for all my sins, iniquities, trespasses and transgressions and to cover them with the Blood of the Lord Christ Jesus, and to cleanse me of all unrighteousness according to Your Word, *1 John 1:9* and *John 14:14*, in Christ Jesus' Holy Name, I ask you to do this.

Heavenly Father, I ask you to heal me, _____, _____, and _____ in Jesus' Name according to your Word: "Jesus is the Lord of my life. Sickness and disease have no power over me. I am forgiven and free from sin and guilt. I am dead to sin and alive unto righteousness" according to Colossians 1:21-22. "You have given me abundant life." I receive that life through Your Word and it flows to every organ of my body bringing life, healing, and health according to John 10:10; John 6:63. "Jesus bore my sickness and carried my pain." Therefore I give no place to sickness or pain. For God sent His Word and healed me. Psalms 107:20. "He sent His word and healed me, and delivered me from my destructions." Psalms 107:19-20.

Heavenly Father, I attend to Your Word. I incline my ears to Your sayings. I will not let them depart from my eyes. I keep them in the midst of my heart, for they are life and healing to all my flesh. *Proverbs 4:20-22.* As You were with Moses, so are You with me. My eyes are not dim; neither is my natural vigor diminished. Blessed are my eyes for they see and my ears for they hear. *Deuteronomy 34:7.* *"No evil will befall me, neither shall any plague come near my dwelling. For You have given angels charge over me. They keep me in all ways."* In my pathway is life, healing, and health. *Psalms 91:10 -11; Proverbs 12:28.* *"Jesus took my infirmities and bore my sicknesses. Therefore I refuse to allow sickness to dominate my body.* The life of God flows within me, bringing healing to every fiber of my being. *Matthew 8:16; John 6:63.* I am redeemed from the curse. *Galatians 3:13* is flowing in my Blood stream. It flows to every cell of my body, restoring life and health. *Mark 11:23-24; Luke 17:6*. The life of *1 Peter 2:24* is a reality in my flesh, restoring every cell of my body. My body is the temple of the Holy Ghost. I make a demand on my body to release the right chemicals and hormones. My body is in perfect chemical balance. My pancreas secretes the proper amount of insulin for life and health. *Mark 11:23-24*.

Heavenly Father, through Your Word You have imparted Your life to me. That life restores my body with every breath I breathe and every word I SPEAK. *John 6:63; Mark 11:23-24*. That which God has not planted is dissolved and rooted out of my body in Jesus' Name. *1 Peter 2:24* is engrafted into every fiber of my being and I am alive with the life of God. *Mark 11:23-24; John 6:63*. Growths and tumors have no right in or on my body. They are a thing of the past, for I am delivered from the authority of darkness. *Colossians 1:13-14*. Every organ and tissue of my body function in the perfection that God created it to function. I forbid any malfunction in my body in Jesus' Name. *Genesis 1:28, 31*.

Heavenly Father, as I give voice to Your Word, the law of the Spirit of life in Christ Jesus makes me free from the law of sin and death. Your life is energizing every cell of my body. *Romans 8:11* Arthritis, you must go. Sickness must flee. Diseases must leave. Harmful bacteria, viruses, and fungi I command them to die, in the Name of Jesus Christ of Nazareth. Tumors cannot exist in me, for the Spirit of God is upon me. Sickness, fear, and oppression have no power over me for God's Word is my confession *Mark 11:23, 24*.

Thank you, Father, that I have a strong heart. My heart beats with the rhythm of life. My blood flows to every cell of my body, restoring life and health abundantly *Proverbs 12:14; 14:30*. I command my blood cells to destroy every disease, germ and virus that tries to inhibit my body. I command every cell of my body to be normal in Jesus' Name. *Romans 5:17*.

Heavenly Father, I speak to the bones and joints of my body. I call you normal in Jesus' Name. My bones and joints will not respond to any disease, for the Spirit life of *1 Peter 2:24* permeates every bone and joint of my body with life and health. I make a demand on my bones to produce perfect marrow. I make a demand on the marrow to produce pure blood that will ward off sickness and disease. My bones refuse any offense of the curse. *Proverbs 16:24*. I make a demand on my joints to function perfectly. There will be no pain or swelling in my joints. My joints refuse to allow anything that will hurt or destroy their normal function. *Proverbs 17:22*. I demand, command, and declare all these things in the Name of the Lord Jesus Christ of Nazareth.

Heavenly Father, in Jesus' Holy Name I speak the Word of Faith to my body. I demand that every internal organ perform a perfect work, for you are the temple of the Holy Spirit; therefore body, I charge you in the Name of the Lord Jesus Christ and by the authority of His Holy Word to be healed and made whole in Jesus' Name. *Proverbs 12:18*.

Heavenly Father, I resist the enemy in every form that he comes against me – I require my body to be strong and healthy, and I enforce it with Your Word. I reject the curse, and I enforce life in this body. *James 4:7*. I will not die but live and declare the works of

God. *Psalms 118:17.* You have forgiven all my iniquities; You have healed all my diseases; You have redeemed my life (lives) from destruction; You have satisfied my mouth with good things so that my youth is renewed as the eagles. *Psalms 103:2-5.* Lord, You have blessed my food and water and have taken sickness away from me. Therefore I will fulfill the number of my days in health. *Exodus 23:25-26.*

Lord Jesus, I ask you to do all of these things according to *John 14:14*; and Heavenly Father I ask You to give me Divine healing, Divine health, the manifestation of Divine healing and Divine health, in the Name of the Lord Jesus Christ of Nazareth; according to *John 16:23*, **Amen**

Heavenly Father, according to Your Word "You are not a respecter of persons." I receive my healing, in Jesus' Holy Name. I forbid the enemy from trying to steal my healing. I bind my mind with the mind of Christ. I bring every thought captive to the obedience of Jesus Christ. Heavenly Father, fill me overflowing with Your Holy Spirit. In Jesus' Holy Name I thank You for healing me. **Amen**

PRAYER FOR PHYSICAL HEALING II

Heavenly Father, I come to you now in the Name of my Lord and Savior, Jesus Christ of Nazareth. [If two or more are gathered in His Name, add this to the prayer. Heavenly Father, we come to You now in the Name of our Lord and Savior, Jesus Christ and we come to You in one accord, according to *Matthew 18* in the Name of the Lord Jesus Christ of Nazareth. Heavenly Father, it says in *Matthew 18*, when two or more are gathered together in Your Name that You will be in our midst. And whatever will be done for us on earth, will also be done as it is in Heaven.]

Heavenly Father, I come and I lift up _____ to You today. In the Name of the Lord, Jesus Christ of Nazareth, I rebuke any affliction, any infirmity, any inflammation, any sickness, any disease, any disorder, any syndrome of any kind, any abnormal cells, any radical cells, any abnormal growth, any radical growth at this time, I rebuke it and loose them from _____ in the Name of Jesus Christ of Nazareth. I curse any infection in _____'s body and command it to die at the roots and leave _____'s body in a normal way. I curse any abnormal cell, radical cell, abnormal growth or radical growth in _____'s body, and command them to die at the roots and leave _____'s body in the Name of Jesus Christ of Nazareth.

Heavenly Father, I rebuke any disease in _____'s body in the Name of Jesus Christ of Nazareth. I banish it in the Name of Jesus Christ of Nazareth. Heavenly Father, it says in *Matthew 18* whatsoever I bind or loose on earth shall be bound or loose in Heaven, in the Name of Jesus Christ of Nazareth; I bind all Satan's evil, wicked, demon, lying, perverse, unclean, demonic or religious strongmen, including all spiritual strongmen of infections, viruses, cancers, abnormal cells, radical cells, abnormal growths, radical growths, lesions of any kind, spasms of any kind, pains of any kind, trauma, shock, sicknesses, disorders, and diseases of any kind, afflictions of any kind, infirmities or inflammations of any kind, in any part of _____'s body. Including _____'s eyes, ears, nose, mouth, gums, backbone, spine, muscles, ligaments, tissues, blood, blood vessels, arteries, heart, lungs, back, bladder, liver, colon disorders and diseases, stomach disorders and diseases, intestinal disorders and diseases (prostate disorders and diseases), kidney disorders and diseases, bladder disorders and diseases, urinary tract disorders and diseases, thyroid disorders and diseases, neurological disorders and diseases, lymphatic disorders and diseases, chemical disorders and diseases, heart disorders and diseases, lung disorders and diseases, brain disorders and diseases, breast disorders and diseases, skin disorders and diseases, reproductive organ disorders and diseases, senility, schizophrenia, paranoia, forgetfulness, and I command them to unlink, unchain, and banish them from _____, every organ, every cell, every gland, every muscle, every ligament, every bone in _____'s body, in the Name of Jesus Christ of Nazareth, and to go wherever Jesus sends them in the Name of Jesus Christ of Nazareth. Lord Jesus, I ask You to force out of _____, all sickness, all disease, all affliction, all infirmity, all inflammation, all infections of any kind, all abnormal cells, all radical cells, all abnormal growths, all radical growths, lesions of any kind, cysts of any kind, spasms, sicknesses, disorders and diseases of any kind, and force them away from her/him in the Name of Jesus Christ of Nazareth.

Heavenly Father, I ask You now in the Name Jesus Christ to release Your healing virtue, Your miracle virtue into _____'s body in the Name of Jesus Christ of Nazareth; release Your healing virtue, Your miracle virtue, Your healing anointing, Your miracle anointing into _____'s body, from the top of her/his head to the soles of her/his feet in the Name of Jesus Christ of Nazareth. Heavenly Father, we ask You to make _____whole, make her/him whole, Lord, in the Name of Jesus Christ of Nazareth. Father, I ask You to restore every organ, every cell, every gland, every muscle, every ligament, every bone in her/his body and bring everything in total alignment, complete alignment, the way you created her/him, in the Name of Jesus Christ of Nazareth.

Heavenly Father, I apply the Blood of Jesus over every organ, every cell, every gland, every muscle, every ligament, every bone in her/his body whether there is any disease, infection, virus, abnormal cells, radical cells, infirmity or affliction of any kind in the Name of Jesus. Father, I ask You to fill _____ now with Your Holy Spirit, in Jesus' Holy Name. Heavenly Father, I ask You to put a hedge of protection around _____ in the Name of Jesus. Heavenly Father, I apply the Blood of Jesus Christ over _____ from the top of her/his head, to the soles of her/his feet. Heavenly Father, in the Name of the Lord, Jesus Christ of Nazareth, I ask You to fill her/him with Your Holy Spirit; with all the fruits of Your Holy Spirit; Your love, Your joy, Your peace, Your patience, Your kindness, Your gentleness, Your faithfulness, and Your self control, in the Name of Jesus.

Heavenly Father, I thank You that You sent Your son, Jesus Christ, to the cross for me to take all my sicknesses, afflictions, infirmities, inflammations, infections, virus, and abnormal cells, etc. to the cross with Him. I thank You for the stripes that Jesus took on the way to the cross were not only for my sicknesses and diseases, but also for my sins, transgressions, iniquities, and trespasses. And I thank You that according to *Isaiah 53:4 -5* that by the stripes Jesus took on the cross that I am healed and made whole. In the Name of Jesus Christ of Nazareth, I declare that I am healed and made whole according to *Isaiah 53:4-5*, by the stripes of Jesus Christ of Nazareth. **Amen**

PRAYER FOR PHYSICAL HEALING III

Heavenly Father, it is written in Your word in *John 15:7-8*, that if I abide in You and Your Word abides in me, I shall ask what I will and it shall be done for me. So that You my Heavenly Father will be glorified and I will bear much fruit.

Heavenly Father, You know the desires of my heart and I ask You to give me the desires of my heart.

I pray Heavenly Father, that you give me total healing and total deliverance from all sicknesses, diseases of any kind, infirmities, afflictions, infections, viruses, inflammations, disorders of any kind in every cell in our bodies, in every gland in our bodies, in every organ in our bodies, abnormal cells, radical cells, abnormal growths, radical growths, cancers, tumors, spasms, lesions, or cysts in any parts of our bodies.

I ask You Heavenly Father, to give me total restoration of every cell, every ligament, every organ, every gland, every muscle and every bone in my body in the Name of Jesus according to *John 16:23*. To God be the glory. In Jesus Name we pray. **Amen**

PRAYER FOR VICTORY IN JESUS

Heavenly Father, I thank you that we have received from Jesus Christ the victory over all diseases, afflictions, infirmities, hindrances, persecutions, torments and lies that the enemy is trying to send our way now or in the future. We claim victory and deliverance from all demonic spirits, curses, hexes, vexes, enchantments, witchcraft prayers, psychic prayers, or spells. We thank you that Jesus Christ is victorious through the power of His might against all the wiles of the devil; against principalities and powers and rulers of darkness of this world and against spiritual wickedness in high places *Ephesians 6:10-12*. We claim our victory in faith through our salvation and His shed Blood of all these things now. We declare according to *Job 22:27-28* that we are victorious through the shed Blood of Jesus Christ, in His Holy Name we pray. **Amen**

PRAYER FOR GOD TO EMPOWER MEDICATION AND REMOVE ADVERSE SIDE EFFECTS OF MEDICATIONS

Heavenly Father, I ask You to empower any medication, supplement, vitamin, or herb that I, or _____ am taking to do the work that You intend it to do. I pray that You will destroy and nullify any allergic reactions and/or adverse side effects that any medication, supplement, vitamin, herb, or combinations of any of these things may cause in me, or _____.

Lord Jesus, I ask You to destroy any adverse side effects of radiation treatments and chemotherapy treatments.

Lord Jesus, I ask You to destroy any adverse side effects from any organ, any cell, any gland; from my vision, sight, mind, hearing; from any part of my body, or _____'s body; and I ask You to do this according to *John 14:13-14*.

Lord Jesus, I ask You to destroy any adverse side effects of the medication of _____,
_____, _____, _____, _____, _____, or any supplement or vitamin that I
am taking, that is having any adverse side effects in any organ, any cell, any gland, or
any part of my body.

I ask You this according to *John 14:13-14*, in the Name of the Lord Jesus Christ of Nazareth.

I pray that You will destroy and nullify any adverse side effects, specifically of ____,
____, ____, and ____, in me, or ____.

Heavenly Father, give me clarity of vision, clarity of sight, clarity of thought, clarity of
mind, clarity of hearing and knowing Your Voice according to *John 16:23*, in Jesus
Christ's Mighty Name, **Amen**

PRAYER OF REPENTANCE

Heavenly Father, we come before You today to ask Your Forgiveness and seek Your
direction and guidance. We know Your Word says, *"Woe to those who call evil good
and good evil,"* Isaiah 5:20, but that's exactly what we have done. We have lost our
Spiritual equilibrium and inverted our values. We confess that; we have ridiculed the
absolute truth of Your Word and called it pluralism; We have worshipped other gods
and called it multiculturalism; We have endorsed perversion and called it an alternative
lifestyle; We have exploited the poor and called it the lottery; We have neglected the
needy and called it self-preservation; We have rewarded laziness and called it welfare;
We have killed our unborn and called it choice; We have shot abortionists and called it
justifiable; We have neglected to discipline our children and called it building self-
esteem; Some of us have abused power and called it political savvy; We have coveted
our neighbor's possessions and called it ambition; We have polluted the air with profanity and pornography and called it freedom of expression; We have ridiculed the time –
honored values of our forefathers and called it enlightenment. Search us, O God, and
know our hearts today; try us and see if there be some wicked way in us; cleanse us
from every sin and set us free according to Your Will.

I ask this in the Name of Your Son, The Living Savior, Jesus Christ. **Amen**

PRAYER FOR FORGIVENESS OF OTHERS

Heavenly Father, I come to You now in the Name of my Lord and Savior Christ Jesus. I
forgive {___, ___, etc.} for anything that they have ever done or said to me, I bless
them in the Name of Jesus Christ and I ask You to forgive and bless them in the Name
of Jesus Christ according to *John 14:14*.

Heavenly Father, I ask You to forgive me for any hard feelings I had towards them and
fill me with Your love for {___, ___, etc.} I ask these things according to *John 14:14*.
In the Name of Jesus Christ I pray with thanksgiving. **Amen**

"But be doers of the Word [obey the message,] and not merely listeners to it, betraying yourselves [into deception by reasoning contrary to the Truth]. James 1:22

BAPTISM OF THE HOLY SPIRIT

Heavenly Father, I come to You now in the Name of my Lord and Savior Christ Jesus. (Note - if two or more praying: Heavenly Father, _____ and I come to You in one accord in the Name of Christ Jesus of Nazareth. We come two or more in agreement touching heaven and earth and You said it will be done, so according to *Matthew 18:19*. We ask You in the Name of Jesus Christ of Nazareth.)

Heavenly Father, I plead the Blood of my Lord and Savior Jesus Christ over me and I thank You for the most wonderful gift of salvation. Lord Jesus You promised me another gift, the gift of the Holy Spirit. So I ask You Lord Jesus, to baptize and fill me (____) in and with Your Holy Spirit, just as You filled Your disciples on the day of Pentecost. Christ Jesus, I (____) want to be a disciple of Yours, filled with the Holy Spirit just as Your disciples were. I (____) will try to do what You tell me (him/her) to do, I (____) forgive all those who have ever caused me (him/her) pain, trauma, shock, harm, rejection, or shame, and I ask You to forgive them. I also ask You to forgive me (____) for holding a judgment against them.

Christ Jesus, Breathe in me (____) Your Holy Spirit. Thank You Lord, for hearing my prayer. I lift up my hands unto You Jesus worshiping and praising You in the Spirit. I give thanks, praise, and glory to You forever with all my heart .

Christ Jesus, I thank You that You may grant me out of the rich treasury of Your glory to be strengthened and reinforced with mighty power of my inner man by the Holy Spirit. That You, Jesus Christ, through my faith may dwell in my heart that I may be rooted deep in love and founded securely on love. That I may have the power and be strong to apprehend and grasp with all the saints what is breadth and length and height and depth of Your love. Ephesians 3:16-18 (Amplified Bible). I pray in Christ Jesus' Holy Name; with thanksgiving. **Amen**

Thank You Lord Jesus that You have baptized me with Your Holy Spirit and fire. Luke 3:16.

Thank You Lord Jesus that I am filled with Your Holy Spirit and begin to speak with other tongues, as the Spirit gives us utterance. Acts 2:4.

Thank You Lord that You poured out Your love into our hearts by Your Holy Spirit whom You have given us. Romans 5:5

Thank You Lord, that You, who know our hearts, bear witness to us, giving us the Holy Spirit. Acts 15:8.

Thank You Lord that You anointed us with the Holy Spirit and with
power, and we will go about doing good, and healing all who are
oppressed by the devil; for You are with us. Acts 10:38.

Thank You Jesus that we will do greater works than You. John 14:12.

"I baptize you with water. But one more powerful than I will come, the
thongs of whose sandals I am not worthy to untie. He will baptize you
with the Holy Spirit and with fire. Luke 3:16.

PRAYER FOR WISDOM

Heavenly Father, I come to You now in the Name of my Lord and Savior Christ Jesus. I thank you that Your Word gives knowledge, instruction, wisdom, and understanding to all who pays attention to its truths. You promised to impart wisdom to me if I will listen to Your Words and attain unto Your wise counsels. I, therefore, enter Your presence with trust, knowing that You will give me wisdom according to *II Chronicles 1:10*. Heavenly Father, fill me with the spirit of wisdom so that I will be able to discern Your will. With You, Lord, there is both strength and wisdom according to *Job 12:13*.

Heavenly Father, let my mouth speak Your wisdom, Lord, because of the righteousness You have imparted to me according to *Psalms 37:30*. In the hidden part of my life, make me know Your wisdom according to *Psalms 51:6*. Teach me to number my days, so that I may gain a heart of wisdom according to *Psalms 90:12*.

Heavenly Father, Your wisdom and knowledge makes me happy, because the gain of it is better than fine gold. By wisdom You founded the earth, and by knowledge You established the heavens according to *Proverbs 3:13-20*.

Christ Jesus, I thank You that my eyes of Your understanding are continually being enlightened; that I may know Your calling, and the riches of Your glory and Your inheritance for Your saints. I thank You for Your exceeding greatness. I believe, trust and rely on You only. Heavenly Father, I believe that Jesus Christ is Your Son, that He died on the cross for my sins, I believe that You, Heavenly Father raised Jesus Christ from the dead and He now sits at Your right hand in heaven according to *Ephesians 1:17-23*.

Heavenly Father, thank You for sending Jesus who represents Your power and wisdom to us. Because I am in Him – and desire to always abide in Him. He has been made unto me wisdom, and righteousness, sanctification, and redemption. It is this reality that causes me to glory in You forever according to *I Corinthians 1:22-31*. In the Name of Jesus Christ of Nazareth I pray with thanksgiving. **Amen**

PRAYER FOR ISRAEL

Heavenly Father, I come to You now in the Name of my Lord and Savior Christ Jesus. I pray for Israel. Thank You that all Israel will be saved according to *Romans 11:26*. Thank You that Israel will hope in the Lord for with You there is loving kindness, and with You Lord there is abundant redemption, and You will redeem Israel from all his iniquities according to *Psalms 130:7-8*.

Thank You Father that You have taken away Israel's punishment, You have turned back Israel's enemy. Thank You that the king of Israel is with Israel; never again will Israel fear any harm.

Thank You Father that You are with Israel, You are mighty to save, You will take great delight in Israel. You will quiet Israel with Your love, You will rejoice over Israel with singing. Heavenly Father, thank You that the sorrows for the appointed feasts; You will remove from Israel, they are a burden and a reproach to Israel. Thank You that You will rescue the lame and gather those who have been scattered. You will give Israel praise and honor in every land where they have been put to shame. At that time You will gather Israel; at that time You will bring Israel home according to *Zephaniah 3:15-20*.

Heavenly Father, thank You that You will give honor and praise among all the peoples of the earth when You restore Israel's fortunes before her very eyes. In the Name of Jesus Christ, I pray with thanksgiving. **Amen**

PRAYER FOR AMERICA

Heavenly Father, I come to You now in the Name of my Lord and Savior, Jesus Christ. Heavenly Father, I thank you that I can abide under the shadow of my Almighty God. I thank You that a thousand may fall at my side, and ten thousand at my right hand, but none will come near me. I thank You that You have given Your angels charge over me to keep me in all of my ways.

Heavenly Father, I pray for the President of this nation, all of the Executive Branch of this nation and all members of Congress of this nation, all of the leadership of all local, state, regional, and federal agencies, commissions and governments of this nation. I ask You to guide and direct the leadership of this nation in every way.

Lord, I thank You for Your protective hand that has shielded my nation. Thank You Lord for hearing the prayers and requests of Your people on behalf of this nation. Heavenly Father, I pray in the Name of Your Son, Jesus, asking You to give us divine protection for Your people of this nation, according to *John 16:23*. I'm asking You, Lord God, to ensure the safety of Your people and to keep me and our nation from harm's way and provide protection from plans of destruction that have been plotted against us. I pray that you would stop any strategies of destruction that would try to come against Your people and this nation. I pray Father, that you would extend a hand of protection against all of the destructive forces of terrorism against Your people and this nation. I pray that You will protect me and this nation from evil attacks or acts of terrorism, and stop the aggressors or terrorists that attempt to bring destruction against me or this nation. May the knowledge of terrorist's planned attacks be revealed to those who provide our national and international security. I pray that You would give wisdom and discernment to those who provide protection for Your people and this nation. Help everyone in authority to be alert to signs of wrongdoing in this nation. I pray that You will provide insight to national, international and local authorities of this nation, to act swiftly, to avert all danger, protecting American lives and property. I pray that you will provide instruction in the development of effectual and efficient anti-terrorist strategies and provide our nation with an arsenal of weapons that will give my nation an advantage against any aggressor coming against this nation or Your people. Guide the authorities of this nation in efforts to seek out and eradicate terrorists. Enable the military forces of this nation to become swift, powerful and accurate in any action of intelligence gathering and retaliation. I submit this to Your Hand, Lord. I give You the Praise and I give You the Glory, that You hear my prayers and my supplications. Heavenly Father, I pray that every potential act of terrorism against this nation or Your people will be exposed. Heavenly Father, I ask You to loose Your mighty warring and guardian angels to expose and destroy any potential acts of terrorism against any city, any town, or any of Your people of this nation. Lord Jesus, I ask You to destroy any plans that Satan and any physical and spiritual enemies of this nation have against any city, any town, or any of Your people in this nation. I ask You to expose and destroy all terrorist cells that are located in this nation. I ask You to bless and strengthen this nation. I ask You to loose in great abundance Your mighty warring and guardian angels over this nation to guard and protect us. Lord Jesus, I ask You to cause confusion in the minds of all terrorists who are plotting against this nation, or any of Your people in this nation. I ask you to do all of these things according to John 14:14. In the Name of the Lord Jesus Christ of Nazareth, I pray with thanksgiving. In Jesus' Name, we pray.

Heavenly Father, You are our Refuge and Stronghold in times of trouble. So I declare with my mouth that Your people of this nation will dwell safely in this land, and prosper abundantly. I are more than conquerors through Christ Jesus. I declare that no weapon formed against me shall prosper. **Amen**

PRAYER FOR WORLD LEADERS

Heavenly Father, I come to You now in the Name of my Lord and Savior Christ Jesus. I pray for our world leaders that Your Spirit rests upon them.

I believe that skillful and godly wisdom has entered into the hearts of our world leaders and that they will do Your will, Heavenly Father, that they have hearts and ears attentive to Your godly counsel. Lord make them women and men of Your integrity, that we may lead a quiet and peaceful life in all godliness and honestly. I pray that the wicked world leaders shall be cut off and rooted out.

Heavenly Father, You are our Refuge and Stronghold in times of trouble. So we declare with our mouths that Your people dwell safely in this land, and we prosper abundantly. We are more than conquerors through Christ Jesus.

We give thanks unto You Lord that the good news of the Gospel is published in our land. The Word of the Lord prevails and grows mightily in the hearts and lives of the people. We give thanks for this land and the leaders You have given us, in Jesus' Name I pray. **Amen**

PRAYER FOR THE LOST

Heavenly Father, I come to You now in the Name of my Lord and Savior Christ Jesus. I pray for the lost of the world this day and that every man, woman, and child from here to the farthest corners of the earth be saved. As I intercede, I use my faith, believing that thousands this day have the opportunity to make Jesus their Lord.

I ask the Lord of the harvest to thrust the perfect laborers across these lives this day to share the good news of the Gospel in a special way so that they will listen and understand it, that it will touch their hearts. In the Name of Jesus Christ, I pray with thanksgiving. **Amen**

PRAYER TO ABIDE IN HIS LOVE

Heavenly Father, I come to You now in the Name of my Lord and Savior Christ Jesus. I am abiding in Your Word, holding fast to Your teachings and living in accordance with them. It is my desire to be Your true disciple.

Heavenly Father, because You are the Vine and I am a branch living in You, I bear much fruit. Apart from You, I can do nothing. Your Son, Jesus, said *"If you live in Me and My Words remain in you and continue to live in your hearts, ask whatever you will, and it shall be done for you" John 15:7.* When I bear much fruit, You, Father, are honored and glorified. By Your grace that I have received, I will show and prove myself to be a true follower of Your Son, Jesus. He has loved me, just as You, Father, have loved Him. I am abiding in that love.

Heavenly Father, You have assured me that if I keep Your commandments, I will abide in Your love and live in it, just as Your Son, Jesus, obeyed Your commandments and lived in Your love. He told me these things, that Your joy and delight may be in me and that my joy and gladness may be full measure, complete and overflowing. This is Your commandment: that we love one another just as You have loved us.

Heavenly Father, thank You for Your Word for this truth sets me free. I am born of You and I do not deliberately, knowingly or habitually practice sin. Your nature abides in me; and I cannot practice sinning because I am born of You. I have hidden Your Word in my heart that I might not sin against You.

Heavenly Father, may Christ Jesus through my faith dwell in my heart. It is my desire to be rooted deep in love and founded securely on love, that I may have the power and be strong to apprehend and grasp with all the saints (Your devoted people, the experience of that love) what is breadth and length and height and depth of it. I pray in the Name of Jesus, that I may know this love that surpasses knowledge, that I may be filled to the measure of all Your fullness. Now to You Who is able to do immeasurably more than I ask or imagine, according to Your power that is at work within me, to You be glory in the Church and in Christ Jesus throughout generations, forever and ever. **Amen**

Psalms 107:20 Prayer

Heavenly Father, I come to You now in the Name of my Lord and Savior Christ Jesus. I pray for myself and everyone that I prayed for today and I ask that You will send forth Your Word to heal us. I ask You to deliver us from our destruction.

Heavenly Father, I thank You for sending Your Word forth to heal us. I thank You for healing us. I thank You for delivering us from our destruction. In the Name of Jesus Christ of Nazareth I pray. **Amen**

Job 22:27-28 Prayer

Heavenly Father, I come to You now in the Name of my Lord and Savior Christ Jesus. I thank You that the prayer I make to You, that You will hear me and I will pay my vows.

Heavenly Father, I thank You that when I decree (declare) a thing; that You will establish it for me and light will shine on my ways according to *Job 22:27-28*. In the Name of Jesus Christ of Nazareth, I pray with thanksgiving. **Amen**

Prayer Over Buildings, Churches, Restaurants, Houses

Heavenly Father, I ask You to loose Your angels into this building, every area of this building and I ask You to force out all evil, wicked, demon, lying and perverse spirits and send them wherever You want to. I plead the blood of Jesus over this building, everything and everybody in this building and every opening coming into this building and I ask You Lord Jesus to render powerless, nullify and cancel the power of all evil, wicked, demon, lying and perverse spirits that try to enter into this building, the presence of anyone or anything in this building. I ask You to do these things according to *John 14:13* and *14*. Heavenly Father, please cover this building, everybody and everything in it with Your Glory and Your Presence. In Jesus' Name, **Amen**

Prayer For Cleansing A Home.

Heavenly Father, I come to You now in the Name of my Lord and Savior, Christ Jesus. In the Name and authority of the Lord Jesus Christ and by the power of His shed Blood, I now renounce all opportunities for ground held by Satan's wicked demons in relation to our home and property. I bind with chains and fetters of iron all wicked spirits and their schemes and assignments, against this home and property. I ask my Lord Jesus Christ to evict them from this home and property, with any controlling powers of darkness, and to send them where they may never control or harm any person again.

Heavenly Father, in the Name and authority of the Lord Jesus Christ and by the power of His shed Blood, I now renounce all past use of this property for false religions, occult practices, divination, magic, sorcery, witchcraft, spiritualistic healings and such. I ask the Lord Jesus Christ to remove all curses, spells, hexes, witchcraft spells, voodoo spells, satanic spells, and occult evil.

Heavenly Father, In the Name and authority of the Lord Jesus Christ and by the power of His shed Blood, I now renounce all expressions of anger, bitterness, rebellion, and lack of submission to God's will exercised by persons who live on this property or in this home at the present or who previously lived here. I ask the Lord Jesus Christ to remove all anger, bitterness, rebellion, stubbornness, and spirits of separation seeking to rule this home.

Heavenly Father, in the Name and authority of the Lord Jesus Christ and by the power of His shed Blood, I now renounce all expressions of pride and control exercised by persons who live on this property or in this home at the present or who previously lived here. I ask the Lord Jesus Christ to remove all prideful spirits and all controlling spirits.

Heavenly Father, In the Name and authority of the Lord Jesus Christ and by the power of His shed Blood, I now renounce all acts of immorality, impurity, indecency, strife, jealousy, selfishness, drunkenness, drug abuse, envy exercised by people who lived on this property or in this home at the present or who previously lived here. I ask the Lord Jesus Christ to remove all immoral, impure, indecent, strifeful, jealous, selfish, drunkenness, drug abuse and envious spirits.

Heavenly Father, In the Name and authority of the Lord Jesus Christ and by the power of His shed Blood, I now renounce all generational claims against this home and property including ground obtained through worship of false gods, practice of sorcery, fortune telling, consulting with mediums, freemasonry, or other secret organizations. I ask the Lord Jesus Christ to remove all demonic spirits associated with these wicked acts.

Heavenly Father, I ask that You do these things according to *John 14:14* in the Name of Jesus Christ of Nazareth.

Heavenly Father, I dedicate this home and property to You, it shall be a house of prayer, a house of praise and worship to You my Lord. In the Name of Jesus I pray with thanksgiving. **Amen**

PRAYER TO DESTROY CURSES

Heavenly Father, I come to You now in the Name of my Lord and Savior Christ Jesus.

Lord Jesus Christ I confess all of my sins of _____, _____, _____, and _____. I repent fully and turn away from any ways, thoughts, deeds and actions that have led me to where I am now. I choose by faith to receive my forgiveness and healing from all sins, in Jesus Christ's Holy Name. Lord Jesus Christ, according to *John 14: 14*, You said if I asked, that You would do this thing for me, so by Your will for my life I ask You to: sever, remove and destroy all curses, word curses, and generational curses coming from my sins, prayers of others, or my generational line out of, off of, and away from me. Lord I ask You to cast these evil things along with their effect, side effects and stings into the Abyss. Lord Jesus Christ I ask you to sever, remove and destroy all curses and generational curses out of, off of, and away from my: spouse, parents, grandparents, children, grandchildren and any future generations. Lord I ask You to cast these evil things along with their effect, side effects and stings into the Abyss and keep these generational curses from coming back on us, in Jesus Christ's Holy Name and to God be the Glory, **Amen**

Note: Remember to include step parents, step children, half brothers & sisters, step grandparents, etc., as needed.

Lord Jesus, I ask You to break and destroy any curses, side effects, effects, influences or stings of any curses that have been placed on me, anyone that I have prayed for today our: children, grandchildren, marriages, homes, cars, trucks, offices, properties, buildings, businesses, ministries, finances... in the Name of Jesus Christ of Nazareth according to *John 14:14*. I ask You to destroy any witchcraft prayers, charismatic witchcraft prayers, psychic prayers, side effects, effects, influences, or stings of any witchcraft prayers, or charismatic witchcraft prayers, psychic prayers, that have been prayed over me, about me, over, or about anyone that I have prayed for today, our: children, grandchildren, marriages, homes, cars, trucks, offices, properties, buildings, businesses, ministries, finances. I ask You to destroy them now in the Name of Jesus Christ of Nazareth. I ask You to destroy any false prophecies spoken into or over me, into anyone or over anyone that I have prayed for today, our: children, grandchildren, marriages, homes, cars, trucks, offices, properties, buildings, businesses, ministries, finances. I ask You to destroy them now in the Name of Jesus Christ of Nazareth. Lord Jesus, I ask You to destroy any hexes, vexes, witchcraft spells, voodoo spells, satanic spells, incantations, chains, fetters, snares or traps that have been placed on me, anyone that I have prayed for today, our: children, grandchildren, marriages, homes, cars, trucks, offices, properties, buildings, businesses, ministries, finances. I ask You to destroy them now in the Name of Jesus Christ of Nazareth. I ask You to destroy any words, declarations, decrees, effects, side effects, stings and influences spoken into me or over me, into anyone or over anyone that I have prayed for today, that do not conform to Your Will or Your destiny for our lives, or the way You want us to believe and think. I ask You to do all these things according to *John 14:14* in the Name of the Lord Jesus Christ of Nazareth. **Amen**

CANCELLATION OF WITCHCRAFT OR PRAYERS OF MANIPULATION

Heavenly Father, I come to You in Jesus Christ's Holy Name. I ask You Lord Jesus Christ according to *John 14:13* and *14* to destroy any witchcraft prayers or psychic prayers or ungodly soulish prayers that have been prayed over me to control or manipulate me spiritually or naturally. **Amen**

BREAKING WORD CURSES SPOKEN OVER YOURSELF AND OTHERS

Heavenly Father, I come to You now in the Name of my Lord and Savior Christ Jesus. I repent of the word curses I have spoken over myself and over _____ (my child, my finances, my health, my mind, my spouse, my relationship to You). Heavenly Father, please forgive me for speaking these word curses according to *1 John 1:9*. I ask You to destroy and break these word curses according to *John 14:14* in Jesus Christ's Holy Name.

I am standing on your Word. You said You would give me the Keys to the Kingdom, that whatsoever I would bind on earth would be bound in heaven and whatsoever I would loose on earth would be loosed in heaven. In the Name of Jesus Christ, I bind my will to the Will of God, I bind myself and everyone that I prayed for today to the Will of God and I pray you will make me constantly aware of Your will for my life. I bind my mind, _____'s mind to the mind of Christ that we will be aware of how Jesus would have us think and believe.

Heavenly Father, in Jesus' Name, I banish every wrong thought I have placed or others have placed into our minds. I banish every wrong thought I have placed into _____'s mind and every evil imagination that exalts itself against the knowledge of God. In the Name of Jesus, I banish the power and effects of any wrong words spoken to, about or by us. In the Name of Jesus Christ of Nazareth, I pray with thanksgiving. **Amen**

PRAYER FOR OUR CHILDREN IN SCHOOL

Heavenly Father, I come to You in the Name of my Lord and Savior Jesus Christ. I ask You to forgive me, all my family, all my classmates, my teacher Mr./Mrs. _____ and _____, my principle Mr. / Mrs. _____, and all my friends for all of our sins and cleanse us of all unrighteousness.

Heavenly Father, I ask You to loose your angels into our homes, school buses, schools, and playgrounds to force out all of Satan's demonic spirits and strongmen and to force them to go wherever You wish to send them.

Heavenly Father, I ask You to cover me, my classmates, teachers, principal, school, home, playground, and family with the blood of Jesus Christ to protect us. I ask You to loose Your angels around us to protect us and guard us from the enemy.

Heavenly Father, I ask You to bless me and every person I have prayed for today in the Name of our Lord and Savior Jesus Christ. **Amen**

PRAYER TO KEEP US FROM HARM

Heavenly Father, I come to You now in the Name of my Lord and Savior Christ Jesus. I ask You Lord Jesus Christ of Nazareth according to *John 14: 13-14*, to protect me and everyone I have prayed for today and for our homes, cars, lands, properties, (vehicles,) animals, pets, work places, finances, churches, businesses, and ministries, all that You have placed us in charge over, keep us from any harm, destruction, pestilence, diseases, distresses, stress, natural disasters, attacks of the enemy directly or indirectly, evil people, that we not be taken advantage of, trickery of any type, dysfunctionality, distractions, illusions, delusions, deceptions, snares, and any undue hardship.

Lord God, cause us to be extremely sensitive to Your Holy Spirit and be extremely sensitive to the leading of Your Holy Spirit, becoming the sons of God, cause us to realize it! Protect us on our right and on our left, be our rearward guard, go before us, that we possess the gates of the enemy and take back what was stolen from us and help us to learn to walk upright in Your Righteous council all the days of our lives. That our desire and will be the accomplishing of Your total Will in our lives, Word upon Word, precept upon precept, line upon line, unto the full measure of the maturity of Christ, the Hope of Glory. So, that we are an honor and a praise unto You all the days of our lives, that our lamps will not be hid but shine forth like bright stars in the midst of a dark, wicked, and perverse generation. The Word of God clearly states that we be found redeeming the time and the lives of those who will receive it. You have called us to be victorious and we hearken to Your call, help us to have victorious dominion as Your priests and kings, Your humble servants, and to God be the Glory, Honor and Praise, in Jesus Christ's Holy Name. **Amen**

PRAYER FOR A PERSON EXPERIENCING LOSS OF A LOVED ONE

Heavenly Father, I come to You now in the Name of my Lord and Savior Christ Jesus.

Heavenly Father, in the Name of Jesus, I approach Your throne of grace, bringing _____ before You. We recognize that grieving is a human emotional process, and we give her/him the space that she/he needs to enter into the rest that you have for her/him. Lord, Jesus bore _____'s grief and carried her/his sorrows and pains. We know Heavenly Father that Your Spirit is upon Jesus to heal _____'s broken heart. May _____ be gentle with herself/himself, knowing that she/he is not alone, for You Almighty One is with her/him and You will never forsake her/him.

Heavenly Father, I ask You to give _____ an expedient manifestation of Your healing according to *John 16:23*. Your Word says that we are to rejoice with those who rejoice and to weep with those who weep. I pray that my love will give _____ comfort, joy and encouragement in Jesus Christ's Holy Name.

Heavenly Father, I ask You to fill _____ with Your precious Holy Spirit. I ask You to fill her/him with all Your fruits of Your Holy Spirit which includes love, joy, peace, patience, gentleness and goodness, with longsuffering, with meekness, faithfulness and self control. Heavenly Father, in Jesus' Holy Name I ask You to fill _____ with Your Holy Ghost anointing and power, fill her/him with Your presence, in the Name of Jesus Christ of Nazareth, I pray with thanksgiving. **Amen**

PRAYER TO RECEIVE FORGIVENESS & CLEANSING OF SINS

Heavenly Father, I come to You now in the Name of my Lord and Savior Christ Jesus. Holy Spirit I pray that You will quicken me to hear my Heavenly Father's Voice and lead me in prayer. Heavenly Father, I bow and worship before You. I come to You with praise and with thanksgiving. I come to You in humility, in fear, and in trembling. I come to You in gratitude, in love, and through the precious Blood of Your Son Jesus Christ of Nazareth.

Lord Jesus Christ according to Your Word in *1 John 1: 9*, You said if I confess my sins You are faithful and just to forgive me of my sins and cleanse me from ALL unrighteousness. So Lord Jesus Christ I come to You now, I receive my forgiveness and cleansing from all unrighteousness: spot, wrinkle and blemish free, totally blameless, from the top of my head to the soles of my feet, at the dendritic and quantum level, in Jesus Christ's Holy Name. **Amen**

CASTING OUT EVIL SPIRITS

Heavenly Father, I come to You now in the Name of my Lord and Savior Christ Jesus. Holy Spirit I pray that You will quicken me to hear my Heavenly Father's Voice and lead us in prayer. Heavenly Father, I bow and worship before You. I come to You with praise and with thanksgiving. I come to You in humility, in fear and in trembling. I come to You in gratitude, in love, and through the precious Blood of Your Son, Jesus Christ of Nazareth.

Lord Jesus Christ, I ask You according *to John 14: 13-14*, to: force out, drive out, cast out Satan and all foul, wicked, demon, tormenting, lying, hindering, seducing, perverse, unclean spirits; any evil strongmen, any religious, and controlling spirits, all familiar spirits, any spirit contrary to the Holy Spirit, spirits of sickness, disease, infirmities, infection, pains, trauma, shock, aches, arthritis, crippling arthritis, sinusitis, acute sinusitis, any spirits contrary to Divine health along with their effects, side effects and stings, out of my spirit, mind, will, emotions, ego, libido, imaginations, thoughts, and all subconscious areas, and physical beings, every object on me, my homes, cars, lands, properties, animals, vehicles, and work places. I ask You to bind and cast these evil things in the Abyss; deaf, dumb, blind, mute, and unable to gesture, keep them there until they are judged and then thrown into the Lake of Fire, in Jesus Christ's Holy Name. **Amen**

PRAYER FOR THE COVERING BLOOD OF JESUS

Heavenly Father, I come to You now in the Name of my Lord and Savior Christ Jesus.

I plead the Blood of Jesus, the Blood Covenant, and *Psalms 91* over, through, around and about me, my spirit, mind, will, emotions, ego, libido, imaginations, thoughts, and all subconscious areas and physical beings, all spiritual and natural doors and openings coming into my life and properties, the atmosphere above, around about me and my homes, cars, lands, properties, animals, (vehicles,) and work places, in Jesus' Name. **Amen**

PRAYER FOR RENDERING THE ENEMY HARMLESS & UNABLE TO RETURN

Heavenly Father, I come to You now in the Name of my Lord and Savior Christ Jesus.

Lord Jesus Christ, I bind and command not to manifest themselves in our possession all evil spirits and their effects, side effects and stings, powerless and harmless, unable to come back through any opening to me, my presence, the presence of our homes, cars, lands, properties, animals, vehicles, and work places, this day and all the days of my life, in Jesus Christ's Holy Name. **Amen**

LOOSING ANGELS FOR PROTECTION

Heavenly Father, I come to You now in the Name of my Lord and Savior Christ Jesus.

Lord Jesus Christ I ask You according to *John 14:13-14*, to loose now Your angels around me, my homes, cars, lands, properties, animals, (vehicles,) and work places, in great abundance, to guide, guard, protect and minister to me. I ask You Lord Jesus Christ that Your angels will continuously force out, drive out, and keep out all demonic spirits from me, and my homes, cars, lands, properties, animals, (vehicles,) and work places, the rest of this day, into tomorrow afternoon, in Jesus Christ's Holy Name. **Amen**

PRAYER FOR FINANCES

Heavenly Father, I come to You now in the Name of my Lord and Savior Christ Jesus. Holy Spirit I pray that You will quicken me to hear my Heavenly Father's Voice and lead me in prayer. Heavenly Father, I bow and worship before You. I come to You with praise and with thanksgiving. I come to You in humility, in fear, and in trembling. I come to You in gratitude, in love, and through the precious Blood of Your Son Jesus Christ of Nazareth.

Heavenly Father, in Jesus Christ Holy Name, I pray Your Word over my finances and I thank You for manifesting Your Word in my life according to *3 John 1:2; "Beloved, I wish above all things that thou mayest prosper and be in health, even as thy soul prospereth; "But thou shall remember the Lord thy God: for it is He that giveth thee power to get wealth, that He may establish His covenant which He swore unto thy fathers, as it is this day."* According to *Deuteronomy 8:1; "...but shall believe that those things which he saith shall come to pass; he shall have whatsoever he saith."* According to *Mark 11:23; "And these are they which sown on good ground; such as hear the Word and receive it, and bring forth fruit, some thirty fold, some sixty, and some a hundred."* According to *Mark 4:20; "He that keepeth his mouth keepeth his life: but he that openeth wide his lips shall have destruction."* According to *Proverbs 13:3; "I can do all things through Christ which strengthen me. But my God shall supply all your needs according to His riches in glory by Christ Jesus."* according to *Philippians 4:13, 19; "But this I say, he which soweth sparingly shall reap also sparingly; and he which soweth bountifully shall reap also bountifully." "Every man according as he purposeth in his heart, so let him give; not grudgingly, or of necessity: for God loveth a cheerful giver." "And God is able to make all grace abound toward you; that ye, always having all sufficiency in all things, may abound to every good work."* according to *2 Corinthians 9:6-8*. I pray in the Name of Jesus Christ with thanksgiving. **Amen**

Heavenly Father, in Jesus' Name and on the authority of Your Holy Word, I call my debts paid in full. Debt, I speak to you in Jesus' Name: be paid and be gone. Dematerialize and cease to exist. I now declare that all my debts, mortgages, and notes are paid in full, cancelled, or dissolved. I pray in Jesus' Holy Name with thanksgiving. **Amen**

PRAYER TO RELEASE GUILT

Heavenly Father, I come to You now in the Name of my Lord and Savior Christ Jesus. According to Your word, *"I acknowledged my sin to You, and my iniquity I did not hide. I said, I will confess my transgressions to the Lord* [continually unfolding the past till all is told] *– then You* [instantly] *forgave me the iniquity of my sin. Selah." Psalms 32:5*. I acknowledge my sins of ____ [Please see "Sin List" on page 181 and ask God's forgiveness for any other sins that may apply to you] and my iniquities. I confess my transgressions and I thank you, Heavenly Father, for taking this guilt of ____ from me. Thank You Lord that I believe in You and from my innermost being will flow rivers of living waters according to *John 7:38*. Thank You Lord that I will confess my transgressions to You and You will forgive the guilt of my sin according to *Psalms 32:5*. In the Name of the Lord Jesus Christ of Nazareth, I pray with thanksgiving. **Amen**

PRAYER FOR FREEDOM

Heavenly Father, I come to You now in the Name of my Lord and Savior Christ Jesus. Holy Spirit, I pray that You will quicken me to hear my Heavenly Father's Voice and lead me in prayer. Heavenly Father, I bow and worship before You. I come to You with praise and with thanksgiving. I come to You in humility, in fear, and in trembling. I come to You in gratitude, in love, and through the precious Blood of Your Son, Jesus Christ of Nazareth.

Heavenly Father, I present to You myself, my family, and my property. By the power of the Blood of the Lord Jesus Christ, I bind the power of Satan's demons and all dominion of darkness seeking entrance into our lives. I bind any demonic assignments spoken or sent against us, and pronounce them to be no effect. *"For this reason the Son of God made manifest, to destroy the works of the devil." 1 John 3:8.*

I declare the ways and works of darkness over all of us to be broken. I bind the satanic forces of nature from harming any property that we possess, in the Name of Jesus Christ.

Heavenly Father, in the Name of Jesus Christ, I ask You to expose and bring into light, negative inner vows and strongholds that contradict Your Word and Will. By the breath of Your Spirit, release Your truth as a sword to expose falsehood, curses of self-rejection, self-hatred, and reactive hatred and bitterness towards others. I take up the sword of Your Word and cut ourselves free from the bondage of generational strongholds and ungodly character defects. In the Name of Jesus Christ, I renounce all relationships dishonoring to the Lord, Heavenly Father, break the power of soul ties over our minds and emotions for ourselves and for those people.

I proclaim our freedom to be the children of Yahweh God, to live as You intended us to live, filled and overflowing with the light and power of Your Holy Spirit, filled with the life and love of Jesus Christ. I claim the full protection of the shed Blood of Jesus Christ, the Son of the living God over our individual lives, our marriages, families, possessions, churches, neighborhoods, towns, and nations. *"You, O Lord are a shield about us. Our glory, and the lifter of our heads." Psalms 3:3.* In Jesus Christ's Holy Name, I pray with thanksgiving. **Amen**

PRAISE THE LORD

Heavenly Father, in the Name of Jesus Christ, I praise Your Holy Name. Thank You Lord, O Lord, You are my God; I will exalt You. I will give thanks to Your Name; for You have worked wonders, plans formed long ago, with perfect faithfulness according to *Isaiah 25:1.* Thank You Lord that You are my strength and my song and You have become my salvation. You are my God, and I will exalt You according to *Exodus 15:2-3.*

Thank You Lord that our mouths will speak the praise of the Lord, all flesh will bless Your Holy Name forever and ever according to *Psalms 145:21.* Praise be to Your glorious Name forever; and may the whole earth be filled with Your glory according to *Psalms 72:19.* The Lord lives; praise be to my Rock; exalted be God my Savior according to *Psalms 18:46.*

Thank You Lord that we will praise You from the rising of the sun to the place where it sets, the Name of the Lord be praised according to *Psalms 113:3.* In Jesus' Holy Name, I pray. **Amen**

PRAYER TO LET GO OF RESENTMENT & BITTERNESS

Heavenly Father, I come to You now in the Name of my Lord and Savior Christ Jesus. Life seems so unjust, so unfair. The pain of rejection is almost more than I can bear. My past relationships have ended in strife, anger, rejection, resentment, and bitterness.

Father, help me to let go of all bitterness and resentment. You are the One Who binds up and heals the broken-hearted. I receive Your anointing that breaks and destroys every yoke of bondage. I receive emotional healing by faith according to Your Word, *Isaiah 53:5, "and with His stripes we are healed".* I thank You for giving me the grace to stand firm until the process is complete.

Thank You for my wise counselor, I acknowledge the Holy Spirit as my wonderful Counselor! Thank You for helping me work out my salvation with fear and trembling, for it is You, Father, Who works in me to will and to act according to Your good purpose.

In the Name of Jesus, I choose to forgive those who have wronged me. I choose to live a life of forgiveness because You have forgiven me. With the help of the Holy Spirit, I get rid of all resentments, bitterness, rage, anger, brawling, and slander, along with every form of malice. I desire to be kind and passionate to others, forgiving them, just as in Christ, You forgave me.

With the help of the Holy Spirit, I make every effort to live in peace with all men and to be holy, for I know that without holiness, no one will see You. I chose to see to it that I do not miss Your grace and that no roots of resentment or bitterness grow up within me to cause trouble. I will watch and pray that I will not enter into temptation or cause others to stumble.

Thank You, Heavenly Father, that You watch over Your Word to perform it and that whom the Son has set free is free indeed. I declare that I have overcome resentment and bitterness by the Blood of the Lord Jesus Christ and by the word of my testimony. **Amen**

PRAYER FOR CHILDREN WITH ADD/ADHD

Heavenly Father, I come to You now in Jesus Christ's Holy Name. I ask You Lord Jesus according to *John 14:14*, to destroy any words that have already been spoken, declared, and decreed over _____ along with any diagnosis of ADD/ADHD. Heavenly Father God, I ask You to give _____ total deliverance and total freedom from all demonic spirits according to *John 16:23*.

I plead the Blood of Jesus over _____ from the top of their head to the soles of their feet. I ask You Lord Jesus according to *John 14:14*, to render powerless and harmless the enemy cannot come back into _____ presence. I ask You Lord Jesus to loose Your angels around about _____ to protect him/her. I ask You Lord Jesus to destroy any curses and generational curses off of _____ and keep them from coming back on him/her. I ask You Lord Jesus to destroy any evil effects, side effects, stings, darts, arrows, sting claws, any instruments of unrighteousness that have penetrated _____, along with their manifestations, influences, symptoms, any false memories, lies of the enemy, evil imprints and impressions, wrong mind sets, trauma, and shock.

I plead the Blood of Jesus, the Blood Covenant, *Psalms 91*, and the Healing Balm of Gilead over all areas of _____'s life and ask You Lord to wash, cleanse, purify him/her spot, wrinkle, and blemish free and heal him/her mentally, physically and emotionally, totally and completely .

Heavenly Father God, I ask You to give _____ the mind of Christ according to *1 Corinthians 2:16* . I ask You Lord Jesus according to *John 14:14* to guide and teach him/her in the use of their new mind. Heavenly Father, I ask you to give me and each person I have prayed for today clarity of vision, clarity of sight, clarity of thought, clarity of mind, clarity of knowing, and hearing Your Voice according to *John 16:23*. **Amen**

I ask You Lord Jesus according to *John 14:14* to help _____ be at peace now mentally and physically from now on and to perceive, excel at understanding, remembering, displaying, and walking in what they are taught. I ask You Lord Jesus Christ to guide, protect _____, and bless him/her with alertness and sharpness of mind all the days of their life. **Amen**

PRAYER TO CLEAN OUT A ROOM, CHURCH, BUILDING

Heavenly Father, I come to You in Jesus Christ's Holy Name. I ask You Lord Jesus Christ according to *John 14:14* to loose Your angels into this _____ (room, church, building, land, car, property, house, facility, place) and force out, drive out all foul, wicked, demon, tormenting, lying, hindering, seducing, perverse, familiar, unclean spirits, and demonic strongmen. Send them where Jesus sends them.

I apply the Blood of Jesus Christ of Nazareth over and through me, this land, this _____ (room, church, building, land, car, property, house, facility, place). Heavenly Father, I ask You to render powerless, harmless, nullify the power of the enemy, any strongmen, messenger of Satan, that tries to enter into the presence of anybody, and anything (room, church, building, land, car, property, house, facility, place); the enemy cannot come back, in Jesus Christ of Nazareth's Holy Name, according to *John 14:14*, **Amen**

PRAYER TO CLEAN OUT CHURCHES, RESTAURANTS, PUBLIC BUILDINGS

Father Jesus, I ask You to release Your angels in the presence of this sanctuary, this building, this restaurant, etc., to force out, drive out, clean out all the wicked, demon, lying, perverse, unclean religious spirits or strongmen, out of this building, out of this sanctuary, out of this restaurant, and off this property to force them to go wherever you want to send them Jesus, and I ask You to do this in the Name of Jesus Christ of Nazareth, according to *John 14:12-14*. To God be the Glory!

Heavenly Father, I plead the blood of Jesus Christ over this building, over this sanctuary, over this restaurant, etc., and every threshold entering into this building, restaurant or sanctuary, and it's protection. And I ask You to render powerless and harmless, nullify the power, destroy the power, cast the power of any other spirit, demonic spirit, strongmen, messengers sent of witchcraft prayer or curse that tries to enter the presence of this building, or tries to enter the presence of anything or anybody in this building, church, sanctuary, restaurant, etc.. I ask You to do this now according to *John 14: 13-14* in the Name of the Lord, Jesus Christ of Nazareth. **Amen**

PRAYER OF DELIVERANCE

Heavenly Father, I come to You now in the Name of my Lord and Savior Christ Jesus. Holy Spirit, I pray that You will quicken me to hear my Heavenly Father's Voice and lead me in prayer. Heavenly Father, I bow and worship before You. I come to You with praise and with thanksgiving. I come to You with humility and humbleness, in fear and trembling, and in gratitude, and in love, and through the precious Blood of Your Son, Jesus Christ of Nazareth.

Standing on the Word of God, and in the Name of the Lord Jesus Christ, I bind all Satan's evil spirits, occult spirits, spirits of sin, spirits of trauma and familiar spirits, demonic forces, satanic powers, principalities, attributes, aspects, clusters, endowments, and satanic thrones: I bind all kings and princes of terrors. I bind all demonic assignments and functions of destruction from any of the above demonic entities from outer space, the air, water, fire, the ground, the netherworld, and the evil forces of nature. I bind all interplay, interaction, communication and all their games between satanic and demonic spirits, out of and away from my spirit, mind, body and soul and away from every individual's spirit, soul, mind, and body that I have prayed for today. I expose all of you demonic forces and spirits as weakened, defeated enemies of Jesus Christ. I sever all demonic spirits from any demonic ruler above these demonic spirits. In the Name of Jesus Christ, I revoke any orders given to any of these demonic spirits and demonic forces as it relates to my life and the lives of all I have prayed for today. I bind all enemies of Jesus Christ present together, all demonic entities under the one and highest authority. I banish you from me and everyone that I prayed for today, I banish you to where Jesus Christ sends you. Your assignments and influences in my life and the lives of the people I have prayed for today are broken!! In the Name of the Lord Jesus Christ. **Amen**

Heavenly Father, I ask that You send the Holy Spirit, the holy angels of God, to surround, and protect me and everyone that I have prayed for today, and to seek out and cleanse us with Your holy light on all areas vacated by the forces of evil. I ask the Holy Spirit to permeate our spirits, minds, souls and bodies, creating a hunger and thirst for God's Holy Word, and to fill us to overflowing with the life and love of Jesus Christ, and His Holy Spirit.

In the Name of Jesus Christ, I bind all spells, hexes, curses, voodoo practices, witchcraft, occult, Masonic and satanic rituals, occult, Masonic and satanic blood covenants, occult, Masonic and satanic blood sacrifices, demonic activity; evil wishes, coven rituals, all occult, Islamic, and coven fasting prayers (not of the Lord) and curse-like judgments that have been sent our way, and/or have been passed down through the generational bloodline. I banish them to where Jesus Christ sends them. I ask forgiveness for, and renounce, all negative inner vows made by myself and by those for whom I am praying. I ask that Jesus Christ release us from these vows, and from any bondage they may have held in. That You Lord will not remember the iniquities of our forefathers against us. *Psalms 79:8*

In the Name of the Lord Jesus Christ, and by the power of God's Holy Word, I take the sword of the Spirit and cut myself and everyone that I have prayed for today, free from all generational- inherited sins, weaknesses, character defects, personality traits, cellular disorders, genetic disorders, learned negative inner vows, and spiritual and psychologi-cal ties. I cut all bonds that are not of the Lord, and put His cross between us, our mates (and any relationships that our mates have had with others in the past), our children, our parents, our grandparents, our siblings. I cut all bonds of the relationships of each one of us that are not of the Lord, back to the beginning of time. By the Sword of the Spirit, and in the Name of Jesus Christ, I say that we are cut free, and we are free indeed. We are now free to become the children of God as the Lord intended us to be. In the Name of Jesus Christ.

In the Name of the Lord Jesus Christ, and by the power of God's Word, and the shed Blood of Jesus Christ, and the Holy Spirit, I bind all evil spirits of _____, _____, _____ and _____ [Please look at the "Demon List" on page 183 and banish any foul spirits that you feel may apply to you.] in all of us. I command them to go where Jesus Christ sends them.

Lord Jesus, I ask that You release the fullness of Your Holy Spirit to flood the places vacated by the darkness in my mind, body and soul, and all the people's minds, bodies and souls that I have prayed for today. Please fill us with Your perfect love, joy, peace, truth, power, charity, humility, forgiveness, faithfulness, goodness, kindness, whole-ness, wellness, health, trust, self control, a good self image, discipline, obedience, a sound mind, prosperity, order, relinquishment, acceptance of ourselves and others. Free us from all fear, guilt, shame, and all addictions, and fill us to overflowing with the light and life of You. In the Name of Jesus Christ. Thank You Lord; that You will awaken our sleeping spirits, and bring us into the light. Thank You Lord that You will transform us by the renewing of our minds daily in Christ Jesus. Thank You Lord; that You will pour out Your Spirit on us, and reveal Your Word to us. Thank You Lord that You will give Your angels charge over us in all our ways.

Thank You Lord that we believe in You, and from our innermost beings shall flow riv-ers of living waters. Thank You Lord that You will direct our hearts into the love of God and the steadfast of Jesus Christ. In the Name of Jesus Christ of Nazareth I pray with thanksgiving. **Amen**

PRAYERS FOR SPIRIT, SOUL, AND BODY

THE SPIRIT OF MAN

Heavenly Father I come to You in Jesus Christ's Holy Name. I come in humility, in fear and trembling acknowledging my sins against You and others. I truly repent with Godly sorrow that I have hurt You through my ways. I choose to forgive those who I perceive have hurt or harmed me, or others, my friends or loved ones. I ask You to forgive them and bless them the way You forgive them and bless. I ask You to forgive me of my sins against You and cleanse me from all unrighteousness. Lord let not Your Holy Spirit depart from me. It hurts me Lord to know that I have hurt You. I am so very sorry. I repent, I turn, I choose not to ever do this again. Help me Lord, please Lord, to not sin against You. Lord cause me to go in Your paths of Righteousness, not seeking my own. Restore me to walk in Your courts Oh Heavenly Father, renew a right spirit within me, with a right heart, a contrite and humble heart, to know You and serve You all the days of my life. Cause me Lord to walk on the High places with You Lord!

THE SOUL OF MAN

I command every high and lofty thought, vain imagination, every thought that exalts itself against You to come down now to the obedience of the Mind of Christ in me. I command them to cease their laboring in the Name of Jesus. Soul be still in the Name of Jesus! Lord Jesus Christ I ask You according to *John 14:14* to supply Your anointing to and destroy all evil bondages, yokes, chains, fetters, anklets, bands, all evil works roots, fruits, tentacles and links, out of, off of, and away from me, along with any darkness, darts, arrows, stings, claws, spears, barbs, lies of the enemy, anything not Your Truth, evil imprints, evil impressions, wrong mind sets, pains, aches, false memories, and wrong mind sets. I ask You Holy Spirit to convict me and reveal to me what You desire and need me to be free of. I plead the Blood of Jesus Christ, the Blood Covenant, *Psalms 91*, and the Healing Balm of Gilead over, in, through and about me, my houses, cars, lands, properties, vehicles, animals, work places, finances, and everywhere I traffic or go today as a hedge of protection against the enemy. I ask You Lord to render powerless and harmless the enemy cannot hear me or come near me the rest of this day and into tomorrow afternoon, amen. Lord, fill me with Your peace that passes all understanding, cause me, and help me to think on things that are good, and pure, and from above(of You).

THE BODY OF MAN

I ask You Lord to rebuke all: infirmity, affliction, inflammation, sickness, disease, disorder, syndrome of any kind, abnormal cells, radical cells, abnormal growth, radical growth, and cancer, out of and away from me at this time, I curse those things to die and cease to exist, in Jesus Christ's Holy Name. I rebuke it and loose them from me in the Name of Jesus Christ of Nazareth. I curse any infection in my body and command it to die at the roots and leave my body in a normal way. I curse any abnormal cell, radical cell, abnormal growth or radical growth, and cancer in my body, and command them to die and leave my body in the Name of Jesus Christ of Nazareth. Heavenly Father, I rebuke all abnormal effects, side effects, and stings, any adverse effects, side effects, and stings in my body in the Name of Jesus Christ of Nazareth. I banish it in the Name of Jesus Christ of Nazareth. Heavenly Father, it says in *Matthew 18* whatsoever I bind or loose on earth shall be bound or loose in Heaven, in the Name of Jesus Christ of Nazareth. I bind all viruses, cancers, abnormal cells, radical cells, abnormal growths, radical growths, lesions of any kind, spasms of any kind, pains of any kind, trauma, shock, sicknesses, disorders, and diseases of any kind, afflictions of any kind, infirmities or inflammations of any kind, in any part of my body, I bind ___, ___, and ___ (Ask the Holy Spirit to direct you). I ask You now in the Name Jesus Christ to release Your healing virtue, Your miracle virtue into my body in the Name of Jesus Christ of Nazareth; release Your healing virtue, Your miracle virtue, Your healing anointing, Your miracle anointing into my body, from the top of my head to the soles of my feet. I ask You to make me whole, restore every organ, every cell, every gland, every muscle, every ligament, every bone in my body and bring everything in total alignment, complete alignment, the way you created me, in the Name of Jesus Christ of Nazareth. Heavenly Father, I apply the Blood of Jesus over every organ, every cell, every gland, every muscle, every ligament, every bone in my body whether there is any sickness, disease, infection, virus, abnormal cells, radical cells, infirmity or affliction of any kind, in the Name of Jesus. Father, I ask You to fill me now with Your Holy Spirit, in Jesus' Holy Name. Heavenly Father, I ask You to put a hedge of protection around me in the Name of Jesus **Amen**

PRAYER FOR YOUR DIVINE PURPOSE

Dear Lord, help me, oh Gracious Father to not be caught up in religion, but to be caught up in spirit; Your Holy Spirit that I might be more effectual in my prayers and be obedient to You. I want to serve Your Divine purpose, Lord; and do what is good and right in Your sight.

Allow me, Dear Lord, to live in Your Light and the Love that You have for me. Show me how to be helpful to Your Kingdom. Show me how to live a life of constant praise to You. Bless Jesus Christ's Holy Name. **Amen**

PRAYER FOR THE WORD OF PROVISION

(Read straight through as a prayer.)

But you shall earnestly remember the Lord your God, for it is He who gives you the power to get wealth, that He may establish His covenant which He swore to your fathers as at this day. (Duet 8:18)

A good man leaves an inheritance to his children's children and the wealth of the sinner finds its way into the hands of the righteous for whom it was laid up. (Prov. 13:22)

For to the person who pleases Him God gives wisdom and knowledge and joy; but to the sinner He gives the work of gathering up, that he may give to one who pleases God. (Ecc. 2:26)

And I will give you the treasures of darkness and hidden riches of secret places, that you may know that it is I, the Lord, the God of Israel, Who calls you by your name. (Isa. 45:3)

For the scepter of wickedness shall not rest upon the land of the righteous. Do good O'Lord to those who are good and to those who are righteous in their hearts. (Psalm 125:3-4)

Yea, the Lord shall give that which is good; and our land shall yield her increase. (Psalm 85:12)

And my God will liberally supply (fill to the fullest) your every need according to His riches in glory in Christ Jesus. (Phil. 4:19)

For You would that we prosper and be in good health even as our souls prosper. (3 John 2)

Let those who favor my righteous cause and have pleasure in my uprightness shout for joy and be glad, and say continually, let the Lord be magnified, Who takes pleasure in the prosperity of His servant. (Psalm 35:27)

The young lions lack food and suffer hunger, but they who seek (inquire of and require) the Lord [by right of their need and on authority of His Word] none of them shall lack any beneficial thing. (Psalms 34:10)

Blessed be the Lord, who daily loads us with benefits, even the God of our salvation. (Psalm 68:19)

For the Lord God is a sun and shield; the Lord bestows present grace and favor and future glory, honor, splendor and heavenly bliss! NO GOOD THING WILL HE WITHHOLD FROM THOSE WHO WALK UPRIGHTLY. (Psalm 84:11)

Then the Lord said to me, "You have seen well, for I am alert and active, watching over My word to perform it. (Jeremiah 1:12)

I will cry to God Most High, Who performs on my behalf and rewards me, Who brings to pass His purposes for me and surely completes them. (Psalm 57:2)

The Lord will perfect that which concerns me. (Psalm 138:8)

OUR GOD IS AN AWESOME GOD!

PRAYER OF IMPARTATION

Heavenly Father I come to You now in Jesus Christ's Holy Name. I apply the Blood of Jesus Christ over me and I ask You Lord Jesus Christ according to *John 14:14*, to render powerless and harmless the enemy cannot transfer onto me, in Jesus' Name.

[Anoint the head, forehead, or shoulder lightly, leave your hand in contact as you speak.] "Lord Jesus, I impart every blessing, anointing, gifts, and impartations that You have imparted or given to me, Lord Jesus, into _____ in the Name of the Lord Jesus

Christ of Nazareth. What I have received from You Lord Jesus, I freely give to
_____, according to Your Will in the Name of Jesus Christ of Nazareth, **Amen**

Heavenly Father, I ask You to stir the gifts in _____ and increase the anointing on
_____ with out measure to do Your Work and do Your Will in the Name of the Lord
Jesus Christ, **Amen**

PRAYERS OF PRIESTLY BLESSING TO ANOINT A BROTHER OR SISTER IN CHRIST

Heavenly Father I come to You now in Jesus Christ's Holy Name. I apply the Blood of
Jesus Christ over me and I ask You Lord Jesus Christ according to John 14:14, to render
powerless and harmless the enemy cannot transfer onto me, in Jesus Christ's Holy
Name.

[Anoint their forehead with oil, leave your hand in contact as you speak.] "I ask You
Lord according to *Psalms 92:10* (KJV) to anoint _____ in the Name of the Father,
the Son, and Holy Spirit, in Jesus Christ's Holy Name."

[Anoint their ears, leave your hand in contact as you speak.] "Lord, anoint his/her ears
to hear Your Voice, not that of a stranger, that he/she would hear you clearly, in a definite way that he/she would know that they know it is You!"

[Anoint over their eye brows, leave your hand in contact as you speak.] "Lord give him/
her eyes to see into the spiritual realm what You want him/her to see."

[Anoint their nose, mid-ridge, leave your hand in contact as you speak] "Lord quicken
_____'s spiritual senses to the spiritual realm and the things that are going on around
him/her at all times."

[Anoint their head, forehead, or shoulder lightly, leave your hand in contact as you
speak.] "Lord Jesus, I impart every blessing, anointing, gifts, and impartations that You
have imparted or given to me, Lord Jesus, into _____ in the Name of the Lord Jesus
Christ of Nazareth. What I have received from You Lord Jesus I freely give to
_____, according to Your Will in the Name of Jesus Christ of Nazareth, **Amen**

Heavenly Father, I ask You to stir the gifts in _____ and increase the anointing on
_____ without measure to do Your Work and do Your Will.

[Anoint their hands starting with the right, the outside top of the thumb, anoint the inside of the hand, the outside of the hand, then repeat with the left hand, leave your hand
in contact as you speak.] "Heavenly Father, Lord Jesus Christ, I ask You to anoint and
bless _____'s hands and what he/she puts his/her hands to, to do Your Work and to
do Your Will for the Kingdom of God, that he/she will be a blessing in their work place,
their home, their spouse, their children, and bless _____ too Lord, wherever he/she
goes."

[Anoint their knees, leave your hand in contact as you speak.] "Lord I ask You to anoint and keep _____ in Your paths of Righteousness, guide him/her and direct him/her in Your Paths & Ways."

[Anoint their feet, that is the top over the tips of the shoes, the underneath side of the tips of his/her shoes, and the backside of the heel of the shoes, leave your hand in contact as you speak.] "Lord I ask You that everywhere _____ goes today that he/she will possess the gates of his/her enemies, and the lands there of. Every place his/her feet shall go, that You would go before him/her, protecting him/her, that any weapon formed against him/her shall not prosper, but the enemy will be thrown into total confusion and flee from him/her in seven different directions!"

[Place your hand over his/her head, ask the Lord to bless him/her. Leave your hand in contact as you speak.] "Lord Jesus Christ, I ask You according to *John 14:14* to bless and anoint brother/sister _____, fill him/her with Your Peace and Presence to go forth and do the Work of the Kingdom, as they are lead by Your Holy Spirit, to God be the glory, in the Name of Jesus Christ of Nazareth, **Amen**

PRAYER OF WORSHIP

Heavenly Father, I come to You in Jesus Christ's Holy Name. Lord God, Creator of Heaven and Earth, as Your son (daughter), I come to You to worship You as You desire, in Spirit and in Truth. According to *John 4:42*, I know that Jesus is indeed the Christ, the Savior of the world. Your Spirit witnesses to my spirit, the Truth that Jesus is the Christ and I believe in Him. Lord God, according to *John 9,* You seek those who worship You and do Your will (*Matt. 7:21*) out of the love you have placed in my heart for You. Lord create in me a clean heart, a broken and contrite heart, a right heart, repentant in all my ways. Let nothing be done in strife or vain glory, but in lowliness of mind, knowing that with You Father God, all things are possible, but with man, the flesh, they shall fall short of Your Glory. Lord we do not come to worship just to be doing something, but we come to You out of the intimate love relationship we have with You through the Blood and the Cross. You have created within us a heart of Thanksgiving. We choose to, and abide in, the Spirit of Truth, so that we are in a continued state of Fellowship and Worship with You, Lord God. According to what David said in *Psalms 42:1-2, "As the deer pants for the water brooks, so my soul pants for Thee, O God. My soul thirsts for You, for the living God."* "My soul yearns (overwhelmingly desires), yea, even pines for the courts of the LORD: my heart and my flesh cry out for the living God." Lord let this be our hearts cry. Let that fire burn ever increasingly in me (each of us). Uphold me with thy free Spirit and let God be magnified! Lord if there be any wicked way within me let it be exposed and taken out of the way. *(Psalms 84:2)* Lord let no murmuring, complaining, backbiting nor evil be found in me, that my life be a glory, an honor and a praise unto You. Circumcise my heart. Fill me with Your Spirit, Your tender mercies and loving-kindness, that I sing praises to You all of my days. Create in me a heart of worship for I rejoice only in You. You are my joy and the lifter of my head! Through Your Spirit, lead me in rivers of Your worship and truth. Let my hands be lifted up to You as I go through this day and make my life (lives) be a living sacrifice (*Romans 12:1-2*), a sweet savoring aroma, that You would be glorified, honored, and my life be a praise, in the everyday things of life, unto You Lord Jesus Christ and Heavenly Father.

Heavenly Father I come to You in Jesus Christ's Holy Name. Father God, Lord Jesus Christ, Holy Spirit, I praise You and worship You. I come to You in love and admiration, through the Precious Blood of Jesus Christ. Holy Spirit I ask You to pray to my Lord and Savior Jesus Christ to renew a right spirit within me that the mind of Christ arise within me and over all areas of my life. I yield all that I am to You and ask that true praise and worship come forth from my inner man, that I worship my Heavenly Father and the Lord Jesus Christ in Spirit and in Truth. Allow your prayer language, Tongues to flow, worship Him with all You are because He is Worthy! Hallelujah!

In true worship comes true oneness with the Father! The cares and things of this life fall away and we truly walk in the light as He is in the light and we have fellowship with the Father, the Son, and the Holy Spirit. Here is where the glory of God is birthed in us and He starts manifesting His Glorious Presence and Communion takes place. In Him we live, and move, and have our being! In true worship we see ourselves as we truly are, in need of Him, and how gloriously wonderful He IS. **Amen**

PRAYER OF ACKNOWLEDGEMENT, SUBMISSION, & POSITION

Heavenly Father God, I come to You in Jesus Christ's Holy Name. I acknowledge that Jesus Christ is the Preeminent One, Who I acknowledge has all Authority and Power in Heaven, and Earth, over, in, and through my life. I willfully bow, surrender and submit all areas of my life, all that I am and all that I have unto You Heavenly Father, Son, and Holy Spirit, the One True and Living God, Creator of Heaven and Earth, under Your Lordship, my Lord, Savior, and Master!

I renew and give my Total Allegiance to You, Lord Jesus Christ, Father, Son, and Holy Spirit, fresh and anew, today and for the rest of my life, to do Your work, to do Your will and obey You at all times. I give my permission, my life, and all that is in it, as a living sacrifice, unto You which is my reasonable service, that first and foremost, all that I am would be a glory, honor, and praise unto You, Heavenly Father, Son, and Holy Spirit, in Jesus Christ's Holy Name.

I commit my life and all that is in it, to You, to do Your Good Works, and to have and be in Your total Desire, Will, Way, and Presence. I will, I am, and I will be, transformed into Your total likeness by Your might and power, in Jesus Christ's Holy Name.

Come Lord Jesus Christ, take Your rightful place on the Throne of my life, I give it to You, for eternity and I ask You Lord, to bind all that I am to all that You are, in Jesus Christ's Holy Name. Lord extend Yourself through me, in all areas of my life fully and completely that I be a glory, honor, and praise unto You.

I decree and declare You to be on the Throne of my life, in and over all areas of my life. Lord Jesus Christ, You are the Author and the Finisher of my faith: in all, through all, and above all, of my life. Thy Kingdom come Your will be done! **Amen.**

PRAYER TO STOP EVIL SPIRITS THAT FOLLOW

Heavenly Father I come to You in Jesus Christ's Holy Name. I ask You Lord Jesus Christ according to *John 14:13 & 14* to force out, drive out, all foul, wicked ,demon, tormenting, lying, hindering, seducing, perverse, unclean, familiar, foul spirits, anything that traffics in darkness, bind back all evil spirits that are following me, _____, _____, _____, and _____, or may try to follow me throughout this day and into tomorrow, and send them into the Abyss, along with their replacements or other evil spirits, bound deaf, dumb, blind, and mute, unable to gesture, and keep them there until they are judged and thrown into the lake of fire, **Amen**

PRAYER TO STOP EVIL SPIRITS TRANSFERRING, INFLUENCING, AND MANIFESTING

Heavenly Father I come to You in Jesus Christ's Holy Name. I plead the Blood of Jesus Christ of Nazareth over, in, and through this building. I ask You Lord Jesus Christ according to *John 14:13 & 14* that You force out, drive out, all foul, wicked ,demon, tormenting, lying, hindering, seducing, perverse, unclean, familiar, foul spirits, anything that traffics in darkness, from this place and any evil spirit that has a right to be here on this land and property, in this building or place, I ask You to bind these evil spirits, that they cannot transfer, they cannot influence me, that they cannot manifest in any way, shape, or form. Lord Jesus Christ I ask You to bind the enemies' ears deaf and eyes blind, and totally unaware to my presence this day and into tomorrow afternoon, **Amen**

PRAYER TO BIND DEMONIC SPIRITS FROM ANSWERING WRONG PRAYERS

Heavenly Father I come to You in Jesus Christ's Holy Name. I ask You Lord Jesus Christ according to John 14:13 & 14 to bind Satan and all demonic spirits, ears deaf and eyes blind to any prayers or words declared, decreed, or spoken that have been spoken, are being spoken, or will be spoken about me, my family members, and those that I pray and intercede for, that the enemy cannot learn or discern what is said or we are doing. I ask You Lord Jesus that You throw the enemy into confusion and that they will remain in confusion, so that they will not be able to come against us. I ask You Lord to dry up the wrong prayers being spoken null and dead and totally ineffective at their root source. Lord I ask that a Spirit of Conviction and Repentance be loosed to anyone praying wrong prayers and that You would forgive them and help them to learn how to pray properly, according to Your Word, according to *John 14:13 & 14*, **Amen**

PRAYER TO CALL ON GOD

Heavenly Father I come to You in Jesus Christ's Holy Name. I surrender myself to You, Heavenly Father, Son, and Holy Spirit. Your Word says in *Jeremiah 33:3* to call upon You and You will show me great and mighty things that I cannot understand. Lord God I come to You and cry out, I call unto You Creator of the Universe, I ask You to show me great and mighty things, of the unfathomable riches of Your glory and splendor, all that You are, help me to plumb the depth of Your Being and know You, I worship You, I praise Your Holy Name, Blessed be Your Holy Name. **Amen**

PARENTS PRAYER FOR A TEENAGER

Heavenly Father, in the Name of Jesus, I affirm Your Word over my child/children. I delight myself in You according to *Psalms 37:4* knowing that You will give me the desires of my heart. I commit _____, my child/children; to You and affirm Your Word over them from *Isaiah 54:13* that tells me my children shall be taught by the Lord and great shall be the peace of my children. I thank You that You deliver _____ out of rebellion into right relationship with us, his/her parents. In *Exodus 20:12*, Your Word teaches us that the first commandment given with promise is to the child who obeys his/her parents in the Lord. Father, You said in *Deuteronomy 5:16* that all will be well with my child/children and _____ will live long on the earth. I affirm this promise on behalf of my child, asking You to give _____ an obedient spirit that he/she may honor (esteem and value as precious) his/her father and mother.

Father, forgive me for mistakes made out of my own unresolved hurts or selfishness, which may have caused _____ hurt. I ask full and true repentance for the mistakes I have made in raising my children. I release the anointing that is upon Jesus to bind up and heal our broken hearts and the broken hearts of our children. Give us the ability to understand and forgive one another as God for Christ's sake has forgiven us. Thank You for the Holy Spirit Who leads us into all truth and corrects erroneous perceptions about past or present situations.

Thank You for teaching us to listen to each other and giving _____ an ear that hears admonition, for then he/she will be called wise. I affirm that I will speak kind, excellent and Godly things and that any words coming out of my mouth will be the right words and will be used for Your glory Lord Jesus *Colossians 3:21*. Father, I promise to train and teach _____ in the way that he/she is to go, and when _____ is old he/she will not depart from sound doctrine and teaching, but will follow it all the days of his/her life. In the Name of Jesus, I command the spirit of rebellion to be far from the heart of my child and confess that he/she is willing and obedient, free to enjoy the reward of Your promises. I ask that _____ shall be peaceful, bringing peace and to be a blessing to others. Father, according to Your Word we have been given the ministry of reconciliation, and I release this ministry and the word of reconciliation into this family. I refuse to provoke or irritate or belittle my child; I will not be hard on _____ or require perfection lest he/she becomes discouraged, feeling inferior and frustrated. I will not break his/her spirit, in the Name of Jesus and by the power of the Holy Spirit. Father, I forgive my child for the wrongs he/she has done and stand in the gap until he/she begins to understand Your love and Your grace causing them to come out of the spirit of rebellion which is the snare of the enemy, *Ephesians 6:1-3*. We should not abandon hope in Your love and commitment to all Your creation. We know You Jesus, died for our children, even before they were born. Although It may seem to us that our children's journey into selfishness, self-destruction and secularism is never-ending, but God we know You are at work in our children's lives in ways we may never understand. We ask you, Heavenly Father, for a quiet assurance that this process of conversion will take place and the inner peace that only You, Lord Jesus can gives us, will now manifest in our lives, in the Name of Jesus. Help us to be strong like Mary, the mother of Jesus, as she wept and felt deep pain as she witnessed her Son's journey knowing God's plan; as You knew Your plans for our children, even before they were born, *Jeremiah 1:2*. Help us O Lord, to know and understand that we must let God control difficult situations and always be mindful to trust You. Heavenly Father, help us to remember always that our children have belonged to you from the beginning. Help us Lord to understand that we are here to nurture them and guide them in Your ways while they are in our care. Lord, we have been mindful to raise them up in the way they should go, having made some mistakes of the flesh as we are not perfect. We did what we thought was right at the time and we know that you, Lord, knows our heart and honors that effort. It is so difficult, Lord, to understand them and to be the way they would like us to be. Even though it is difficult to understand we continue giving Glory to You and put our complete trust and expectancy in Your Word. Thank You for watching over Your word and performing it, turning and reconciling the heart of our rebellious child back to us and our hearts back to our child. We declare the power of the enemy over our children, null and void according to *Psalms 55:12-14*. Lord, help us to sleep at night knowing that You, Heavenly Father, will be holding each one of our children in Your loving hands. **Amen**

PRAYER FOR RELEASE FROM ADDICTION FOR THE BELIEVER

Dear Heavenly Father, I stand in faith on the authority I have as a believer in Jesus Christ, and a co-heir to His kingdom. Your Word says that Satan has come down with great wrath, knowing that he has only a short time. This disease is a spiritual disease that has become a curse on an entire generation. We know Lord that You are the only answer. We know Lord that the enemy comes to steal our lives, to kill and destroy our families. He is a liar and the father of lies and there is no truth in him *John 10:10, John 8:44*. In the name of Jesus Christ, I bind every evil spirit and every evil plan the enemy has planned to keep me in this addiction. I cancel Satan's plan and call forth Your plan for my life, Lord Jesus. God's Word says that God has plans for good and not evil *Jeremiah 29:11* for me and I claim God's plan for my life right now. Father, I ask that Your will be done in this situation, as it is done in heaven. I give thanks and praise to You dear Heavenly Father and I bind and declare it unlawful and evil based on God's Word because we have His authority through Jesus Christ to execute this judgment on the forces of Satan *Psalm 149:5-9*. Our faith in Your Word releases the power from heaven that binds the evil I am facing in this addiction to _____. Heavenly Father, I ask that you will send Your forces to drive back all the forces of the enemies of Christ that are working in this stronghold of addiction. Your Word says that the adversaries of the Lord shall be broken in pieces in Your perfect timing, and will bring salvation, restoration and healing to me *Samuel 2:10*. O Lord, with each new day, help me to be strong and continue to trust you. Bring into my eyes and heart an honesty that sees my true situation and find support in your goodness and guidance. I declare release from my addiction and receive my renewed joy in living from this day forward *Psalms 21:1-3*. Help me to recognize your hand in all things. Please help me O'Lord, to seek peace and patience as I work through the issues that bind me *Galatians 5:21-23*. I pray also for those that have bore the hurt of watching my life depreciate. May they forgive me for the many hurts I have hurled at them because I could not control my physical and emotional needs over this addiction (*Matthew 6:14-15*). To You O'Lord, I lift up my soul. Let me not be ashamed for I put my trust in You. I ask that I may be with Your spirit today. Cleanse my mind of all darkness and fill it with love and light. Almighty God, You sent Jesus to set the captives free (*Isaiah 61*). I know Your power and I know Your might. I ask that You deliver me from all addictions and bondages that has kept me from being and doing my best. This sin is repulsive and I can no longer tolerate it. I know Lord that You and only You can and will deliver me from this evil. I ask You Lord to be a place of refuse during this grueling time. Send me Your help. Let me arm myself with strength and hope and help of others that will companion with me and give me sound and Godly advice. I believe in miracles and according to Your Word in *Psalms 149:5-9*, I have the authority through Jesus Christ to execute judgment on the forces of satan and release power from heaven to bind the evil that I am facing in this addiction of _____. Heavenly Father, I ask that You send Your angelic warriors to drive back the enemy of Christ that are working in this stronghold of addiction. Your Word says in *1 Samuel 2:10* that the adversaries of the Lord shall be broken in pieces and You will bring salvation, restoration and healing to me. From heaven You will thunder against them and You will give strength to Your children and exalt the horn of Your anointed. In Jesus Name we pray, **Amen**

PRAYER TO HUMBE YOURSELF BEFORE THE LORD

We give our heart to You Lord
Please teach us to be humble
We give our feet to You Lord
Please help us not to stumble
Our eyes belong to you Lord
To see Your Holy way
Help us to look straight ahead
And seek You every day
With our ears let us hear Lord
Every time You call
We give ourselves to You Lord
We will obey Your Law
We give our hands to You Lord
We lift them up in praise
We will worship You Lord
All our blessed days
Our mouth we give to You Lord
We shout with victory
We belong to You Lord
Now we are living free.
Amen

PRAYER FOR MEMBERS OF THE ARMED FORCES

Dear Heavenly Father, our troops have been sent into war, _____ as peace-keepers and conquers. We petition You, Lord, according to *Psalm 91*, for the safety of our military personnel. We ask You Lord to comfort them in the midst of this turmoil and to show them that they are not forgotten by America or by You, Lord.

This is no small task that our armed forces will walk away from and forget about in a couple of hours. This is for keeps, a life-or-death fight to the finish against the devil and all his angels. We look beyond human instruments of conflict and rebuke, in Jesus Name, all the forces and authorities and rulers of darkness and powers in the spiritual realm (*Colossians 2:15*). As children of the Most High God we enforce the triumphant victory of our Lord Jesus Christ.

We know Lord that all power and authority both in heaven and earth belong to You. We petition heaven to turn our troops into a real peacekeeping force by pouring out the glory of God through our men and women in that part of the world. Let them take everything the Master has set out for them, well-made weapons of the best materials. (*Ephesians 6:12*) Use them as instruments of righteousness to defeat the plans of the devil.

Lord, we plead the power of the blood of Jesus, asking You to manifest Your power and glory. We entreat You on behalf of the citizens in these countries on both sides of the conflict. They all have experienced pain and heartache; they are victims of the devil's strategies to steal, kill and destroy *John 10:10*). We pray that they will come to know Jesus Who came to give us life and life more abundantly.

We stand in the gap for the people of the war-torn, devil-overrun land. We expect an overflowing of Your goodness and glory in the lives of those for whom we are praying (*Ezekiel 22:30*). May they call upon Your name and be saved.

Heavenly Father, provide for and protect the families of our armed forces. Preserve marriages; cause the hearts of the parents to turn toward their children and the hearts of the children to turn toward the fathers and mothers *(Malachi 4:6*). We plead the blood of Jesus over our troops and their families. Provide a support system to under gird, uplift and edify those who have been left to raise children by themselves. Jesus has been made unto these parents wisdom, righteousness and sanctification. Through Your Holy Spirit, comfort the lonely and strengthen the weary.

You Lord, make known Your salvation; Your righteousness You openly show in the sight of the nations. (*Psalm 98:2, Luke 2:30-31*)

Heavenly Father, we are looking forward to that day when the whole earth shall be filled with the knowledge of the Lord as the waters cover the sea. In Jesus' Name we pray, **Amen**

PRAYER FOR YOU TO KNOW GOD'S PLAN REGARDING MARRIAGE

Unto You, O Lord, do I bring my desire to find a godly husband (wife). Lord, I trust in, lean on, rely on and am confident in You. Let me not be put to shame or be disappointed; let not my enemies, the spirits of rejection, hurt, inferiority, or unworthiness triumph over me (*Psalm 25*).

Heavenly Father, it is written, "For I know the thoughts and plans that I have for you", says the Lord, "thoughts and plans for welfare and peace and not for evil, to give you hope in your final outcome. Then you will call upon Me, and you will come and pray to Me, and I will hear and heed you. Then you will seek Me, inquire for, and find Me when you search for Me with all your heart. I will be found by you," says the Lord .. (*Jeremiah 29:11-14* AMP)

Heavenly Father, I am looking for Your plan, Your answer for my life. It is my desire to be married. But I must be sure in my decision that I am living as You intend and than I am accepting whatever situation You have put me into. According to Your Word, marriage will bring extra problems that I may not need to face at this time in my life.

Lord you weigh the spirits, the thoughts and the intents of the heart (*Proverbs 16:2*), therefore, I give them wholly to You. I ask that You cause my thoughts to become agreeable to Your will, and so shall my plans be established and succeed. Because You Lord, are my Shepherd and I have everything I need!

I trust to You my life, Lord, that You will let me rest in the meadow grass and lead me beside the quiet streams. You will give me new strength and help me do what honors and glorifies you the most.

Heavenly Father, help me to not be afraid, and to know that You are close beside me, guarding and guiding me all the way as I seek Your will for my life. Lord teach me to always pray and not to faint, lose heart, or give up that I may know Your will for my life. I ask You Lord to give me strength to accept Your will even if that means that it is not Your will for me to be married at this time (*Luke 18:1*). In Jesus Name I pray.
Amen

PRAYER FOR PEACE IN A TROUBLED MARRIAGE

Heavenly Father, in the Name of Jesus, we bring _____ before You. We pray and confess Your Word over them, and as we do, we use our faith, believing that Your Word will come to pass.

Therefore we stand in the gap for _____ and we pray and confess that _____ will let all bitterness, indignation, wrath, rage, bad temper, resentment, brawling, clamor, contention, slander, abuse, evil speaking or blasphemous language, all malice, spite and ill will be banished from them. We pray that _____ have become useful and helpful and kind to each other, tenderhearted, compassionate, understanding, loving-hearted, forgiving one another readily and freely as You Father, in Christ, forgave them (*Ephesians 4:31*).

We ask Lord that they will walk in love, esteeming and delighting in one another as Christ loved them and gave Himself up for them, a slain offering and sacrifice to You, God, so that it became a sweet fragrance (*Ephesians 5*).

Satan, we render you helpless in your activities in the lives of _____. We come against the spirit of separation and divorce, and we command you from your assignment against them. Satan, your power is broken from their marriage in the name of Jesus (*2 Timothy 2:26*).

Heavenly Father, we thank You that _____ will be constantly renewed in the spirit of their minds, having a fresh mental and spiritual attitude. They have put on the new nature and are created in God's image in the true righteousness and holiness (*Ephesians 4:23*). They have come to their senses and escaped out of the snare of the devil who has held them captive and henceforth will do Your will, which is that they love one another with the God-kind of love, united in total peace and harmony and happiness.

Lord we know that whatever you forbid and declare to be improper and unlawful on earth must be what is already forbidden in heaven, and whatever you permit and declare proper and lawful on earth must be what is already permitted in Heaven (*Matthew 18:18*).

Therefore, Lord, I ask you to speak to their hearts and heal their hurts so they may be reconciled to making this marriage work. In Jesus Name We Pray. **Amen**

PRAYER FOR THE RESTORATION OF A MARRIAGE

Heavenly Father I thank You that You will hear my prayer, for I come in the Name of Jesus and on the authority of Your Word. I come boldly to the throne of grace to receive mercy and find grace for your help in restoring my marriage. I take my place standing in the gap for my husband/wife against the devil and his demons until the salvation of God is manifested in his/her life. Father I have forgiven them of their sins and transgressions, just as you have forgiven me. I stand firm knowing that the Holy Spirit will convict and convince him/her of their sin, unrighteousness and judgment.

Help me Lord to remain sane and sober-minded, temperate and disciplined because I love my husband/wife and my children and I commit myself to them. May I steadfastly remain self-controlled, chaste, good-natured and kindhearted, adapting myself so the Word of God may not be exposed to reproach, blasphemed or discredited.

Heavenly Father, I pray that _____, will be delivered from this present evil age by the Son of the Living God, and whom the Son has set free is free indeed (*Galatians 1:4*). I ask Lord that we be delivered from the spirit of rejection and accepted in the beloved to be holy and blameless in His sight (*Colossians 3:12-15*). Lord I come humbly before you and ask that You heal this broken marriage as Jesus came to heal the brokenhearted.

You have promised us in Your Word, that if we believe on the Lord Jesus Christ, that we will be saved, and also our household (*Acts 16:31*). Help us Lord to submit one to another as we submit ourselves to You.

Heavenly Father, I ask You to rebuke any plans of the enemy to keep this family from being together. We know Lord that Satan comes to steal, kill and destroy but we stand firm and confident knowing that he has no power over You, Lord Jesus (*John 10:10*).

Thank You, Father, for hearing my prayer on behalf of this family as we strive for the love of God to reign supreme in our home, and for the peace of God to act as umpire in all situations.

As for me and my house, we will serve the Lord. (*Joshua 24:15*) May our family know that You are Lord, spirit, soul and body and that you watch over Your Word to perform it, in Jesus Name we pray (*Acts 16:31*). **Amen**

IN A PINCH PRAYER

(WHEN THINGS ARE FLYING AROUND YOU!)

This warfare prayer is based on the authority and power in the Name of Jesus, the Blood of Jesus, the Word of God, and the Power of the Holy Spirit! The believers authority is taken to prayer to overcome and to drive out the powers of darkness!

> *"For the word of God is quick, and powerful, and sharper than any two edged sword, piercing even to the dividing asunder of soul and spirit, and of the joints and marrow, and is a discerner of the thoughts and intents of the heart." Hebrews 4:12 KJV*

In the Name of Jesus Christ of Nazareth I command you (*Luke 10:19, Mark 16:17*) devil and all evil spirits in the sound of my voice to loose from me and leave my presence. By the Blood of the Lamb and the Word of my testimony (Rev.12:11) I overcome you devil and evil spirits, in the Name of Jesus Christ Who died on the cross for my sins and the sins of this world. I am a Blood bought child of God (*Col 1:14*) and Satan, you are trespassing, you have no right to come near me, my land, animals, or property, including the atmosphere about me. I plead the Blood of my Lord and Savior Jesus Christ of Nazareth as a thick hedge of protection against all evil spirits, as a wedge between us that you cannot penetrate. I speak the Blood against you Satan, in Jesus Christ's Holy Name. It is written in God's Word that no weapon formed against me can prosper, I stand on the Word of God, He is my Shield and my Buckler (*Psalms 35:2*). He says in *Deuteronomy 33:27* that He thrusts out the enemy and says to me destroy them! Lord Jesus Christ I ask You according to *John 14:13-14,* to "destroy the enemy". Satan, you are a defeated foe! You have been defeated and by the authority and power given to me in *Luke 10:19* I command you to leave (*Mark 16:17*), I banish you to the Abyss, the dry waste place, with all your minions in the Name of Jesus Christ of Nazareth. Lord Jesus Christ I ask according to *John 14:13-14* to destroy all the dark destruction that came with the enemy, cleanse me in Your precious Blood, heal me, restore me, and seal me up in Your Glory. I ask You to shut all demonic doors that need to be shut and seal them so that the evil spirits can never come through them again. Lord Jesus, I ask You to loose Your angels over me and this place to guard and protect me, the animals, and this land from the enemy from coming back here. **Amen** [After this I encourage you to take your time and go back and pray the warfare prayers in this book.]

PRAYER TO HELP AGAINST ANGER

Lord Jesus I truly regret my sin of anger, I come to You in humility and lowliness of mind. I acknowledge my sin of anger and I repent, I turn from that way to walk in Your chosen paths of Righteousness. I ask You to forgive me and cleanse me of all unrighteousness, pride, self-centeredness, hate, rage, bitterness, resentment, strife, contention, taking offense, giving offense, misplaced hostility, indifference and all forms of anger in my life.

Lord Jesus, Your Word says that Your anointing destroys all yokes of bondage (*Isaiah 10:27*) so I ask You now to cause Your anointing to break and destroy any yokes and strongholds of pride, self-centeredness, hate, rage, bitterness, resentment, strife, contention, taking offense, giving offense, misplaced hostility, indifference, and all forms of anger in my life along with all of their works, roots, fruits, tentacles and links that are in my life, the lives of anyone that I have prayed for today according to *John 14:14,* in the Name of the Lord Jesus Christ. Amen!

I ask You Lord to force out all spirits of pride, self-centeredness, hate, rage, bitterness, resentment, strife, contention, taking offense, giving offense, misplaced hostility, indifference, control, and anger from me, and any replacements of evil spirits trying to come back from the Abyss, bound till they are judged and thrown into the Lake of Fire. Lord Jesus fill me in all these areas that were set free with Your Love and Your Holy Spirit. **Amen.**

Affirmations And Lists

IMPORTANCE OF AFFIRMATIONS

Affirming God's Word over yourself and others is crucial because it speaks life into your spirit, body and soul. Take to heart the forthcoming scriptures and you will understand the importance of speaking out loud all or some of the following scriptures over yourself every day. If you speak negative over yourself and others, you are speaking the words of the enemy and those words will hold you in bondage.

Faith comes more quickly when you hear yourself quoting, speaking, and saying the things God said. You will more readily receive God's Word into your spirit by hearing yourself say it OUT LOUD everyday than if you hear someone else say it. Hearing yourself speak the Word of God out loud everyday for thirty days will change your life. *"So then faith cometh by hearing and hearing by the word of God" Romans 10:17.*

> *"death and life are in the power of the tongue." Proverbs 18:21 Amplified*
>
> *"for the tongue can kill or nourish life." Proverbs 18:21 NLT*
>
> *"I say unto you, that every idle word that men shall speak, they shall give account thereof in the day of judgment. For by thy words thou shalt be justified and by thy words thou shalt be condemned." Matthew 12:36-37*
>
> *"For with the heart a person believes (adheres to, trusts in and relies on Christ) and so is justified (declared righteous, acceptable to God), and with the mouth he confesses, declares openly and speaks out freely his faith and confirms (his) salvation." Romans 10:10 AMP*

AFFIRMATIONS FOR YOU

- I recognize by faith that God is worthy of all honor, praise, and worship as the Creator and Sustainer and End of all things. As my Creator I confess that God made me for Himself. In this day I therefore choose to live for Him according to *Revelation 5:9, 10, and 4:11; Isaiah 43:1, 7, 21.*
- I recognize by faith that God loved me and chose me in Christ before time began according to *Eph. 1:1-7.*
- I recognize in faith that God has proven His love to me in sending His Son to die in my place, whereby every provision has already been made for my past, present, and future needs through His representative work whereby I have been quickened, raised, seated with Christ in the heavenlies and anointed with the Holy Spirit according to *Rom. 5:6-11; 8:28-39; Eph. 1:3; 2:5-6.*

151

- I recognize by faith that since I have received Christ as my Lord and Savior, I believe God's Word that He has received me, adopted me into His family whereby He has assumed every responsibility for me.
- My body is a temple for the Holy Spirit, redeemed, cleansed, healed, delivered, and sanctified by the Blood of Jesus Christ.
- My members, the parts of my body, are instruments of righteousness, yielded to God for His service and for His glory.
- Satan has no place in me, no power over me, no unsettled claims against me. All has been settled by the Blood of Jesus Christ.
- I have overcome Satan by the Blood of the Lamb and by the word of my testimony, and I love not my life unto the death. (I crucify my flesh, myself, my ego, my way, etc.) My body is for the Lord and the Lord is for my body.
- Through the blood of the Lord Jesus Christ, I am redeemed out of the hand of Satan.
- Through the blood of the Lord Jesus Christ, all my sins are forgiven.
- The blood of the Lord Jesus Christ, God's son, continually cleanses me from all sin.
- Through the blood of the Lord Jesus Christ, I am justified, made righteous, just as if I'd never sinned.
- Through the blood of the Lord Jesus Christ, I am sanctified, made holy, set apart unto God.
- The blood of the Lord Jesus Christ cleanses my conscience from dead works to serve the Living God.
- Blessed be the God and Father of our Lord Jesus Christ, who hath blessed us with all spiritual blessings in heavenly places in Christ Jesus.
- I confess with my mouth and I believe in my heart that God has raised Jesus Christ from the dead and that He (Jesus Christ) is Lord.
- "No weapon formed against me shall prosper, and every tongue which rises against me in judgment You shall condemn. This is the heritage of the servants of the LORD, and their righteousness is from Me," Says the LORD.
- I am crucified with Christ: nevertheless I live; yet not I, but Christ liveth in me: and the life which I now live in the flesh I live by the faith of the Son of God, who loved me, and gave Himself for me.
- I am washed, sanctified and justified in the Name of the Lord Jesus Christ and by the Spirit of God.

- My body is a temple of the Holy Spirit, who is in me, whom I have received from God. I am not my own; I was bought with a price.
- I desire to walk in the Spirit and not fulfill the lust of the flesh.
- I am saved from wrath by Him and justified by the Blood of the Lamb.
- I submit myself to God who gives more grace to the humble, and He will lift me up.
- Behold, the Lord Jesus Christ has given unto me power to tread on serpents and scorpions, and over all the power of the enemy: and nothing shall by any means hurt me.
- I cast down vain imaginations and every high thing that exalteth itself against the knowledge of God, and I bring every thought captive to the obedience of the Lord Jesus Christ.
- I yield no ground to Satan; I take back all that I have ever surrendered to him in the past and acknowledge that the Lord Jesus Christ is the Lord of all my life.
- Thanks be to God, which giveth us the victory through our Lord Jesus Christ.
- Jesus Christ is the same yesterday, today, and forever. **Amen**

AFFIRMATIONS FOR OUR CHILDREN/GRANDCHILDREN

- Heavenly Father, in the Name of Jesus Christ of Nazareth; I thank You and praise You for the promises in Your Word concerning my children (grandchildren). I affirm now that all my children (grandchildren) shall be taught of the Lord and great shall be the peace of my children (grandchildren) according to *Isaiah 54:13*
- I thank You and praise You for the Salvation of my children (grandchildren) and pray that they will love the Lord God with all their heart, with all their soul and with all their mind, might and strength and love their neighbor as thyself; according to Your Word in *Deuteronomy 6:5, Mark 12:30 and Matthew 22:37-39.*
- According to Your Word in *2 Corinthians 5:21*, my children (grandchildren) are the righteousness of God in Him. And they are the head and not the tail as promised in *Deuteronomy 28:13*. He who began a good work in my children (grandchildren) will continue it until the days of Jesus Christ, as found in *Philippians 1:6.*
- I thank You, Heavenly Father, that my children (grandchildren) honor their father and mother according to *Deuteronomy 5:16*. And I do not

provoke my children (grandchildren) to wrath but bring them up in the training and admonition of the Lord as instructed in *Ephesians 6:4*.

- According to *Philippians 2:3-4*, We pray that nothing will be done by our children (grandchildren) through selfish ambition or conceit. I praise God, the Father in Heaven; that He is able to make all grace abound to my children (grandchildren), that they will always have all sufficiency in all good things, and may have abundance for every good work according to His Word in *2 Corinthians 9:8*.

- As written in *Ephesians 5:17*, my children (grandchildren) are not unwise but understand what the will of the Lord is. In *Colossians 4:6*, the Word says their speech is always with grace, seasoned with salt that they might know how to answer each one. According to *Psalms 34:10*, my children (grandchildren) seek the Lord and shall not lack any good thing. The Lord pours out His Spirit on my offspring and His Blessing on my descendants as written. In *Isaiah 49:25-26*, it is written that the Lord contends with those who contend with my children (grandchildren).

- Heavenly Father, according to Your Word in *Psalms 112:2-3*; my children (grandchildren) will be mighty on this earth and the generation of the upright will be Blessed and the Lord gives me increase more and more, me and our children (grandchildren). Behold how good and pleasant it is for my children (grandchildren) to dwell together in unity as promised in Your Word in *Psalms 133:1*. According to Your Word in *2 John 1:2*; my children (grandchildren) prosper in all things and are in health, even as their souls prosper.

- In *2 Peter 1:3-4*, Your divine power has given to my children (grandchildren) all things that pertain to Life and Godliness...and they have been given exceedingly great and precious promises. The Lord blesses my children (grandchildren) and keeps them. He makes His face to shine upon my children and grandchildren and He is gracious unto them. He lifts up His countenance upon them and gives them peace, according to His Word in *Numbers 6:23-26*.

- Thank You Heavenly Father that my children (grandchildren) are kindly affectionate to one another with brotherly love, in honor giving preference to one another as promised in Your Word in *Romans 12:10*. According to Your Word in *1 John 2:20*, my children (grandchildren) have an anointing from the Holy One and they know all things. To God be the Glory. **Amen**

I AM IN CHRIST AFFIRMATIONS

- I am: God's child for I am born again of the incorruptible seed of the Word of God. *1 Peter 1:23.*
- I am: Forgiven of all my sins and washed in the Blood. *Ephesians 1:7, Hebrews 9:14, Colossians 1:14, 1 John 1:9.*
- I am: A new creature in Christ. *2 Corinthians 5:17.*
- I am: The temple of the Holy Spirit. *1 Corinthians 6:19.*
- I am: Delivered from the power of darkness and translated in God's kingdom. *Colossians 1:13.*
- I am: Redeemed from the curse of the law of sin and death. *1 Peter 1:18-19, Galatians 3:13.*
- I am: Blessed. *Deuteronomy 28:2-12, Galatians 3:9.*
- I am: A Saint. *Romans 1:7, 1 Corinthians 1:2, Philippians 1:1.*
- I am: The head and not the tail, above and not beneath. *Deuteronomy 28:13.*
- I am: Holy and without blame before Him in love. *1 Peter 1:16, Ephesians 1:4*
- I am: The Elect of God. *Colossians 3:12, Romans 8:33.*
- I am: Established to the end. *Romans 1:11.*
- I am: Made near to My Heavenly Father by the Blood of Christ. *Ephesians 2:13.*
- I am: Set free. *John 8:31-33.*
- I am: Strong in the Lord. *Ephesians 6:10.*
- I am: Dead to sin. *Romans 6:1, 11 and 1 Peter 2:24.*
- I am: More than a conqueror. *Romans 8:37.*
- I am: Joint heir with Christ. *Romans 8:13.*
- I am: Sealed with the Holy Spirit of promise. *Ephesians 1:13.*
- I am: In Christ by His doing. *1 Corinthians 1:30.*
- I am: Accepted in the Beloved. *Ephesians 1:6.*
- I am: Complete in Him. *Colossians 2:10.*
- I am: Crucified with Christ. *Galatians 2:20.*
- I am: Alive with Christ. *Galatians 2:20.*
- I am: Free from condemnation. *John 5:24.*
- I am: Reconciled to God. *2 Corinthians 5:18*
- I am: Qualified to share in His inheritance. *Colossians 1:12.*
- I am: Firmly rooted, built up, established in my faith and overflowing with thanksgiving. *Colossians 2:7.*

- I am: Born of God and the evil one does not touch me. *1 John 5:18.*
- I am: His faithful follower. *Revelation 17:14, Ephesians 5:1.*
- I am: A fellow citizen with the saints of the household of God. Ephesians 2:19.
- I am: Built upon the foundation of the apostles and prophets, Jesus Christ Himself being the chief corner stone. *Ephesians 2:20.*
- I am: Overtaken with blessings. *Deuteronomy 28:2 and Ephesians 1:3.*
- I am: His disciple because I have love for others. *John 13:34-35.*
- I am: The light of the world. *Matthew 5:14*
- I am: The salt of the earth. *Matthew 5:13.*
- I am: The righteousness of God. *2 Corinthians 5:21, 1 Peter 2:24*
- I am: A partaker of His Divine Nature. *2 Peter 1:4.*
- I am: Called of God. *2 Timothy 1:9.*
- I am: An ambassador for Christ. *2 Corinthians 5:20*
- I am: God's workmanship created in Christ Jesus for good works. *Ephesians 2:10.*
- I am: The apple of my Father's eye. *Deuteronomy 32:10.*
- I am: Healed by the stripes of Jesus. *1 Peter 2:25, Isaiah 53:6*
- I am: Being changed into His image. *2 Corinthians 3:18, Philippians 1:6*
- I am: A child of God. *John 1:12, Romans 8:16.*
- I am: Christ's friend. *John 15:15.*
- I am: Chosen and appointed by Christ to bear His fruit. *John 15:16.*
- I am: A slave of righteousness. *Romans 6:16.*
- I am: Enslaved to God. *Romans 6:22.*
- I am: A son/daughter of God. *Romans 8:14-15, Galatians 3:26 and 4:6.*
- I am: A temple of God, His Spirit dwells in me. *1 Corinthians 3:16, 6:19*
- I am: Joined to the Lord and I am one with him. *1 Corinthians 6:17*
- I am: A member of Christ's Body. *1 Corinthians 12:27, Ephesians 5:30.*
- I am: Reconciled to God and I am a minister of reconciliation. *2 Corinthians 5:18-19*
- I am: One in Christ. *Galatians 3:26, 28.*
- I am: An heir of God since I am a son/daughter of God. *Galatians 4:6-7.*
- I am: Righteous and holy. *Ephesians 4:24.*

- I am: A citizen of Heaven and seated in Heaven right now. *Philippians 3:20, Ephesians 2:6.*
- I am: An expression of the Life of Christ because He is my life. *Colossians 3:4.*
- I am: Chosen and dearly loved by Christ. *Ephesians 1:4, 1 Peter 2:9.*
- I am: A son/daughter of light and not of darkness. *1 Thessalonians 5:5.*
- I am: A Holy brother/sister, partaker of a Heavenly Calling. *Hebrews 3:1*
- I am: One of God's living stones and I am being brought up as a spiritual house. *1 Peter 2:5*
- I am: A Chosen Race, a Royal Priesthood, a Holy Nation, a people for God's own possession to proclaim the excellence of Him. *1 Peter 2:9-10.*
- I am: An alien and stranger to this world I temporarily live in. *1 Peter 2:11.*
- I am: The enemy of the Devil. *1 Peter 5:8.*
- I am: Now a child of God, I will resemble Christ when He returns. *1 John 3:1-2.*
- I am: Not the great I AM but by the grace of God I am what I am. *1 Corinthians 15:10.*
- I am: Justified, completely forgiven and made righteous. *Romans 5:1.*
- I am: Dead with Christ and dead to the power of sin's rule over my life. *Romans 6:1-6.*
- I am: Dead, I no longer live for myself but for God. *2 Corinthians 5:14-15*
- I am: Bought with a price, I am not my own, I belong to God. *1 Corinthians 6:19-20*
- I am: Established, anointed and sealed by God in Christ. *2 Corinthians 1:21*
- I am: Given the Holy Spirit as a pledge, a guarantee of my inheritance. Ephesians 1:13-14.
- I am: Crucified with Christ and it is no longer I who lives, but Christ. *Galatians 2:20.*
- I am: Chosen in Christ before the foundation of the world. *Ephesians 1:4.*
- I am: Predestined (determined by God) to be a son/daughter. *Ephesians 1:5.*

- I am: Sanctified and I am one with the Sanctifier, Christ. He is not ashamed to call me brother/sister. *Hebrews 2:11.*
- I have: Received the Spirit of God into my life that I might know the things given to me by God. *1 Corinthians 2:12*
- I have: Been redeemed, forgiven and I am a recipient of His lavish grace. *Ephesians 1:7.*
- I have: Been raised up and seated with Christ in the Heavenlies. *Ephesians 2:6.*
- I have: Christ Himself in me. *Colossians 1:27.*
- I have: Been firmly rooted in Christ and I am now built up in Him. *Colossians 2:7.*
- I have: Been buried, raised and made alive with Christ. *Colossians 2:12 -13.*
- I have: Been raised up with Christ, my life is now hidden with Christ in God. For Christ is now my life. *Colossians 3 1-4.*
- I have: Been given a spirit of power, love and self discipline. *2 Timothy 1:7.*
- I have: Been saved and called (set apart) according to God's doing. *2 Timothy 1:9.*
- I have: A right to come boldly before the throne to find mercy and grace in time of need. *Hebrews 4:16.*
- I have: Been given exceedingly great and precious promises by God which I am a partaker of His Divine Nature. *2 Peter 1:4.*
- I have: The mind of Christ. *Philippians 2:5, 1 Corinthians 2:16*
- I have: Obtained an inheritance. *Ephesians 1:11.*
- I have: Overcome the world. *1 John 5:4.*
- I have: Everlasting life and will not be condemned. *John 5:2*
- I have: The peace of God which passes all understanding. *Philippians 4:7.*
- I have: Received power; power of the Holy Spirit, power to lay hands on the sick and see them recover, power to cast out demons, power over all the power of the enemy. *Mark 16*
- I may: Approach God with boldness, freedom and confidence. *Ephesians 3:12.*
- I live: By the law of the Spirit of Life in Christ Jesus. *Romans 8:2.*
- I walk: In Christ Jesus. *Colossians 2:6.*
- I can: Do all things in Christ. *Philippians 4:13.*

- My life: Is hid with Christ in God. *Colossians 3:3.*
- I shall: Do even greater works than Christ Jesus. *John 14:12.*
- I shall: Overcome because greater is He who is in me then he who is in the world. *1 John 4:4.*
- I press: Toward the mark for the prize of the high calling of God. *Philippians 3:14.*
- I always: Triumph in Christ. *2 Corinthians 2:14*

NAMES OF GOD

"O Magnify the Lord with me, and let us exalt His Name together."
Psalms 34:3

"I will bow down toward Your holy temple and will praise Your Name for Your love and Your faithfulness, for You have exalted above all things Your Name and Your Word." Psalms 138:2

God's Names are dynamic; they are full of power; and He reveals great truths about Himself that can be found only in His Names. Pray to God and ask Him to give you insight into each of His Names. Ask Him to teach you about His character and attributes. Study the following list of God's Names. Ask God to show you how to apply them in your life. Use God's Names to cry out to Him in every need. Scriptures tells us. *"Our help is in the Name of the Lord, Who made heaven and earth." Psalms 124:8.*

- *Adonai-Jehovah Genesis 12:2, 8*
- *Advocate 1 John 2:1*
- *All and All Colossians 3:11*
- *Anchor Hebrews 6:19*
- *Angel of His Presence Isaiah 63:9*
- *Apostle and High Priest Hebrews 3:1*
- *Arm of the Lord Isaiah 51:9*
- *Author of our Faith Hebrews 12:2*
- *Balm of Gilead Jeremiah 8:22*
- *Banner for the Nations Isaiah 11:12*
- *Blessed and Only Potentate 1 Timothy 6:15*
- *Bright and Morning Star Revelations 22:16*
- *Captain of Our Salvation Hebrews 2:10*
- *Captain of the Host of the Lord Joshua 5:14*
- *Chief Cornerstone 1 Peter 2:6*

- *Chief Shepherd 1 Peter 5:4*
- *Christ the Power of God 1 Corinthians 1:24*
- *Consuming Fire Hebrews 12:29*
- *Cover from the Tempest Isaiah 32:2*
- *Deliverer Romans 11:26*
- *Emmanuel – God With Us Matthew 1:23*
- *Faithful and True Revelation 19:11*
- *Father of Mercies 2 Corinthians 1:3*
- *Flame Isaiah 10:17*
- *Fountain of Living Waters Jeremiah 17:13-14*
- *Friend who sticks closer than a brother Proverbs 18:24*
- *Glorious Lord Isaiah 33:21*
- *God of All Comfort 2 Corinthians 1:3*
- *God of All Grace 1 Peter 5:10*
- *God of Hope Romans 15:13*
- *God of Peace Romans 15:33*
- *God of My Life Psalms 42:8*
- *God of Truth Deuteronomy 32:4*
- *God the Judge of All Hebrews 12:23*
- *Governor Matthew 2:6*
- *Great High Priest Hebrews 4:14*
- *Great King Over All the Earth Psalms 47:2*
- *Great King above all gods Psalms 95:3*
- *Great Light Isaiah 9:2*
- *Great Shepherd of the Sheep Hebrews 13:20*
- *Head of Every Man 1 Corinthians 11:3*
- *Head Over All Things Ephesians 1:22*
- *Health of My Countenance Psalms 42:11*
- *He Who Shall Have Dominion Numbers 24:19*
- *Hiding Place from the Wind Isaiah 32:2*
- *High and Lofty One Isaiah 57:15*
- *Holy and Awesome Psalms 111:9*
- *Holy One of God Luke 4:34*
- *Hope of Glory Colossians 1:27*
- *I AM John 8:58*
- *Jehovah-Elyon – The Lord Most High Psalms 7:17*

- *Jehovah-Jireh – The Lord Will Provide Genesis 22:8*
- *Jehovah-Mekaddishkem –The Lord Our Sanctifier Leviticus 20:8*
- *Jehovah-Nissi – The Lord My Banner Exodus 17:15*
- *Jehovah-Rohi – The Lord My Shepherd Psalms 23:1*
- *Jehovah-Rapha – The Lord My Healer Exodus 15:26*
- *Jehovah-Sabaoth – The Lord of Hosts 1 Samuel 1:3*
- *Jehovah-Shalom – The Lord of Our Peace Judges 6:24*
- *Jehovah-Shammah – The Lord Is There Ezekiel 48:35*
- *Jehovah-Tsidkenu – The Lord Our Righteousness*
- *Jeremiah 23:6*
- *Jesus Christ the Righteous 1 John 2:1*
- *Judge of the Living and the Dead Acts 10:42*
- *King in His Beauty Isaiah 33:17*
- *King of Kings Revelation 17:14*
- *King Over All the Earth Zechariah 14:9*
- *Lamb in the Midst of the Throne Revelation 7:17*
- *Lamb of God John 1:29*
- *Lamb Slain Revelation 5:12*
- *Lamb without Blemish 1 Peter 1:19*
- *Life Giving Spirit 1 Corinthians 15:45*
- *Light of the World John 8:12*
- *Lion of the Tribe of Judah Revelation 5:5*
- *Lord Romans 10:13*
- *Lord and Savior Jesus Christ 2 Peter 3:18*
- *Lord of Both the Dead and Living Romans 14:9*
- *Lord God Almighty Revelation 4:8*
- *Lord God of Truth Psalms 31:5*
- *Lord God Omnipotent Revelation 19:6*
- *Lord Jesus Christ of Nazareth Luke 4:34*
- *Lord Mighty in Battle Psalms 24:8*
- *Lord Most High Psalms 47:2*
- *Lord of All Acts 10:36*
- *Lord of All the Earth Zechariah 6:5*
- *Lord Jehovah Psalms 83:18, Isaiah 26:4*
- *Lord of Hosts Psalms 24:10*
- *Lord of lords Revelation 17:14*

- *Lord Our Maker Psalms 95:6*
- *Lord Our Righteousness Jeremiah 23:6*
- *Lord Over All Romans 10:12*
- *Lord Strong and Mighty Psalms 24:8*
- *Lord Your Redeemer Isaiah 43:14*
- *Love 1 John 4:8*
- *Man of War Exodus 15:3*
- *Mediator 1 Timothy 2:5*
- *Mediator of a Better Covenant Hebrews 8:6*
- *Mediator of the New Covenant Hebrews 12:24*
- *Messiah John 4:25*
- *Mighty God Isaiah 9:6*
- *Mighty One Psalms 45:3*
- *Mighty One of Israel Isaiah 30:29*
- *ost High – Highest Psalms 18:13*
- *Most Holy Daniel 9:24*
- *My Fortress Psalms 144:2*
- *My Help Psalms 115:11*
- *My Helper Hebrews 13:6*
- *My High Tower Psalms 144:2*
- *My Hope Psalms 71:5*
- *My Lord and My God John 20:28*
- *My Strength and My Power 2 Samuel 22:33*
- *My Rock of Refuge Psalms 31:2*
- *My Salvation Psalms 38:22*
- *My Shield 2 Samuel 22:3, Psalms 144:2*
- *My Song Isaiah 12:2*
- *My Support – My Stay Psalms 18:18*
- *Our Great God 2 Chronicles 20:12*
- *Our Passover 1 Corinthians 5:7*
- *Our Peace Ephesians 2:14*
- *Overcoming Lamb Revelation 17:14*
- *Priest Forever Hebrews 5:6*
- *Prince of Life Acts 3:15*
- *Prince of Peace Isaiah 9:6*
- *Redeemer Isaiah 59:20*

- *Refiner and Purifier Malachi 3:3*
- *Refuge from the Storm Isaiah 25:4*
- *Resting Place Jeremiah 50:6*
- *Restorer Psalms 23:3*
- *Rewarder Hebrews 11:6*
- *Rock Deuteronomy 32:4*
- *Rock That Is Higher Than I Psalms 61:2*
- *Rod of Your Strength Psalms 110:2*
- *Ruler Micah 5:2*
- *Ruler Over The Kings Of The Earth Revelation 1:5*
- *Sanctuary Isaiah 8:14*
- *Shadow of a Great Rock in a Weary Land Isaiah 32:2*
- *Shepherd Genesis 49:24*
- *Shepherd of Israel Psalms 80:1*
- *Shelter of His People Psalms 91:1*
- *Shield Psalms 3:3, Psalms 115:11*
- *Shield of Your Help Deuteronomy 33:29*
- *Shiloh (Peacemaker) Genesis 49:10*
- *Son of God John 1:34*
- *Son of the Highest Luke 1:32*
- *Son of the Most High God Mark 5:7*
- *Spirit of Justice Isaiah 28:5-6*
- *Strength of My Life Psalms 27:1*
- *Strength to the Needy Isaiah 25:4*
- *Strong Lord Psalms 89:8*
- *Strong Tower Psalms 61:3*
- *Stronghold Nahum 1:7*
- *Sun and Shield Psalms 84:11*
- *Sure Foundation Isaiah 28:16*
- *Surety Hebrews 7:22*
- *Sword of Your Excellency Deuteronomy 33:29*
- *Testator Hebrews 9:16*
- *That Eternal Life 1 John 1:2*
- *That Spiritual Rock 1 Corinthians 10:4*
- *The Alpha and the Omega Revelations 22:13*
- *The Beginning and the End Revelations 22:13*

- *The Root and the Offspring of David Revelations 22:16*
- *The Way, the Truth, the Life John 14:6*
- *Trap and a Snare Isaiah 8:14*
- *Tried Stone Isaiah 28:16*
- *True Bread of Heaven John 6:32*
- *True Light John 1:9*
- *Tower of Salvation 2 Samuel 22:51*
- *True God 1 John 5:20*
- *Understanding Proverbs 8:14*
- *Upholder of All Things Hebrews 1:3*
- *Vine John 15:5*
- *Wisdom Proverbs 8:12*
- *Wonderful Isaiah 9:6*
- *Wisdom of God 1 Corinthians 1:24*
- *Witness to the People Isaiah 55:4*
- *Word John 1:1*
- *Word of God Revelation 19:13*
- *Word of Life 1 John 1:1*
- *Worthy Lamb Revelation 5:12*
- *Your Confidence Proverbs 3:26*
- *Your Everlasting Light Isaiah 60:20*
- *Your Exceeding Great Reward Genesis 15:1*
- *Your Holy One Acts 2:27*
- *Your Keeper Psalms 121:5*
- *Your King Zechariah 9:9*
- *Your Maker Isaiah 54:5*
- *Your Shade Psalms 121:5*
- *Your Shield Genesis 15:1*

THE WORD OF GOD; A SCRIPTURAL REFERENCE BY SUBJECT

What a treasure we have in God's Word! The Holy Bible is relevant to today's issues and gives solid guidance for daily living. Study the following Scriptures and ask God to show you how to apply each one in your life.

CONCERNING US AND GOD'S GIFTS

- *Abundant Life John 10:10*
- *Alertness Mark 14:38*
- *Attentiveness Hebrews 2:1*
- *Boldness Acts 4:29*
- *Citizenship Romans 13:1-7*
- *Cautiousness Proverbs 19:2*
- *Cleanliness 2 Corinthians 7:1*
- *Compassion 1 John 3:17*
- *Consecration Romans 12:1-2*
- *Contentment 1 Timothy 6:6-8*
- *Courage Psalms 27:14*
- *Creativity Romans 12:2*
- *Decisiveness James 1:5*
- *Deference Romans 14:21*
- *Dependability Psalms 15:4*
- *Determination 2 Timothy 4:6-7*
- *Diligence Colossians 3:23*
- *Discernment 1 Samuel 16:7*
- *Discretion Proverbs 22:3*
- *Duty Luke 20:21-25*
- *Endurance Galatians 6:9*
- *Enthusiasm 1 Thessalonians 5:16, 19*
- *Faith Mark 11:22-24*
- *Faithfulness Matthew 25:23*
- *Forgiveness Ephesians 4:31-32*
- *Freedom John 8:32, 36*
- *Fruitfulness John 15:8*
- *Generosity 2 Corinthians 9:6*

165

- *Gentleness 1 Thessalonians 2:7*
- *Godliness Titus 2:11-14*
- *Gratefulness 1 Corinthians 4:7*
- *Happiness Matthew 5:3-12*
- *Holiness 1 Peter 1:13-16*
- *Honesty 2 Corinthians 8:21*
- *Honor 1 Peter 2:17*
- *Honor to Parents Matthew 15:4*
- *Hope 1 Peter 1:13*
- *Hospitality Hebrews 13:2*
- *Humility James 4:6*
- *Initiative Romans 12:21*
- *Joy Luke 10:20*
- *Joyfulness Proverbs 15:13*
- *Justice Micah 6:8*
- *Kindness Colossians 3:12-13*
- *Labor John 9:4*
- *Love 1 Corinthians 13:3*
- *Loyalty John 15:13*
- *Obedience John 14:15-24*
- *Orderliness 1 Corinthians 14:40*
- *Overcoming John 16:33*
- *Patience Hebrews 10:36*
- *Peacefulness John 14:27*
- *Perseverance Mark 13:5-13*
- *Persuasiveness 2 Timothy 2:24*
- *Prayer Ephesians 6:18*
- *Punctuality Ecclesiastes 3:1*
- *Pure Thinking Philippians 4:8*
- *Purity Matthews 5:27-32*
- *Resourcefulness Luke 16:10*
- *Responsibility Romans 14:12*
- *Resolution Ephesians 6:10-18*
- *Reverence Proverbs 23:17-18*
- *Righteousness Matthews 6:33*
- *Security John 6:27*

- *Self-control Galatians 5:24-25*
- *Sensitivity Romans 12:15*
- *Sincerity Philippians 1:9-10*
- *Steadfastness 1 Corinthians 15:58*
- *Stewardship 2 Corinthians 9:6-7*
- *Temperance 1 Thessalonians 5:6-8*
- *Thriftiness Luke 16:11*
- *Thoroughness Proverbs 18:15*
- *Tolerance Philippians 2:2*
- *Trust Proverbs 3:5-6*
- *Truth Ephesians 4:14-15, 25*
- *Victory 1 John 5:4*
- *Virtue 2 Peter 1:3*
- *Watchfulness Mark 13:34-37*
- *Wisdom Proverbs 9:10*
- *Worship John 4:23-24*
- *Zeal John 2:13-17*

CONCERNING OUR STRENGTH TO OVERCOME SIN

- *Adultery Matthew 5:27-28, 32*
- *Adversity Romans 8:28*
- *Afraid Psalms 34:4, 56:3*
- *Alcohol Ephesians 5:18*
- *Anger Ephesians 4:26-27, 31-32*
- *Anxiety Philippians 4:4-7*
- *Apprehension Matthew 6:31-33*
- *Astrology Deuteronomy 18:9-14*
- *Backbiting Hebrews 12:14-15*
- *Backsliding Psalms 51*
- *Bereaved 2 Corinthians 1:3-4*
- *Burdens 1 Peter 5:6-11*
- *Conceit Luke 18:9-14*
- *Contention Proverbs 13:10. 22:10*
- *Confusion 2 Corinthians 10:3-6*
- *Covetousness Exodus 20:17, Romans 7:7*

- *Crisis Psalms 121*
- *Criticism Romans 12*
- *Cursing James 3:10*
- *Daydreaming 2 Corinthians 10:3-6*
- *Death Psalms 116*
- *Deceit Colossians 2:8*
- *Defeated Romans 8:31-39*
- *Depression Isaiah 61:1-3. Psalms 34*
- *Despair 2 Corinthians 4:8*
- *Destruction Psalms 103; Proverbs 18:12*
- *Disaster Threatens Psalms 91*
- *Discouragement Isaiah 42; Psalms 23*
- *Disobedience John 15:14*
- *Divorce Mark 10:2-12*
- *Doubt Proverbs 3:5-6; Hebrews 11*
- *Drugs 2 Corinthians 7:1*
- *Drunkenness Luke 21:34-36*
- *Envy Proverbs 14:30*
- *Excuses Luke 14:15-24*
- *Faith Falls Psalms 42:5*
- *Fantasy 2 Corinthians 10:3-6*
- *Fatigue Isaiah 40:31*
- *Faultfinding Matthew 7:1-5*
- *Fear 2 Timothy 1:7; Luke 12:5*
- *Fear of Rejection Ephesians 1*
- *Fornication 1 Corinthians 6:18-20*
- *Friends Fail 2 Timothy 4:16-18*
- *Gluttony Proverbs 23:2*
- *Gossip Proverbs 13:3*
- *Greed Matthew 19:24*
- *Grief Isaiah 53:3-4*
- *Guilt Romans 8:1*
- *Hatred 1 John 2:11*
- *Heartache Matthew 5:3-12*
- *Heartbreak Psalms 147:3*
- *Heaviness Isaiah 61:1-3*

- *Hurting John 14*
- *Idleness Proverbs 19:15*
- *Idolatry 1 John 5:21*
- *Inadequacy Philippians 4:13*
- *Incest Leviticus 20:11,12,14*
- *Inferiority Philippians 4:13*
- *Impure Thought 2 Peter 2:10*
- *Insomnia Proverbs 3:24*
- *Intolerance 1 Corinthians 13*
- *Irritability 1 Corinthians 13*
- *Jealousy Proverbs 6:34*
- *Judging Romans 14:10-13*
- *Laziness Hebrews 6:12, Proverbs 19:15*
- *Legalism Galatians 3*
- *Lethargy Proverbs 21:24-26*
- *Loneliness John 14; Psalms 23*
- *Lying Revelation 21:8*
- *Lust Matthew 5:28*
- *Manipulation 2 Peter 2*
- *Masturbation Romans 1:24-28*
- *Materialistic 1 John 2:15-17*
- *Mocking Proverbs 17:5*
- *Murder Exodus 20:13*
- *Negativism 2 Corinthians 1:20*
- *Nervousness Philippians 4:6*
- *Obsessive Behavior Galatians 5:16-25*
- *Occult Deuteronomy 18*
- *Overly Sensitive 1 Corinthians 13*
- *Passivity Matthew 10:33*
- *Pouting Matthew 6: 14-15*
- *Prejudice James 2: 1-13*
- *Pressure Proverbs 3:25-26*
- *Pride Proverbs 16:18*
- *Profane 1 Timothy 1:9*
- *Protection Psalms 27*
- *Quarreling Ephesians 4:25-32*

- *Rape 2 Corinthians 7:1*
- *Rebellion 1 Samuel 15:23*
- *Rejection John 14*
- *Resentment Hebrews 12*
- *Restlessness Psalms 46:10*
- *Retaliation Romans 12*
- *Revenge Matthew 5:43-48*
- *Sadness Nehemiah 8:10*
- *Scorning Proverbs 22:10*
- *Selfishness 2 Corinthians 9:1-14*
- *Self-pity Philippians 4:8-9*
- *Self-righteousness Luke 18:9-14*
- *Self-rejection Psalms 139:14*
- *Self-will Isaiah 53:6*
- *Sensuality Galatians 5:16-26*
- *Sexual Impurity Proverbs 6:24-35*
- *Sin Psalms 66:18; 1 John 1:9; John 8:34-36*
- *Slow to Forgive Matthew 18:21-35*
- *Sorrow Isaiah 53*
- *Spite Isaiah 50:6*
- *Stealing Exodus 20:15*
- *Strife James 3*
- *Stubbornness 1 Samuel 15:23*
- *Submission 1 Peter 2:13-17*
- *Suicide Exodus 20:13*
- *Suspicion Exodus 20:16*
- *Swearing Colossians 3:8*
- *Temper 2 Peter 1:5-8*
- *Tempted Matthew 26:41*
- *Timidity Acts 4:29*
- *Too Quick to Speak James 3:1-13*
- *Unbelief Hebrews 3:12-13*
- *Unforgiveness Matthew 18:21-35*
- *Vanity Galatians 5:26*
- *Violence Ezekiel 45:9*
- *Weariness Hebrews 12:3; 2 Thessalonians 3:13*

- *Witchcraft Galatians 5:20*
- *Withdrawal Ezekiel 18:17*
- *Workaholic Romans 10:3; Ephesians 2:8-9*
- *Worldliness 1 John 2: 15-17*
- *Worry Isaiah 35:3-5; 26:3-4*

HEALING SCRIPTURES LIST

Jesus is the Lord of my life. Sickness and disease have no power over me. I am forgiven and free from sin and guilt. I am dead to sin and alive to righteousness. Colossians 1:21, 22

Jesus bore my sins in His Body on the tree; therefore I am dead to sin and alive unto God and by His stripes I am healed and made whole. 1 Peter 2:24; Romans 6:11; 2 Corinthians 5:21

Jesus bore my sickness and carried my pain. Therefore I give no place to sickness or pain. For God sent His Word and healed me. Psalms 107:20

No evil will befall me, neither shall any plague come near my dwelling. For You have given Your angels charge over me. They keep me in all my ways. In my pathway is life, healing and health. Psalms 91:10,11; Proverbs 12:28

Jesus took my infirmities and bore my sicknesses. Therefore I refuse to allow sickness to dominate my body. The Life of God flows within me bringing healing to every fiber of my being. Matthew 8:17; John 6:63

My body is the temple of the Holy Spirit. I make a demand on my body to release the right chemicals. My body is in perfect chemical balance. My pancreas secretes the proper amount of insulin for life and health. 1 Corinthians 6:19

Growths and tumors have no right to my body. They are a thing of the past for I am delivered from the authority of darkness. Colossians 1:13, 14

Every organ and tissue of my body functions in the perfection that God created it to function. I forbid any malfunction in my body in Jesus' Name. Genesis 1:28, 31

Your Word is manifest in my body, causing growths to disappear. Arthritis is a thing of the past. I make a demand on my bones and joints to function properly in Jesus' Name. Mark 11:23; Matthew 17:20

Thank You Father that I have a strong heart. My heart beats with the rhythm of life. My blood flows to every cell of my body restoring life and health abundantly. Proverbs 12:14; 14:30

My heart beat is normal. My heart beats with the rhythm of life, carrying the life of God throughout my body restoring life and health abundantly. John 17:23; Ephesians 2:22

I command my blood cells to destroy every disease, germ and virus that tries to inhabit my body. I command every cell of my body to be normal in Jesus' Name. Romans 5:17; Luke 17:6

I make a demand on my joints to function perfectly. There will be no pain or swelling in my joints. My joints refuse to allow anything that will hurt or destroy their normal function. Proverbs 17:22

You have forgiven all my iniquities; You have healed all my diseases; You have redeemed my life from destruction; You have satisfied my mouth with good things so that my youth is renewed as the eagles. Psalms 103:2-5

You have given me abundant life. I receive that life through Your Word and it flows to every organ of my body bringing healing and health. John 10:10; John 6:63

I am redeemed from the curse. Galatians 3:13 is flowing in my blood stream. It flows to every cell of my body, restoring life and health. Mark 11:23; Luke 17:6. My affliction will leave and not come back again. Nahum 1:9

FINANCIAL SUCCESS SCRIPTURES LIST

As I give, it is given unto me, good measure, pressed down, shaken together, and running over. Luke 6:38.

My God makes all grace abound toward me in every favor and earthly blessing, so that I have all sufficiency for all things and I abound to every good work. 2 Corinthians 9:8.

I am blessed in the city, blessed in the field, blessed coming in, and blessed going out, my laying down, my rising up. I am blessed in the basket and blessed in my bank accounts, investments, health, and relationships; they flourish. The blessings of the Lord overtake me in all areas of my life and I receive them. Deut 28:1-14.

I am like a tree planted by rivers of water. I bring forth fruit in my season, my leaf shall not wither, and whatever I do will prosper. Psalms 1:3.

The blessings of the Lord makes truly rich, and He adds no sorrow with it. Proverbs 10:22

The Lord has opened unto me His good treasure and blessed the work of my hands. He has commanded the blessing upon me in my storehouse and all that I undertake. Deuteronomy 28:8 and 12.

God delights in my prosperity. He gives me power to get wealth that He may establish His covenant upon the earth. Deuteronomy 8:18, 11:12

God has given me all things that pertain to life and godliness, and I am well able to possess all that God has provided for me. Numbers 13:30, 2 Peter 1:3-4.

I delight myself in the Lord, and He gives me the desires of my heart. Psalms 37:4.

The Lord rebukes the devourer for my sake, and no weapon that is formed against me will prosper. All obstacles and hindrances to my prosperity are now dissolved. Malachi 3:10-11; Isaiah 54:17.

The Lord is my shepherd, and I do not want. Jesus came that I might have life and have it more abundantly. Psalms 23:1; John 10:10.

A Believer's Scriptural Authority Against Demonic Spirits

Luke 10: 17-19, "Then the seventy returned with joy, saying, Lord, even the demons are subject to us in Your Name. And He said to them, I saw Satan fall like lightning from heaven. Behold, I give you the authority to trample on serpents and scorpions, and over all the power of the enemy, and nothing shall by any means hurt you."

Mark 16: 17-18, 20, "And these signs will follow those who believe: In My Name they will cast out demons; they will speak with new tongues; they will take up serpents; and if they drink anything deadly, it will by no means hurt them; they will lay hands on the sick, and they will recover." Verses 20, "And they went out and preached everywhere, the Lord working with them and confirming the word through the accompanying signs."

Psalms 149: 5-9, "Let the saints be joyful in glory; let them sing aloud on their beds. Let the high praises of God be in their mouth, and a two-edged sword in their hand, To execute vengeance on the nations, and punishments on the peoples; To bind their kings with chains, and their nobles with fetters of iron, To execute on the written judgment... this honor have all His saints." Praise the LORD!

James 4: 7-8, "Therefore submit to God. Resist the devil and he will flee from you. Draw near to God and He will draw near to you ..."

2 Corinthians 10: 3-5, "For though we walk in the flesh, we do not war according to the flesh. For the weapons or our warfare are not carnal but mighty in God for pulling down strongholds, casting down arguments and every high thing that exalts itself against the knowledge of God, bringing every thought into captivity to the obedience of Christ, and being ready to punish all disobedience when your obedience is fulfilled."

1 John 4: 1-3, "Beloved, do not believe every spirit, but test the spirits, whether they are of God; because many false prophets have gone out into the world. By this you know the Spirit of God: Every spirit that confesses that Jesus Christ has come in the flesh is of God, and every spirit that does not confess that Jesus Christ has come in the flesh is not of God. And this is the spirit of the Antichrist, which you have heard was coming, and is now already in the world."

Matthew 10: 1, "And when He had called His twelve disciples to Him, He gave them power over unclean spirits, to cast them out, and to heal all kinds of sickness and all kinds of disease."

Mark 6: 13, "And they cast out many demons, and anointed with oil many who were sick and healed them."

Hebrews 2: 14-15, "Inasmuch then as the children have partaken of flesh and Blood, He Himself likewise shared in the same, that through death He might destroy him who had the power of death, that is, the devil, and release those who through fear of death were all their lifetime subject to bondage."

Romans 16:20, "And the God of peace will crush satan under your feet shortly."

Psalms 91:13, "You shall tread upon the lion and the serpent, the young lion and the serpent you shall trample underfoot."

Joshua 10:24, "...Joshua called for all the men of Israel, and said to the captains of the men of war who went with him, "Come near, put your feet on the neck of these kings." And they drew near and put their feet on their necks."

1 John 3:8, "...For this purpose the Son of God was manifested, that He might destroy the works of the devil."

1 John 4:4, "You are of God, little children, and have overcome them, because He who is in you is greater than he who is in the world."

Ephesians 3:18-21, (That you) "may be able to comprehend with all the saints what is the width and length and depth and height – to know the love of Christ which passes knowledge; that you may be filled with all the fullness of God. Now to Him who is able to do exceeding abundantly above all that we ask or think, according to the power that works in us, to Him be glory in the church by Christ Jesus throughout all generations, forever and ever." Amen!

Colossians 1:11-14, (That you may be) "strengthened with all might, according to His glorious power, for all patience and longsuffering with joy; giving thanks to the Father who has qualified us to be partakers of the inheritance of the saints in the light. He has delivered us from the power of darkness and conveyed us into the Kingdom of the Son of His Love, in whom we have redemption through His Blood, the forgiveness of sins."

Hebrews 4:12, "For the word of God is living and powerful, and sharper than any two-edged sword, piercing even to the division of the soul and spirit, and of joints and marrow, and is a discerner of the thoughts and intents of the heart."

Acts 16:18, "Paul, greatly annoyed, turned and said to the spirit, "I command you in the Name of Jesus Christ to come out of her." And he came out that very hour.

Acts 26:16-18, "But rise and stand on your feet; for I have appeared to you for this purpose, to make you a minister and a witness both of the things which you have seen and of the things which I will yet reveal to you. I will deliver you from the Jewish people, as well as from the Gentiles, to whom I now send you, to open their eyes, in order to turn them from darkness to light, and from the power of Satan to God, that they may receive forgiveness of sins and an inheritance among those who are sanctified by faith in Me."

John 14:12, "Most assuredly, I say to you, he who believes in Me, the works that I do he will do also; and greater works than these he will do, because I go to My Father."

1Peter 5:8-9, "Be sober, be vigilant; because your adversary the devil walks about like a roaring lion, seeking who he may devour. Resist him, steadfast in the faith ..."

Matthew 17:18-22, "And Jesus rebuked the demon, and it came out of him; and the child was cured from that very hour. Then the disciples came to Jesus privately and said, "Why could we not cast him out?" So Jesus said to them, "Because of your unbelief; for assuredly, I say to you, if you have faith as a mustard seed, you will say to this mountain, "Move from here to there, and it will move; and nothing will be impossible for you. "However, this kind does not go out except by prayer and fasting."

Revelation 12:10-11, "Then I heard a loud voice saying in heaven, "Now salvation, and strength, and the kingdom of our God, and the power of His Christ have come, for the accuser of our brethren, who accused them before our God day and night, has been cast down. "And they overcame him by the Blood of the Lamb and by the word of their testimony, and they did not love their lives to the death."

Daniel 10:11-13, "O Daniel, man greatly beloved ... "Do not fear, Daniel, for from the first day that you set your heart to understand, and to humble yourself before your God, your words were heard; and I have come because of your words. "But the prince of the kingdom of Persia withstood me twenty-one days; and behold, Michael, came to help me, for I had been left alone there with the kings of Persia."

Ephesians 2:1-2, "And you He made alive, who were dead in trespasses and sins, in which you once walked according to the course of this world, according to the prince of the power of the air, the spirit who now works in the sons of disobedience."

John 16:23, ...Most assuredly, I say to you, whatever you ask the Father in My Name He will give you."

Revelation 1:18, "I am he who lives, and was dead, and behold, I am alive forevermore. Amen. And I have the keys of Hades and of Death."

2 Timothy 1:7, "For God has not given us a spirit of fear, but of power and love and a sound mind."

2 Timothy 1:1, "But has now been revealed by the appearing of our Savior Jesus Christ, who has abolished death and brought life and immorality to light through the gospel."

Jude 1:9, "Yet Michael the archangel, in contending with the devil, when he disputed about the body of Moses, dared not bring against him a reviling accusation, but said, "The Lord rebuke you!"

Acts 19: 13-17, "Then some of the itinerant Jewish exorcists took it upon themselves to call the Name of the Lord Jesus over those who had evil spirits, saying, "We exorcise you by the Jesus who Paul preaches."

Also there were seven sons of Sceva, a Jewish chief priest, who did so. And the evil spirit answered and said, "Jesus I know, and Paul I know; but who are you?" Then the man in whom the evil spirit was leaped on them, overpowered them, and prevailed against them, so that they fled out of that house naked and wounded. This became known both to all Jews and Greeks dwelling Ephesus; and fear fell on them all, and the Name of the Lord Jesus was magnified."

Isaiah 47:12-15, "Stand now with your enchantments and the multitude of your sorceries, in which you have labored from your youth – perhaps you will be able to profit, perhaps you will prevail. You are wearied in the multitude of your counsels; let now the astrologers, the stargazers, and the monthly prognosticators stand up and save you from what shall come upon you. Behold, they shall be as stubble, the fire shall burn them; They shall not deliver themselves from the power of the flame ... No one shall save you."

Mark 5:2-8, "And when He had come out of the boat, immediately there met Him out of the tombs a man with an unclean spirit, who had his dwelling among the tombs; and no one could bind him, not even with chains, because he had often been bound with shackles and chains. And the chains had been pulled apart by him, and the shackles broken in pieces; neither could anyone tame him. And always, night and day, he was in the mountains and in the tombs, crying out and cutting himself with stones. When he saw Jesus from afar, he ran and worshiped Him. And he cried out with a loud voice said, "What have I to do with You, Jesus, Son of the Most High God? I implore You by God that You do not torment me." For He said to him, "Come out of the man, unclean spirit!""

Acts 8:7-8, "For unclean spirits, crying with a loud voice came out from many who were possessed; and many who were paralyzed and the lame were healed. And there was great joy in that city."

Matthew 12:43-45, "When an unclean spirit goes out of a man, he goes through dry places, seeking rest, and finds none. "Then he says, "I will return to my house from which I came" And when he comes, he finds it empty, swept, and put in order. "Then he goes and takes with him seven other spirits more wicked than himself, and they enter and dwell there;

and the last state of that man is worse than the first. So shall it also be with this wicked generation."

1 Corinthians 12:4-11, "Now there are diversities of gifts, but the same Spirit. There are differences of ministries, but the same Lord. And there are diversities of activities, but it is the same God who works all in all. But the manifestation of the Spirit is given to each one for the profit of all: for to one is given the word of wisdom through the Spirit, to another the word of knowledge through the same Spirit, to another faith by the same Spirit, to another gifts of healings by the same Spirit, to another the working of miracles, to another prophecy, to another discerning of spirits, to another different kinds of tongues, to another the interpretation of tongues. But one and the same Spirit works all these things, distributing to each one individually as He wills."

Luke 4:18-19, "The Spirit of the Lord is upon Me, because He has anointed Me to preach the gospel to the poor; he has sent Me to heal the brokenhearted, to proclaim liberty to the captives and recovery of sight to the blind, to set at liberty those who are oppressed; To proclaim the acceptable year of the Lord."

Ephesians 6:10-13: "Finally, my brethren, be strong in the Lord and in the power of His might. Put on the whole armor of God that you may be able to stand against the wiles of the devil. For we do not wrestle against flesh and blood, but against principalities, against powers, against the ruler of the darkness of this age, against spiritual host of wickedness in the heavenly places. Therefore take up the whole armor of God, that you may be able to withstand in the evil day, and having done all, to stand."

Ephesians 1:17-23, "That the God of our Lord Jesus Christ, the Father of glory, may give to you the spirit of wisdom and revelation in the knowledge of Him, the eyes of your understanding being enlightened; that you may know what is the hope of His calling, what are the riches of the glory of His inheritance in the saints, and what is the exceeding greatness of His power toward us who believe, according to the working of His mighty power which He worked in Christ when He raised Him from the dead and seated Him at His right hand in the heavenly places, far above all principality and power and might and dominion, and every name that is named, not only in this age but also in that which is to come. And He put all things under His feet, and gave Him to be head over all things to the church, which is His body, the fullness of Him who fills all in all."

Ephesians 3:9-11, "To make all see what is the fellowship of the mystery, which from the beginning of the ages has been hidden in God who created all things through Jesus Christ; to the intent that now the manifold wisdom of God might be made known by the church to the principalities and powers in the heavenly places, according to the eternal purpose which He accomplished in Christ Jesus our Lord.

Colossians 1:15-17, "He is the image of the invisible God, the firstborn over all creation, For by Him all things were created that are in heaven and that are on earth, visible and invisible, whether thrones or dominions or principalities or powers. All things were created through Him and for Him. And He is before all things, and in Him all things consist."

Colossians 2:8-10, "Beware lest anyone cheat you through philosophy and empty deceit, according to the tradition of men, according to the basic principles of the world, and not according to Christ. For in Him dwells all the fullness of the Godhead bodily; and you are complete in Him, who is the head of all principality and powers."

Colossians 2:15, "Having disarmed principalities and powers, he made a public spectacle of them, triumphing over them in it."

Romans 8:35-39, "Who shall separate us from the love of Christ? Shall tribulation, or distress, or persecution, or famine, or nakedness, or peril, or sword? As it is written: "For Your sake we are killed all day long; we are accounted as sheep for the slaughter." Yet in all these things we are more than conquerors through Him who loved us. For I am persuaded that neither death nor life, nor angels nor principalities nor powers, nor things present nor things to come, nor height nor depth, nor any other created thing, shall be able to separate us from the love of God which is in Christ Jesus our Lord."

Sin List

abandonment, abduction, abhorrence of holy things, abhorring judgment, abomination, abortion, abusiveness, accusation, adulterous lust, adultery, afflicting others, aggravation, agitation, aiding and abetting sin, alcoholism, all unrighteousness, anger, animosity, anxiety, apprehension, argumentativeness, arrogance, assaults, astrology, atheism, avariciousness, Baal worship, backbiting, backsliding, bad attitude, bad language, bearing false witness, big talk, being a workaholic, being too quick to speak, believing the lies of the enemy, belittling, bereavement, betraying Jesus, bickering, bigotry, bitterness, black magic, blackmail, blasphemy, blasphemy of the Holy Spirit, boastfulness, boisterousness, bowing down to gods or serving images, bragging, brainwashing, breaking commandments of God, breaking vows and covenants to God, breaking covenants and vows with others, bribery, brutality, burning incense to gods, calamity, carelessness, cares & riches of this world, carnality, casting God away, causing disagreements, causing distress, causing division, causing fear, causing men to err, causing offense, causing poor to fail, changing truth to lies, chanting of charms, cheating, committing willful and/or intentional sin, complaining, complacency against God's will or destiny, conceit, concupiscence, condemnation, condemning the just, causing conflict, confrontation, confusion, conjuration, conspiring against God, consulting wizards and psychics, contempt, contention, controlling, conniving, compulsiveness, contentiousness, contesting and withstanding or resisting God, corruption, counterfeiting Christian work, covering sin, coveting neighbor's spouse, spouse, brother, sister, house, land, automobile, or anything that is our neighbor's; covetousness, cravenness, criticalness, crookedness, cruelty, using crystals, cursing God, cursing, cynicalism, dealing treacherously, deceit, deception, defamation, defeatism, defiantness, defiling, degrading, dejection, demon consciousness, demon worship, denying Jesus and His resurrection, dependencies, depravity, desecration of holy vessels, desires of this world, despair, despising God, His Name and His Word, despising spouse, despising neighbors, despising parents, despitefulness, despondency, destruction of the innocent, saints and holy things; deviousness, disagreements, disbelief, discord, discouragement, discrediting, disdain, disgust, dishonesty, disliking the love of good men, disobedience, disobedient to God, disorderly, disputing, disregard of God's work, disrespectfulness of God, disruptiveness, dissension, distantness, distrust, divining, divining for water with rods, divining for money, division, divorce, domineeringness, double-talking, double mindedness, doubt, dread, driving men from true worship and inheritance, drug abuse, drunkenness, duplicity, drinking blood, eating blood, eating sin offerings, eating unclean food, effeminate behavior, egoism, enchantment, enlarged imaginations, entering into ungodly soul ties, entering into unrighteous agreements, envy, envy produced by lust, escaping, evil hearts, imaginations, exasperation, extortion, failure in duty, failure to glorify God, false burdens, false compassion, falsehood, false praise, false responsibility, fantasizing, fantasy lust, fault finding, fear, fear of accusation, fear of condemnation, fear of disapproval, fear of man, fear of rejection, fear of failure, fear of reproof, fetishes, fighting, flattery, fleshliness, fooling self and/or others, foolishness, following any ways of man, folly, forbidding the preaching of God's Word, forcefulness, forgetting God and His work, fornication, forsaking the assembly, fortune telling, fraud, fretting, frigidity, frustrations, fury, gendering strife, giving judgment for reward, giving offense, giving others alcohol, gloominess, gluttony, gossip, greed, grieving God and the Holy Spirit, grumbling, guilt, hardhearted, harlotry, harshness, hating God, hating God's Word, hating, haughtiness, having other gods before You, headiness, high-minded, holding God's table in contempt, homosexuality, hopelessness, horoscopes, human sacrifice, hypocrisy, idleness, idolatries of any kind, ignorance, ignoring God, ignoring His miracles, ill will, imitating true worship, inhumanity, imaginations, immorality, impatience, impenitence, impetuousness, implacability, imprudence, impurity of thoughts, impurity, inadequacy, incest, incitement, indecision independence, indifferences, inflating, inflexibility, inhospitality, injustice, inquiring of idols, insolence, intemperance, intentional sins, intimidation, intolerances, intellectualism and sophistication, inventing sin, inventing evil, inward wickedness, irrationality, irreverence, jealousy, being judgmental, justifying the wicked, kidnapping, killing, lack of self-control, lawlessness, lasciviousness, laziness, legalism, lesbianism, levitation, lewdness, lying, limiting God, lip service, living contrary to nature, loathing, longing for sin, loneliness, loose morals, looting, loving to curse, loving evil, loving money, loving to be chief, loving human titles, loving human praise, lust, lust of the eye, lust of the flesh, lust of the mind, laying in wait to sin, lying to the Holy Spirit, lying with pleasure and delight, madness, magic, male prostitution, making or buying images, making false vows, making God a liar, making war, maliciousness, manipulation, manslaughter, marauding, masturbation, materialism, meanness, misbelieving, mischief, misery, misleading, misuse of the law, mocking, mulishness, murder, murmuring, murmuring about wages, muttering, necromancy, negativism, nervous habits, nicotine addiction, not having a conscience, not being a good steward of Your money, not fearing God, not giving to the poor, not honoring fathers and mothers, not letting go of wickedness, not loving God with all our heart, soul and mind; not loving our neighbor as our self, not loving our self, not observing and keeping holy the Sabbath day, not praising and worshiping God the way we should and when we should and how we should, not being watchful, occultism, obsessing, obstinacy, offering polluted sacrifices, opposing the gospel, oppressing widows and orphans, oppression, overbearing, pastors destroying and scattering sheep, pedophilia, pendulum, persecuting believers, persecuting the poor, persecution, perversion, perverting the gospel, perverting truth for personal gain, petulance, planning without God, plotting, plundering, polluting God's house and Sabbaths, pompousness, pornography, possessiveness, pouting, prayerlessness, prejudice, presumption, pretending to be a prophet, pretension, pridefulness, pride of life, procrastination, profane God and His holiness, profanity unto God, professing to be wise, prophecy by Baal, prophesying lies, propagating lies, proudness, provoking God, provoking, puffing up, quarreling, quenching the Holy Spirit, questioning God's word, raiding, railing, raging, raping, rationalization, ravaging, rebellion, rebuking the Lord, recklessness, refusing correction, refusing to hear, refusing to repent, refusing to destroy ungodly altars, refusing to be humble, refusing to live in peace, regarding iniquity in your heart, rejecting reproof, rejecting salvation, rejecting God and His Word, rejection, rejoicing in others' adversity, rejoicing in idols, rejoicing in iniquity, repetitiveness, reproaching good men, requiring usury, resentment, restlessness, retaliation, returning evil for good, returning hate for love, reveling, reviling, revenge, rewarding evil for good, rigidity, robbing God, robbery, rudeness, sacrificing children to demons, sadism, scheming, scornfulness, scorning religion, seduction, seeking self gain, seeking pleasures of this world, seizing in an evil way, self-accusations, self-admiration, self-centeredness, self-condemnation, self-corruption, self-criticalness, self-deception, self-delusion, self-destruction, self-exultation, self-glorification, self-hatred, self-importance, self-rejection, selfishness, self-pity, self-righteousness, self-seeking, self-will, serving other gods, setting aside Godly counsel, setting heart to sin, sewing discord, sexual idolatry, sexual immorality, sexual impurity, sexual lewdness, sexual perversion, oral sex, sodomy, shame, shamelessness, silliness, sin consciousness, sinful mirth, sissyness, skepticism, slander, slaughter, slaying, slothfulness, snobbishness, soothsaying, sorcery, sowing seeds of hatred, speaking incantations, speaking folly, speculation, spell-casting, spiritual laziness, spitefulness, stealing, stiff-necked, strife, striving over leadership, struggling, stubbornness, stupidity, suicidal thoughts, suspicion, swallowing up the needy, swearing to false gods, swearing, taking advantage of others, taking a bribe, taking offense, taking God's Name in vain, taking rights away from the poor, teaching false doctrines, temper, temptation, tempting God, theft, threatening disaster, timidity, teaching and tolerating wickedness, tolerating false prophets, tolerating sin and its ways, tolerating wicked men, trafficking with demons, trickery, two-facedness, trusting lies, trusting our own beauty, trusting in our own righteousness, trusting wickedness, tumults, turning to folly, turning aside the way of the meek, turning your back on God, turning from righteousness, turning aside for money, unbelief, unbridled lust, uncleanness, uncompromising, undermining, unequally yoked to non-believers, unfairness, unfaithfulness in trust, unfaithfulness, unforgiveness, unfriendliness, ungratefulness, unholy alliances, unholy habits, unions with menstrual women, unmanly, unmercifulness, unreadiness, unrepenting, unrighteousness of laws, unrighteousness, unruliness of tongues, unsparing, un-submissiveness, unthankfulness, untruthfulness, (being) unwise, unworthiness, using tarot cards, vain imaginations, vain repetitions, vanity, vengeance, viciousness, vile affections, vile speaking, violence, vulgarity, walking after our own devices, walking for unprofitable things, walking after our own thoughts, walking after false gods, walking with heathens, walking with sinners, water witching, white magic, wickedness, willful sin, willful blindness to the truth, winking with evil intent, witchcraft, withdrawal, withholding a pledge, (being) without concern, (being) without natural affection, (being) without mercy, working iniquity, working for praise, worldliness, worrying, worshipping possessions, worshipping our works, worshipping the creation instead of the Creator, worshipping of planets, wrathfulness, wrong doing, zealousness to make others sinful, zealousness in outward show.

DEMON LIST

abandonment, abomination, abortion, abuse, accidents, and accident prone, accusation, accuser of the brethren, aches, addictions, adultery, adulterous lust, adversity, affectation, agitation, aggravation, alcoholism, analysis, anxiety, anger, anguish, animosity, anorexia, anti-Semitism, anti-submissiveness, anxiety, apathy, apprehension, arba, argumentativeness, arrested development, arrogance, atheism, arthritis, automatic writing, Baal, backbiting, bestiality, belittling, busyness, bickering, bitterness, black magic, blasphemy, blindness, burden, boasting, brainwashing, bribes, broken spirit, chaos, cares & riches of this world, carnality, causing offense, cheating, childish/immature behavior, christian science, chronic sickness, complaining, covetousness, cursing, condemnation, confusion, confrontation, conjuring, conceit, concupiscence, contention, continual sorrow, contradiction, control, conniving, complacency, compulsiveness, criticalness, crooked speech, cruelty, cultic art, cursing, cynicism, daydreaming, death, deception, defeatism, deafness, defiance, defilement, dejection, delusion, depression, dependencies, despair, desires of this world, despondency, destruction, dictatorial, diotrophes, disbelief, disgust, discouragement, discomfort, discontentment, disobedience, dissension, disdain, disease, distress, distrust, distraction, driving, division, divination/diviner, domination, doorkeeper spirits, doubt, drug abuse, drug addiction, drunkenness, dread, ego, enchanting, escapism, ego, embarrassment, embezzlement, envy, escape of reality, exasperation, false burdens, false compassion, false responsibility, false teaching, false witness, fantasy, fantasy lust, fatigue, fault finding, fear, fear of rejection, fear of man, fear of disapproval, fear of failure, fear of condemnation, fear of accusation, fear of reproof, fetishes, fighting, financial failure, forgetfulness, fornication, fortune telling, fretting, frigidity, frustration, gall, generational spirits of ____, gloom, gluttony, gout, gossip, greed, grief, guilt, hardhearted, hatred, haughtiness headaches, heaviness, hopelessness, hallucinations, harlotry, horoscopes, hurt, hyperactivity, hypocrisy, idleness, idolatries of any kind, impurity, incest, infirmity, injury, impatience, inadequacy, incantation, incoherence, incubus and succubus, ineptness, indecision, independence, indifference, insomnia, intimidation, intolerance, insecurity, insanity, insensitiveness, intellectualism, intentional sin, irritation, islam, isolation, jealousy, judgmentalness, laboring, lack of knowledge, lasciviousness, legalism, lethargy, leviathan, levitation, listlessness, lofty, loneliness, lust, lust of the eye, lust of the flesh, lust of the mind, lying, madness, magicians, manipulation, masturbation, materialism, material lust, meanness, mental illness, migraine, mind control, mischief, mockery, molestation, morbidity, murder, murmuring, necromancy, nervousness, nervous habits, nicotine addiction, occultism, opposing, oppression, obsession, obstinate, orgies, Orion, pain, paranoia, passivity, pedophilia, pendulums, perfectionism, perplexity, perverse spirit, petulance, perfection, persecution, pornography, possessiveness, pouting, plague, plotting, prejudice, premonitions, presumption, pretension, pride, pride of knowledge, procrastination, provoking, puffed up, quarreling, railing, rape, rage, rebellion, rejection, religious control, restlessness, rationalization, retaliation, retardation, rheumatism, rigidity, resentment, rottenness, rudeness, ruling spirits, sadism, scorn, seduction, shame, slander, self-accusation, self-centered, self-delusion, self-confusion, self-deception, self-rejection, self-seduction, self-pity, selfishness, self-dependent, self-destruction, self-hatred, self-righteousness, self-promotion, self-condemnation, self-criticalness, self-praise, self-torture, self-willed, self-exaltation, self-importance, serpents and scorpions, sexual idolatry, sexual impurity, shame, sharp/bitter words, shield demons, shock, shyness, sciatica, sickness, sin consciousness, skepticism, sleepiness, soothsayer, spirit of chemosh, spiders, spirit of self, spirit of unbelief, stiff necked, strife, stress, stubbornness, struggling, suspicion, suicide, taking offense, tarot cards, temper, tension, tiredness, theatrics, timidity, torment, tragedies, trauma, travail, travailing womb, unbending, uncleanness, unclean spirits, unemployment, unforgiveness, undermining, unfairness, ungodly conduct, unjust gain, unsubmissiveness, unwilling to admit wrong, unwilling to apologize, unwilling to change, unyielding, unworthiness, vagabonds, vanity, violence, wandering, water witching, weariness, white magic, wickedness, willful sin, withdrawal, witches, wizards, wrath, worry, wounded spirit, witchcraft, all unrighteous spirits, demon consciousness, sophistication, intellectualism and Nimrod, high mindedness, Jezebel, Ahab, spirit of Ankh, spirit of Balaam, another Jesus, Baal, Balaam, Cora, Herodian, Python, spirit of Rachel, spirit of Saul, religion, sorcery, voodoo, cults, occultism. All hindering, persecuting, accusing, lying, familiar spirits, seducing spirits, mind binding, mind blocking spirits, anti-christ spirits, generational spirits, all spirits and strongmen of all mental, physical, and emotional illness, sickness, diseases, disorders, death, premature death, infirmities, afflictions, inflammations, viruses, infections, abnormal cells, radical cells, lesions, cysts, pain, shock, trauma, spasms, cramps, abnormal growths, radical growths in or on any parts of our bodies including our eyes, ears, nose, mouth, throat, back, bones, muscles, ligaments, tissues, blood, blood vessels, arteries, colons, intestines, stomach, prostate, thyroid, brains, liver, pancreas, heart, lungs, cardiovascular disorders and diseases, reproductive disorders and diseases, thyroid disorders and diseases, blood pressure disorders and diseases, throat disorders and diseases, breast disorders and diseases, neurological disorders and diseases, lymphatic disorders and diseases, chemical imbalances, hormone imbalances, allergies of any kind, senility, forgetfulness, paranoia, schizophrenia; all spirits of arthritis, crippling arthritis, acute arthritis, sinusitis, acute sinusitis, sciatica, bursitis, tendonitis, discomfort, headaches, migraines, aches, pains, performance spirits; all spirits of disorders and diseases, hypoglycemia of all forms, degenerative diseases of all kinds, all cancers, all tumors, all mind diseases and disorders.

www.ingramcontent.com/pod-product-compliance
Lightning Source LLC
Chambersburg PA
CBHW020517100426

42813CB00030B/3279/J